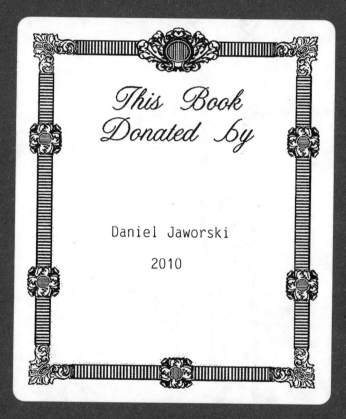

This Book
Donated by

Daniel Jaworski

2010

WAR
STORIES

First published in 2006 by Usborne Publishing Ltd,
Usborne House, 83-85 Saffron Hill, London EC1N 8RT, England.
www.usborne.com

Printed in China

Designed by Sarah Cronin
Illustrated by Ian McNee
Edited by Rachel Firth
Series editor: Jane Chisholm
Cover design by Neil Francis

With grateful thanks to Terry Charman, of the Imperial War Museum, London,
for his most helpful comments on the manuscript.

WAR
STORIES

**TRUE STORIES FROM
THE FIRST AND SECOND WORLD WARS**

PAUL DOWSWELL

Contents

The First World War

THE SECOND WORLD WAR

The world at war

THE FLIMSY BIPLANES, stubby tanks and cavalry officers on horseback of the First World War now seem part of a distant age, like Montgolfier's gaudy hot air balloons and the mighty wooden men o' war of Napoleonic times. But there are still a handful of men alive today who fought in that war. In fact, the last survivor of the 1914 Christmas truce (see p38-46) only died in 2005, a sprightly 109 year old, still willing

★ 7 ★

to reminisce for documentary film-makers about the events of that extraordinary day. Like many other veterans of both world wars, he found it difficult to talk about what had happened to him. Even 90 years on, the memory of the young men who died beside him in France and Belgium moved him to tears.

There are still millions of people alive who lived today through the Second World War. Many grandparents even remember it vividly. Its technology may seem quaint now, but that war introduced the world to computers, jet planes, penicillin, space rockets and nuclear weapons. The end of the war, with its fearful standoff between the western democracies and the Soviet Union, has shaped the history of the world to this day.

The casualties of the two wars are so immense (at least 76 million dead) it is easy to forget the individuals who were caught up in these conflicts. Most were former civilians – farm and factory hands, civil servants, teachers – plucked from their everyday lives and plunged into a terrifying and often lethal ordeal. The wars were on too great a scale to be fought merely by professional standing armies.

Even those that stayed at home were caught up in the Second World War, like no other conflict in history. It was not just the luckless populations of the battle zones, stranded in the scorched earth between advancing and retreating armies. The citizens of London and Hiroshima saw their cities devastated or destroyed by bombers which had flown hundreds or thousands of miles from enemy territory to attack them.

Many of the episodes in this book tell the stories of ordinary men and women – soldiers, sailors, aircrew – caught up in the tide of great battles or campaigns. Some of the stories are about spies – men and women of extraordinary courage who ventured into enemy territory in the certain knowledge that they would be killed if captured.

Even those who survived with no obvious physical or psychological damage were tormented by what they had seen and done. One British veteran of the First World War recalled:

"Us fellows, it took us years to get over it. Years! Long after when you were working, married, had kids, you'd be lying in bed with your wife and you'd see it all before you. Couldn't sleep. Couldn't lie still. Many's the time I've got up and tramped the streets till it came daylight… And many's the time I've met other fellows that were out there doing exactly the same thing. Went on for years that did."

For those that fought in them, the two world wars remained the most intense and vivid experiences of their lives.

Over by Christmas?

1914

IN THE FIRST FOUR DAYS of August 1914, the world's most powerful nations declared war on each other. They lined up in two opposing camps. On one side was Germany and Austria-Hungary, who were known as the Central Powers. On the other was Britain and France, together with their empires, and Russia. They were known as the Allies. In the course of the war, other nations would be drawn into the conflict, too.

The Ottoman empire and Bulgaria joined the Central Powers. Italy, Romania, Japan and China joined the Allies. So did the United States, despite the initial reluctance of a great many of its people. It was to be the first real world war – in that it involved countries from every inhabited continent – although most of the fighting took place on what became known as the Western and Eastern fronts, on either side of Germany.

As news of the outbreak of war spread, crowds began to gather in the hot summer sunshine, congregating in the great squares and parks of Europe's principal cities. Far from being fearful or anxious, they were elated – like football fans anticipating a closely-fought game. Each side expected a war of great marches and heroic battles, quickly decided. The German emperor, the kaiser, told his troops they would be home before the leaves fell from the trees. The British were not so optimistic, although it was frequently claimed that the war would be over by Christmas. Only a few far-sighted politicians realized what was coming, including the British foreign secretary, Sir Edward Grey.

Watching the dusk from his window on August 4, the day Britain declared war on Germany, Sir Edward sighed:

French soldiers march off to fight the Germans. In an echo of a previous age, they wore bright red trousers as part of their uniform – making them all too visible in the battlefields. The trousers were soon discarded.

"The lamps are going out all over Europe; we shall not see them lit again in our lifetime." His melancholy remark had a deep resonance, for the world would never be the same. Grey and his fellow citizens were living in a strong and prosperous country, with a vast empire. The war would provide a rude awakening to the grimier reality of the 20th century, completely undermining Britain's position as the world's most powerful nation.

Almost all the other participants in the war suffered a similar reversal of fortune, or worse. In France, half of all men aged between 20 and 35 were killed or badly wounded; its eminent position in the world would never recover. The Austro-Hungarian empire collapsed, with repercussions that can still be seen in the unstable Balkan nations of today. The Germans ended the war on the brink of a communist revolution, and lost their own monarchy. The war swept away the Russian monarchy too, then brought the communist Bolsheviks to power. With them came 70 years of brutal, totalitarian oppression. Like many countries in Eastern Europe, the Russians have never really recovered from the First World War, and its awful consequences. Only the United

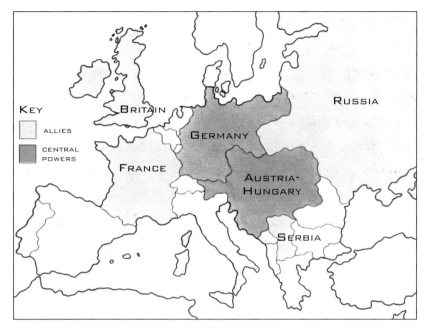

The Allies and Central Powers at the start of the war

States did well out of it. By 1919, it had become the richest, most powerful nation on Earth, and was set to dominate the 20th century.

Quite apart from its consequences, there is something uniquely haunting about the First World War. The Second World War was far worse in terms of its cost in human life: it claimed over four times as many victims. It was also fought with much greater brutality, and came with such horrors as the Holocaust and the mass destruction of cities by aerial bombardment. But it did end with the overthrow of two undoubtedly evil regimes – Nazi Germany and Imperial Japan – and a peace which lasted for the rest of the century. The First World War, for all its terrible cost, produced no positive results at all.

The city crowds that gathered that August had no idea what the next four years had in store. The dreadful waste of life – what British statesman Lloyd George would describe as "the ghastly butchery of vain and insane offensives" – was something hitherto unknown in modern warfare. But, worst of all, when the final shell had been fired, the final gas canister unleashed and the final submarine recalled to port, there was nothing to show for it except an awful air of unfinished business and a tally of 21 million dead. Novelist H.G. Wells called it "the war that will end war", and the phrase had caught on. It was such a gut-wrenchingly horrible conflict, everyone hoped humanity would not be foolish enough to do it again. The Versailles peace treaty officially ended the war in 1919. The proceedings were dismissed as "a 20-year cease-fire" by one of the leading participants, French commander Marshal Foch. He was exactly right. By the early 1920s, people had already begun to refer to "the war that will end war" as the *First* World War.

The causes of the war were many. A system of rival alliances between the different European powers had built up in the previous decades, as individual countries tried to bolster their security and ambitions with powerful allies. But, although alliances provided some security, they also came with obligations. The events that led to war were set in motion in June 1914, when a Serbian student named Gavrilo Princip assassinated the heir to the Austro-Hungarian throne, Archduke Franz Ferdinand. In retaliation, Austria-Hungary swiftly declared war on Serbia. But Serbia was an ally of Russia's. So Russia joined the war against Austria-Hungary, and all the other rival nations, tied to their respective alliances, were dragged into the conflict – whether they wanted to be or not.

But why should a quarrel between Russia and Austria-Hungary over a little-known country in Eastern Europe automatically involve France, Germany and Britain? It was because each was obliged to support the other in the event of war. And there were other long-standing resentments, too. Britain, then the world's greatest empire, maintained her power by means of the world's greatest fleet. So when Germany began to build a fleet to rival the Royal Navy, relations between the two countries deteriorated sharply. The British and French both had vast colonial empires. Germany, similarly prosperous and powerful, had very few colonies and wanted more. They all joined in the fighting to maintain or improve their position in the world.

The reason the conflict was so horrific is easier to explain. The war occurred at a moment in the evolution of military technology when weapons to defend a position were much more effective than the weapons available to attack it. The previous 50 years had seen the development of trench fortifications, barbed wire, machine guns, and rapid-fire rifles. All of this made it simple and straightforward for an army defending its territory. But an army attacking well-defended territory had to rely on its infantrymen, armed with only rifles and bayonets – and they were to be slaughtered in their millions.

Yet all the generals involved in the war had been trained to fight by attacking, so that is what they did. They had also been trained to think of cavalry as one of their greatest offensive weapons. The cavalry – still armed with lances, as they had been for the previous 2,000 years – took part in a few battles, particularly at the start of the war. But these elite troops were quickly massacred. The tactics of Alexander the Great, Ghengiz Khan and Napoleon, all of whom had used cavalry to great effect, were no match for the industrial-scale killing power of the 20th-century machine gun.

There were other ugly additions to the new technology of warfare: poisonous gas, fighter and bomber aircraft, zeppelins, tanks, submarines and, especially, artillery (field guns, howitzers etc.). Armies had long used cannons but, by the time of the First World War, these weapons had reached a new pinnacle of sophistication. They were much more accurate and fired more rapidly than they had done. The shells they fired contained high explosives, shrapnel (metal balls) or gas. Over 70% of all casualties in the First World War were caused by artillery. As artillery could be used both to attack and defend, it gave neither side an advantage. It simply gouged up the battlefield landscape, making fighting even more difficult and dangerous for the hapless participants.

The war began with a massive German attack on France, known as the Schlieffen Plan after its originator, General Alfred, Graf von Schlieffen. The plan called for the German army to wheel through neutral Belgium and seize Paris. The idea was to knock France out of the war as soon as possible. Apart from neutralizing one of Germany's most powerful rivals, this would have two other advantages. First, it would deprive Britain of a base on the continent from which to attack Germany. Second, with their enemies to the west conquered or severely disadvantaged, Germany could then concentrate on defeating the much larger Russian army to the east.

The fighting in late summer and early autumn of 1914 was among the fiercest of the war. Both sides suffered huge losses. At the Battle of the Marne, the German advance was halted less than 24km (15 miles) from Paris. By November, the armies had become bogged down in opposing rows of trenches, which stretched from the English Channel down to the Swiss border. Give or take the odd few miles here and there, the front line would remain much the same for the next four years.

Map of Europe showing the main fronts in 1914

On Germany's eastern border, its armies won crushing victories against vast hordes of invading Russian troops, at Tannenberg in late August, and the Masurian lakes in early September. They had prevented the "Russian steamroller" from overrunning their country. From here on, the German army would gradually advance eastwards.

In 1915, there was an attempt by British and ANZAC (Australian and New Zealand Army Corps) troops to attack the Central Powers from the south, via Gallipoli in Turkey. The strategy was a disaster. Between April and December 1915, around 200,000 men were killed trying to gain a foothold in this narrow, hilly peninsular.

By 1916, the war that was supposed to have ended by Christmas 1914 looked as if it would last forever. Determined, in his own words – "to bleed the French army white" – the German chief-of-staff, General Erich von Falkenhayn, launched an attack on the fortresses of Verdun in February. His strategy was a success in some ways. The French army lost 350,000 men, and never really recovered. But Falkenhayn's own troops suffered 330,000 casualties too, and the French held on to their fortresses. Von Falkenhayn was relieved of his command.

Meanwhile, on May 31, 1916, the German High Seas Fleet challenged the British Royal Navy in the North Sea, at the Battle of Jutland. In an all-out confrontation, 14 British ships, and 11 German ships were lost. If the British navy had been destroyed, then Germany would undoubtedly have won the war. Island Britain would have been starved into submission, as cargo ships would have been unable to sail into British waters without being sunk. The British may have lost more ships at Jutland, but the German navy never ventured out to sea again, and the British naval blockade of Germany remained intact. A pattern was emerging, of titanic struggles, vast casualties, and almost indifferent results. Worse was to come.

On July 1, 1916, another great battle began. The British launched an all-out attack on the Somme, in northern France. The British commander-in-chief, Field Marshal Haig, was convinced that a massive assault would break the German front line. This would enable him to send in his cavalry, and allow his troops to make a considerable advance into enemy territory. The attack – known as "the Big Push" – failed in the first few minutes and 20,000 men were slaughtered in a single morning. Yet the Battle of the Somme dragged on for a further five miserable months.

By 1917, a numb despair had settled on the fighting nations. With appalling stubbornness, Field Marshal Haig launched another attack on the German lines – this time at Passchendaele, in Belgium. Bad weather turned the battlefield into an impenetrable mudbath. Between July 31 and November 10, when the assault was finally called off, both sides had lost a quarter of a million men.

Two other events in 1917 had massive consequences for the outcome of the war. The Russian people had suffered terribly and, in March, a revolution forced Tsar Nicholas II to abdicate. In November, the radical Bolsheviks seized power and imposed a communist dictatorship on their country. One of the first things they did was to make peace with Germany. The Bolsheviks assumed, incorrectly, that similar revolutions would soon sweep through Europe, especially Germany. So, believing that Germany would soon be a fellow communist regime who would treat Russia more fairly, they agreed to a very disadvantageous peace treaty at Brest-Litovsk in March 1918. Germany took vast tracts of land from the Russian empire – including Poland, the Ukraine, the Baltic states and Finland. For Germany, this was a great victory. Not only had they added a vast chunk of territory to their eastern border, they could now concentrate all their forces on defeating the British and French.

But, despite their successes, events were conspiring against Germany. After the Battle of Jutland had failed to win them dominance of the seas, Germany had drifted into a policy of "unrestricted" submarine warfare. This meant that German U-boats would attack any ship heading for Britain – even those belonging to neutral nations. It was a tremendously effective strategy, but it backfired disastrously. The submarine attacks caused outrage overseas, especially in the USA, and became one of the main reasons America turned against Germany. President Woodrow Wilson brought his country in on the side of the Allies on April 6, 1917, but it wasn't until the summer of 1918 that American troops began to arrive on the Western Front in great numbers.

The timing could not have been worse for the German army. The Ludendorff Offensive, named after German commander Erich Ludendorff, began on March 21, 1918. Forty-six divisions broke through weary British and French troops on the Somme, and swept on to Paris. For a while, it looked as if Germany would win the war on the Western Front as well as the Eastern Front. So alarmed were the British that Field Marshal Haig issued an order to his troops on April 12, commanding them to stand and fight until they were killed: "With our backs to the wall and believing in the justice of our cause each one of us must fight to the end," it said.

But the Ludendorff Offensive turned out to be the last desperate fling of a dying army. Faced with stubborn British resistance, and fresh and eager American troops, the German advance ground to a halt. The German army had no more to give. At home, the German population, starved after four years of blockade by the Royal Navy, was on the verge of a revolution. In August 1918, the Allies made a massive breakthrough against the German front lines in northern France, and began an inexorable push towards the German border. Facing mutiny among his armed forces, revolution at home, and an inevitable invasion of home territory, the kaiser abdicated and the German government called for an armistice – a cease-fire. The time was set to be 11:00am on November 11, 1918. Fighting continued right up to the final seconds.

In his memoirs, General Ludendorff recalled the situation with anguish: "[By] 9 November, Germany, lacking any firm guidance, bereft of all will, robbed of her princes, collapsed like a pack of cards. All that we had lived for, all that we had bled four long years to maintain, was gone."

Although there were wild celebrations in Allied cities, many of the soldiers on the Western Front took the news with a weary shrug. "We read in the papers of the tremendous celebrations in London and Paris, but could not bring ourselves to raise even a cheer," wrote one New Zealand artillery man. "The only feeling we had was one of great relief."

The guns fell silent. Grasses, weeds and vines gradually crept over the desolate battlefields, covering the withered trees and ravaged fields, and turning the blackened earth to a pleasanter green. Crude, makeshift burial grounds were replaced by towering monuments and magnificent cemeteries. Many of those killed found a final resting place among long rows of marble crosses, each with a name, rank and date of death engraved upon it. Others, whose torn remains were incomplete and unrecognizable, were buried under crosses marked *known unto God*.

It would be another 10 or 15 years before the charred trucks, shell carriages and tanks were taken away for scrap, and the shell holes filled in. By the time war broke out again in 1939, much of the land was being farmed again; but the faint smell of gas still lingered in corners and copses, rusting rifles and helmets still littered the scarred ground, and shell cases, shrapnel fragments and bones could still be tilled from the battlefields of northern France and Belgium – as they can to this day.

The Angels of Mons

September 1914

IT WAS EARLY AFTERNOON on August 24, 1914. Captain Arthur Osborn of the 4th Dragoon Guards had had a nightmare couple of weeks. Now, waiting to intercept units of German cavalry, he looked at the thundery sky and was reminded of a verse from Revelation 12 in the Bible:

"And the great dragon was cast out…and his angels were cast out with him."

His present surroundings added nothing to his mood. He was in the Belgian mining town of Mons, a marshy area intersected with canals, and littered with towering slag heaps. He and his companions in the British Expeditionary Force (BEF) had been sent to France at the outbreak of war. Facing him, and the other British, French and Belgian troops, were one and a half million German soldiers, hellbent on reaching Paris as part of General Schlieffen's strategy to win a quick victory.

In between marching for days on end, Osborn and his men faced moments of terror when they were caught by advance German units or artillery fire. When their generals commanded them to stand and fight, they confronted hordes of enemy soldiers, advancing in ranks so thick, they seemed to resemble dark clouds sweeping though the green fields towards them. A soldier fighting in such conditions reaches a condition of exhaustion unimaginable to most people. In such a state, men reported seeing imaginary castles on the horizon, towering giants or squadrons of charging cavalry in the far distance – all, of course, hallucinations.

The losses the British troops were taking were disastrous – an average BEF infantry battalion of 850 men would be left with barely 30 by the time the German advance had been halted and the trenches set up. Osborn, and many others like him, could not help but feel they were living in apocalyptic times. It was during their desperate retreat that one of the strangest stories of the war arose: it was whispered that a host of angels had come to the aid of British troops at Mons. Not only had the angels saved the soldiers from certain death, but they had also struck down the attacking Germans. Extraordinary though the story was, it was widely believed for decades after the war ended.

During the early stages of the fighting, the army authorities allowed no real news out from the battlefield and, in consequence, wild and fanciful stories began to circulate. War correspondent Philip Gibbs wrote that the press and public were so desperate to know what was happening that "any scrap of description, any glimmer of truth, and wild statement, rumour, fairy tale or deliberate lie, which reached them from France or Belgium" was readily accepted. "The liars had a great time," he reflected.

In this feverish atmosphere, the story of the Angels of Mons began to circulate among the British public. Like all urban legends, it was always told second-hand – a friend of a friend had learned… a friend had heard of a letter from the front which mentioned… an anonymous officer had reported… The legend blossomed. Sometimes a mysterious, glowing cloud featured in the story, sometimes it was a band of ghostly horsemen or archers, or even Joan of Arc. But most of the time it was a host of angels, that had come to rescue the beleaguered British troops.

Many wild stories from this time were the result of government propaganda, but the origin of this one was more innocent. It was a newspaper article in the September 29 edition of the *London Evening News*, written by freelance journalist Arthur Machen. A fanciful and rather opaque piece of fiction, it tells of a group of British soldiers at Mons, under attack by a vast phalanx of German troops. As the Germans advance towards them, and death seems moments away, one of the soldiers mutters the motto *Adsit Anglis Sanctus Georgius* – May St. George be present to help the English. Just then, according to the story:

> "the roar of battle died down in his ears to a gentle
> murmur… [then] he heard, or seemed to hear thousands

shouting 'St. George! St. George!' And as the soldier heard these voices he saw before him, beyond the trench, a long line of shapes, with a shining about them. They were like men who drew the bow, and with another shout, their cloud of arrows flew singing and tingling through the air towards the German host [a large group of soldiers]."

The story had a potent mixture: England's patron saint and ghostly bowmen, the spirits of those archers, perhaps, who had won a famous English victory against the French at Agincourt in 1415. Perhaps the fiction was believed to be true because it appeared in the news section of the paper – probably due to problems fitting it elsewhere, or a simple misunderstanding by a designer on the paper, rather than any deliberate attempt by the *Evening News* to mislead its readers. The original tale was preposterous enough but, in the weeks and months after it was printed, the retellings became even more fanciful. British newspapers stoked the strange hysteria by reproducing illustrations showing pious British troops praying in their trench, as ranks of ghostly bowmen pour down deadly, glowing arrows on the approaching Germans. As it swept through the country, the tale evolved, with the bowmen becoming angel archers instead.

Machen never claimed his story had a grain of truth to it. "The tale is mere and sheer invention," he freely admitted. "I made it all up out of my own head." He was extremely embarrassed at the effect it had on the British public. But the authenticity of the story was still being debated decades after the war ended. In the late 1920s, one American paper carried a report quoting a German officer who declared the angels were actually motion picture images projected onto the clouds by aircraft. The idea, said the officer, had been to spread terror among the British soldiers, but the plan had backfired badly when the British assumed the ghostly figures were on their side. Curiously, this report took it for granted that the angels had appeared; it was merely offering a logical, if extremely implausible, explanation for why they were seen. And even in the 1970s and 80s, Britain's Imperial War Museum was still being asked about the authenticity of the story.

Nowadays, it is easy to scoff at the naiveté of those who believed such stories. But the fact that the tale was so widely believed tells us much about the society that fought the war. Captain Osborn, who appears at the start of this chapter, was lucky enough to survive, but thousands of other men had been killed in the opening months of the conflict. For those who had lost husbands or sons, there was a great need for consolation. Stories like the Angels of Mons brought reassurance to grieving relatives. For them, it was especially pleasing to note that God was so obviously on the side of the British, rather than the Germans.

Other unlikely stories continued to circulate throughout the war. Some were based on the usual far-fetched tales told by troops on leave from the trenches. It was widely believed, for example, that a renegade, international band of deserters ran loose in No Man's Land, the territory that lay between the opposing trenches. Other stories were deliberately fabricated by a British government propaganda unit, to bolster morale at home and also to lure America into the war on the side of the Allies.

In fact, for most of the time, German military forces behaved no better or worse than any other army. But, during the desperate early stage of the war, the German army had dealt brutally with any resistance from Belgian civilians to the invasion of their country – hostages were shot and villages massacred in reprisals. From the bones of such stories, British propaganda built a picture of the entire German people as a nation of godless barbarians. "Huns" was the term most often used, after the 4th-century soldiers of Attila, who had laid waste Rome and much of Italy.

Sometimes, this propaganda was almost ridiculous in its grotesque imagery. German soldiers, it was reported, had replaced the bells in Belgian church steeples with hanging nuns. Later in the war, stories were planted in the British press saying that the Germans had their own corpse factory, and that German soldiers killed in the fighting were sent there, so their bodies could be made into explosives, candles, industrial lubricants and boot polish.

The reaction such stories produced in Britain was sometimes equally bizarre. German dachshund dogs were stoned in the street. Shops with German immigrant owners were attacked and looted. The British royal family changed their German name of Saxe-Coburg-Gotha to Windsor. But mainly the stories created an atmosphere of intense fear and hatred of the enemy – as they were intended to do. Many of those who rushed to join the army in the opening months of the war were convinced they were fighting for civilization against a barbaric foe who would rape and mutilate their wives and children, should they ever cross the channel and invade Britain.

After the war, people realized that much of the news concerning the war, and their German enemy, had been outright lies. Newspapers would never be so openly trusted again. This attitude still persisted during the Second World War. This meant that in the early stages of that war, when stories of German death camps first broke, they were widely disbelieved. It was too much of an echo of the corpse factory story from 20 years before.

STRANGE MEETINGS
DECEMBER 1914

FOR MOST PEOPLE, Christmas is a time of celebration – presents to be opened with family and friends, heaps of rich food and drink, and optimism for the New Year. So imagine the feelings of men exhausted from four months of heavy fighting: homesick, missing their wives and children, and spending Christmas Eve shivering in muddy, waterlogged trenches. Their lives seemed to be lived out in a dark looking-glass world of cold, hunger and hatred. But Christmas sometimes works a strange magic, even in conditions like these, as it did in the December of 1914.

On Christmas Eve, the German guns on the Western Front fell silent soon after dark. No shells, no murderous chatter of machine gun fire, not even the occasional whine of a sniper's bullet. The British soldiers followed their example. It was a cold, clear night, and stars burned brightly in the sky. The utter silence that fell over the trenches created an eerie atmosphere. Then, along some sections of the trenches, lookouts on the British side saw strange lights flickering and swinging along the German front line. Some shots were fired. But, when officers peered through their trench periscopes or binoculars, they were amazed to see that these lights were illuminated Christmas decorations. There were even some small Christmas trees hung with candles. At first, many soldiers remained suspicious. After all, the British commander-in-chief, Field Marshal French, had issued a stern order to all units warning of a German attack over Christmas or New Year. "Special vigilance will be maintained during these periods," they had been told.

Then the German soldiers started singing carols. Some were unfamiliar to the British soldiers, but others, such as *Stille Nacht* – "Silent Night" – were very well known to them. Then the British soldiers began to sing carols too, the two sides serenading each other with shared Christmas memories. Perhaps it was hearing these familiar songs that led to the amazing events of the following day.

Dawn on Christmas morning brought a thick mist over some sections of the Front but, when it cleared, the most extraordinary scene revealed itself. All along No Man's Land, in some places almost as far as the eye could see, soldiers had ventured out to meet their enemies. They huddled around in small groups, usually based around one man who could speak the other side's language. Sometimes, French was the common language between them. Sometimes, men spoke no language at all, communicating with smiles and gestures. Soldiers swapped cigarettes, chocolate and beer or whiskey. Others, more daringly, exchanged items of equipment – belt buckles, regimental badges, even helmets. Before the war, many Germans had worked in England, and some gave letters

The strain of trench warfare showing on their faces, British and German troops mingle in No Man's Land on Christmas Day, 1914. They exchanged cigarettes, drinks and even items of uniform.

to be posted to friends or girlfriends they had hurriedly left in August. Several photographs were taken, showing groups of German and British troops huddling together, freezing cold but quite relaxed in each other's company.

Sometimes, meetings like these occurred when a truce had been arranged among the officers, to bury the dead left lying between the trenches. Here, burial parties stopped to talk to each other. In other parts of the Front, especially where opposing trenches were very close, soldiers simply called over, promising not to shoot their opponents if they would come out to meet them.

Over on the front line between Frelinghien and Houplines, Leutnant Johannes Niemann of the 133rd Royal Saxon Regiment faced the Scottish Seaforth Highlanders. His soldiers had boldly walked into the pockmarked land between the trenches to talk with their enemy. Now, to Niemann's astonishment, one of the Scottish soldiers had run up from his trench with a soccer ball. Then, within moments, two sets of goal posts were improvised with helmets on the frozen ground.

Niemann remembered the game clearly. Despite the language barrier, and the fact that these same men had been trying to kill each other only the day before, the game was remarkably good-natured. Both sides played with a fierce determination to win, but all kept quite rigorously to the rules, even without the advantage of a referee. The Germans were astonished to discover that these Scottish soldiers wore nothing under their kilts. Whenever a fierce tackle or a strong gust of wind revealed a Scotsman's buttocks, they would hoot and whistle like schoolboys.

The game went on for at least an hour, though soon enough word filtered back to the local German High Command. The senior officers there were strongly disapproving, and Niemann and the other junior officers were ordered to call their men back to their trenches immediately. "Still," Niemann later noted with some pride, "the game finished with a score of three goals to two in favour of Fritz against Tommy."

But not all the encounters were so friendly. Other matches were played with a marked animosity. A boxing match set up between two opposing regimental champions ended with the two men offering to finish each other off in a duel at one hundred paces.

In some parts of the Front, these strange meetings went on over the whole Christmas period. On December 30, one Yorkshire battalion received a message from their German counterparts warning them that they would have to start firing. The message explained, apologetically, that a German general was coming to inspect them that afternoon, and they had to put on a show of belligerence. When a British artillery battery was ordered to destroy a farmhouse just behind the German lines on January 1, they too sent word to the Germans warning them to leave the building.

Other Allied soldiers, such as the French and the Belgians, met their German counterparts too, but in far fewer numbers, and not with anything like the same cordiality. Perhaps the fact that the Germans were fighting from French or Belgian territory made the enmity between opponents more deeply felt and personal.

Field Marshal French's order of the day for Christmas Eve 1914, warning of a possible German attack, had been issued precisely because the Army High Command had feared that such contact with the enemy might occur. It had not been unusual, in earlier wars, for troops to fraternize with the enemy on Christmas Day. In the previous century, it was not unknown for opposing generals to sit down at Christmas dinner together.

The following December, after a year of dreary stalemate and occasional carnage, strict orders went out to both sides forbidding a repeat of the previous Christmas's goodwill.

"Nothing of the kind is to be allowed… this year. The artillery will maintain a slow gun fire on the enemy's trenches commencing at dawn, and every opportunity will be taken to inflict casualties upon any of the enemy exposing themselves," ran one order of the day to a British division.

Not everyone took notice of the order; but the fortunes of those who disobeyed were mixed. One officer in the Coldstream Guards, who went to shake hands with German soldiers who had come unarmed over No Man's Land, was sent home in disgrace. Other British troops, who had walked out to talk to their German opponents, were shelled by their own artillery. And, in most places, the open mixing of the previous year was successfully discouraged. One British officer noted with grim satisfaction that, when the Germans opposite started to sing carols, the British shelled them. Yet, even so, some troops still made friendly gestures to their enemies. On one part of the front line, opposing British and German soldiers lit fires in oil drums with pierced sides, and placed them along the tops of their trenches. "It was a wonderful sight," wrote one Scottish soldier. "I shall never forget it."

But, as the war dragged on, such old-fashioned civility became increasingly rare. As the casualty rate mounted, those who survived lost many of their friends and began to nurse increasingly bitter feelings about their enemy. By 1916 and 1917, such Christmas meetings had become extremely rare, although they did still occur in isolated parts of the Front. By then, for most soldiers, a Christmas truce seemed as distant and unlikely as an end to the war itself. Even so, senior officers on both sides gave orders to step up artillery bombardments over the Christmas period, to ensure any such fraternization would never be repeated.

THE GREAT ZEPPELIN CAMPAIGN

1915–1918

ON THE NIGHT OF MAY 31, 1915, the great dark shadow of German airship *LZ-38* loomed above the clouds over London. The size of an ocean-going liner, it sailed through the sky at a steady 80kmph (50mph). Four powerful engines made such a deafening drone, conversation between Captain Erich Linnarz and his crew was almost impossible.

Through gaps in the clouds, the city could be seen clearly enough. Londoners were not expecting any kind of attack, and the lights of the West End streets and playhouses blazed brightly below. The capital's inhabitants felt perfectly safe. The Western Front was a reassuring distance away. And German warships, which sometimes attacked British coastal towns, lacked the range to hit this far inland.

Linnarz looked around, feeling rather pleased with himself. He later reported, "not a searchlight or anti-aircraft gun was aimed at us before the first bomb was dropped." He gave a curt nod to the bombardier close by in the control cabin, and 150 bombs rained down on the city below. Watching from their lofty perch, the crew could observe their bombs exploding. It was an exhilarating display. Fires broke out and buildings collapsed. In all, 42 people died or were seriously wounded that night – and worse was to come.

The capital was visited by zeppelins, as the huge airships were known, throughout the summer. Named after their German inventor, Ferdinand, Graf von Zeppelin, who had been flying these massive hydrogen-filled behemoths

This near miss from a Zeppelin raid on London has left a huge crater, blown out all the windows and caused extensive damage, but at least the houses are still standing.

since 1897, they seemed to be the perfect weapon. Londoners grew to hate these sinister raiders. Although they did relatively little actual damage, the disruption and harm to morale they caused was formidable. Whenever a raid was on, traffic ground to a halt. People stared fearfully at the sky, and all electric lights were extinguished. When the bombs began to drop, people crouched in alleyways and cellars. They whispered in dread, in case their voices carried up to betray them. They were even afraid to strike a match to light a cigarette, in case the flare caught the attention of a zeppelin bombardier.

Despite its huge size, the zeppelin was almost invulnerable. Its main opponent, the fighter plane, could not fly high enough to attack it. Even when improvements in aircraft design allowed fighters to reach the altitude of a zeppelin, they still couldn't climb very quickly. So the invader would be long gone by the time the fighters got there. When the attacks began, 26 batteries of anti-aircraft (AA) guns were placed around London, and searchlights lit up the night sky with their bright, rapier beams. But these guns were also a new invention. The science of hitting flying machines, even ones as big as zeppelins, was complex. Hitting a moving target at that range, and priming a shell to explode at a particular height, were deadly arts yet to be perfected.

When war first broke out, the German kaiser, Wilhelm II, would not allow the zeppelins to be used over England. He was closely related to the British royal family, and he knew that bombing from the air would bring civilian casualties and severe family disapproval. But it soon became apparent that the war would not be over quickly; instead, it turned into a dreary stalemate with no end in sight, and the kaiser's own generals persuaded him it was his duty to use whatever advantage Germany might have.

So, in early January 1915, the first zeppelins appeared over the east coast of Britain, bringing massive disruption and anxiety. In this early stage of the war, the only threat zeppelin crews faced was the weather. Something so large and so ungainly was always going to be vulnerable to a strong wind. Zeppelins crashed in storms; but nothing the enemy could throw at them had any effect.

These days, we have spy satellites and distant early warning (DEW) radar systems, to give us advanced warning, within seconds, of any potential enemy missile or bomber attack – even from the other side of the world. During the First World War, such technology had scarcely been imagined, let alone made available. Instead, the British had to rely on a network of human spotters placed along the coast – much as they had done for the arrival of the Spanish Armada during the time of Queen Elizabeth I. But the zeppelin spotters had at least the advantage of being able to report their sightings by telephone, rather than a chain of bonfires. They also used a cumbersome device called an orthophone – a huge, trumpet-like listening apparatus designed to detect the distant drone of the zeppelin's engines.

As the war dragged on, the design of fighter aircraft and AA guns raced forward. In 1914, flimsy planes could barely fly the English Channel. But, by 1916, the British had developed both aircraft and AA guns which were capable – at least in theory – of hitting the vast, slow-moving zeppelins. They also armed their aircraft with incendiary bullets, which were fired from machine guns mounted above the plane's cockpit. These projectiles, which glowed white-hot when discharged, were intended to set the highly flammable zeppelins alight. Zeppelin crews carried no parachutes – the available weight these huge machines could lift into the air was limited, and fuel and bombs were given priority over the crew's safety. Once a zeppelin caught fire, the crew had virtually no chance of escape. But such weapons were a great danger to the British pilots too, often exploding when used.

As zeppelin crews reported near-misses and lucky escapes from anti-aircraft fire on the ground, it was quickly decided that night attacks would be safer. As it turned out, they were also tremendously harmful. Curiously, it was the threat of attack, more than any actual damage done, which caused the most harm. If zeppelins were detected in the night sky, the order would be given to extinguish all lights below. This *blackout*, as it became known, caused huge disruption and inconvenience, especially to factories and other local industries. But the blackout was also effective. Zeppelins sent out huge, powerful flares, hoping to find their way by briefly illuminating the land below. But launching such devices gave their position away to night fighter patrols and vigilant AA batteries.

As the zeppelins became more vulnerable to attack, they adopted more effective methods of defending themselves. Machine guns were mounted on top of their vast hulls. Manning them took special courage and stamina. A gunner would be tethered to his precarious position, exposed to both the machine guns of attacking fighter planes, and the freezing high-altitude temperatures and air currents. If he was injured or overcome by either, rescue was impossible.

One ingenious device employed to protect a zeppelin crew was the cloud car. Shaped like a fairground rocket ride, the car and its single passenger would be lowered from the interior of the zeppelin by a long cable that could dangle its load 800m (half a mile) below. The idea was that the zeppelin would lurk inside thick cloud, safely concealed from air and AA attack, while the cloud car dangled in the clear air beneath, too small to be seen in the vastness of the sky. Its passenger, in communication with the zeppelin via a telephone line, would then direct the ship towards its target. It was a hair-raisingly dangerous job. One cloud-car passenger was dashed to death on a cliff when his zeppelin flew too low over the coast. If the cable jammed or snapped, the cloud-car passenger was totally at the mercy of any enemy warplane that might spot him, and he could also be hit by bombs dropped from his own zeppelin. Yet, despite these additional dangers, there was no shortage of volunteers for cloud-car duty. Astonishingly, this was mainly because its passenger was allowed to smoke – an activity expressly forbidden in the zeppelin itself, with its highly inflammable, hydrogen-packaged fuselage.

For almost two years, the zeppelins were able to roam at will over Britain, their greatest foes the weather and their own occasional structural failures. But on September 2, 1916, everything changed. That evening, the crew of German airship *SL-11* and Lieutenant William Leefe Robinson, a pilot of 39 Squadron of the Home Defence Wing, Royal Flying Corps, were about to earn their place in history.

As the wet and dreary day drew to a close, 16 airships from the German navy and army services took to the air and began their long journey through the darkening skies over the North Sea. This was the largest fleet of airships so far assembled by the Germans, and their target was to be the British military headquarters in London.

Not all were zeppelins. Half of the fleet had been manufactured by the rival airship firm Schütte-Lanz, who made their flying machines with wooden, rather than light metal, frames. For the British, however, such differences were academic – the Schütte-Lanz airships were equally formidable. *SL-11*, for example, was 174m (570ft) long and 21m (70ft) high, and could carry a similar number of bombs.

Robinson and his fellow pilots had a new anti-zeppelin weapon in their arsenal; although it was one they had very little confidence in. The British had been using incendiary bullets against airships for as long as they had been trying to shoot them down. However, to date, these bullets had proved ineffective. New, more powerful incendiaries had been developed, but so far the results had been disastrous. The new type of bullet was prone to explode in the weapon firing it, and almost 20 British warplanes had been destroyed trying to use it.

As night fell, radio operators at listening stations picked up a noticeable increase in German wireless communications, suggesting a massive raid was in progress. Spotters along the coast were informed, and began to scan the skies for any incoming airships.

By ten o'clock that evening, the airship fleet had been detected as it approached the Norfolk coast. The massive sound of its combined engines hinted at the size of the attack. London AA gun batteries and airfields were alerted. Over on Sutton's Farm airfield, 30km (20 miles) southwest of London, Lieutenant Robinson prepared his *BE2* biplane for takeoff.

These lumbering two-seater planes were normally used as reconnaissance aircraft, but their wide wings and powerful engines enabled them to fly higher than many of the faster, more agile fighters in the Royal Flying Corps. As the *BE2s* earmarked to intercept zeppelins usually only carried one crew member, rather than two, the lack of extra weight helped the plane climb higher still. Robinson headed off into the moonless sky just after half past eleven. That night, he would be one of six pilots out to try their luck in the dangerous skies over the capital.

These days, flying at over 1.5km (1 mile) every three seconds, modern jet fighters can reach high altitudes in a matter of minutes. In 1916, it took an entire hour for Robinson's *BE2* to reach 3,000m (10,000 ft). Peering through the velvet sky, hoping to spot a looming black hull, he could see nothing. He even switched off his engine, in the hope of hearing the approaching airships.

Just after one in the morning, while flying over the docks at Gravesend, Robinson spotted a zeppelin, the *LZ-98*. Turning in to attack, he unleashed a hail of bullets into the vast body of the airship. Nothing happened – except that, as soon as the crew realized they were being attacked, they executed a standard zeppelin procedure. The *LZ-98* rose swiftly in the air, way out of reach of the *BE2*. But just as Robinson gave up and turned away, he caught sight of something else lurking in the clouds below. A searchlight had illuminated another airship.

It was the *SL-11*, returning home after dropping its bombs on the northern suburbs of the capital. Half an hour earlier, the airship had been the focus of most of the anti-aircraft guns of north and central London. They had failed; but the volume of fire bursting around the *SL-11* had convinced its captain, Hauptmann Wilhelm Schramm, to turn his giant ship around and head further north.

As Robinson wheeled in to face his enemy, the *SL-11* vanished into a bank of clouds. Twenty minutes passed. Then, just when he was contemplating returning home before his fuel ran out, Robinson spotted the airship again. AA guns were firing up at it, and searchlights occasionally caught the huge hull in their beam.

He turned his *BE2* to face the shadow. This time, he was determined not to let his quarry slip away. But, just as he was preparing to fire his machine gun, his plane rocked alarmingly, buffeted by an explosion just underneath him. The AA guns below were also firing up at the airship – and exploding at the height they guessed their target was flying. They had no idea a British plane was up there too. In those days, pilots did not have radios to alert their comrades below, but the Royal Flying Corps did have a procedure for such emergencies. The pilot could fire off a flare to let the AA gunners know he was up there. But Robinson knew this would also warn the airship crew that he was stalking them. So he pressed on, hoping his own plane would not be hit.

The *BE2* approached its target from below, swooping over to the front of the hull. Then, as the vast shadow loomed over him, Robinson began to fire his incendiary bullets into the great, gas-filled body of the ship. His highly detailed account of the attack makes for a vivid read:

"I made nose down in the direction of the zeppelin. I saw shells bursting and night tracer shells flying around it. When I drew closer I noticed that the anti-aircraft aim was too high or too low; also a good many some 800ft [240m] behind… I flew along about 800ft below it from bow to stern and distributed one drum [of ammunition] along it. It seemed to have no effect."

As he began placing a fresh magazine on his machine gun – a tricky process, as he had to fly at the same time – the airship machine gunners opened up. He weaved away into the black night, then headed in for a second attempt. Firing all along the side of the airship, he emptied his entire ammunition drum; and still nothing happened.

On that run, he flew so close to the crew control car, he could see the silhouettes of men inside. Perhaps they were not aware he was attacking them. After all, they were engrossed in their bombing of the territory below, and the roar of their own engines would have prevented them from hearing his tiny plane. By now, Robinson was beginning to feel angry. The incendiaries obviously posed far more danger to the pilot firing them than to the airship they were aimed at. But, risking attack from the guns of both the Germans and his own side, he flew in for a third time, as close as he dared:

"I then got close behind it (by this time I was very close – 500ft [150m] or less below) and concentrated one drum on one part (underneath rear)… I had hardly finished the drum before I saw the part fired at glow. When the third drum was fired there were no searchlights on the zeppelin and no anti-aircraft was firing. I quickly got out of the way of the falling zeppelin and being very excited fired off a few red Very lights* and dropped a parachute flare."

Something awesome had happened inside the body of the airship. The gas bag where he had concentrated his fire had ignited, lighting up the inside of the hull like a magic lantern. Then the stern of the airship burst open in an immense explosion, which tossed his tiny plane like a paper dart in a gale. The fire quickly spread along the entire body of the ship. Once he had regained control of his plane, Robinson could

*Very lights were bright flares, fired from a specially adapted pistol.

see many of the crew throwing themselves out of the zeppelin, to avoid being burned to death.

He let off his flares because he was determined the AA gunners below should know it was he who had downed the airship and not them. As he turned his plane to return to the airbase, he noted that the *SL-11* had crashed into the ground. So bright was the blazing hull that he could make out the shapes of houses all along the outer rim of northeast London.

Robinson had proved it was possible to down these huge machines. Despite the early hour, all over London people rushed out into the streets to sing and dance. Church bells rang, sirens wailed, and ships' horns and motor horns tooted. The airships had caused such dread, for so long; but now it seemed there was a way of hitting back at them.

For the German airship crews still approaching the city over the flatlands of Suffolk and Cambridgeshire that night, the huge blaze lighting up the sky in the far distance was an ominous sight. Their airships were not indestructible after all. Perhaps the demise of *SL-11* affected their performance, because the raid on London that night was not a success. Although the 16 airships dropped a huge number of bombs between them, only four people were killed and another 12 injured. Damage to buildings was put at £21,072. In comparison, 16 trained airmen aboard *SL-11* had lost their lives, and their £94,000 airship had been destroyed.

SL-11 fell to earth behind the Plough Inn pub, by the village of Cuffley, Hertfordshire. The next day, the village was besieged by sightseers, and the country lanes nearby were clogged with cars, carts, bicycles and pedestrians. The burned-out frame of tangled steel and wire, with the broken gondolas and smashed engines, was a startling sight. To the side of the wreckage, a green tarpaulin was laid on the ground to hide the charred remains of those members of the crew who had not leaped to their deaths. Other bodies would be found in the next few days, scattered over the countryside on *SL-11*'s last, doomed flight path.

Robinson's method of attack – a sustained burst of incendiary fire at one concentrated spot – was immediately passed on to all fighter pilots likely to encounter a German airship. Such daring deserved reward. Robinson was presented with the Victoria Cross – the highest award for bravery that can be given to members of the British armed forces. But thereafter, the fortunes of this 21-year-old fighter pilot declined. He was shot down over German-occupied France eight months later, and spent the rest of the war in a prison camp, where he was badly treated because he had shot down the *SL-11*. At the end of the war, he became one of many millions of victims of a massive flu epidemic that swept through the world, and died on New Year's Eve, 1918.

Robinson's victory had an impact far beyond the simple destruction of one airship. The swaggering confidence that airship crews had displayed in their mess halls and barracks was gone. Nights away from flying duty were haunted by dreams of burning airships. Now, they were no longer invulnerable, like the gods of ancient Greece or Rome, casting death and destruction down from the skies. They too were flesh and blood. When death came, as it did with increasing regularity, the entire crew would perish.

From then on, the zeppelin raids grew less frequent and more costly. From the spring of 1917, German Gotha bombers were sent over London instead. They were faster, flew higher, and could defend themselves from fighter planes more effectively. Yet the Germans still nursed high hopes for their magnificent airships. By the end of the war, the latest model zeppelins were even earmarked for a raid on New York. Luckily for the Americans, the war ended before such an attack could be mounted.

THE BATTLE OF JUTLAND
MAY-JUNE 1916

IN LATE MAY 1916, anyone climbing the heathery hills of Hoy in the Scottish Orkney Islands could have peered through the mist of the vast Scapa Flow inlet and seen one of the most magnificent sights in naval history. For here was the home of the British Grand Fleet. Almost as far as the eye could see sat row upon row of battleships, battlecruisers, cruisers, destroyers – and scores of lesser vessels scurrying between these deadly ships with supplies, men and messages. Each ship was spaced at a neat interval and at exactly the same angle to every other – a visible representation of the discipline and tradition of this most prestigious fighting force. And, astonishingly, the power of the British navy did not end with this vast collection of ships. There were other bases too, at Cromarty, Moray Firth and Rosyth, along the eastern coast of Scotland. Each contained a formidable battle squadron of warships, all under the command of Admiral John Jellicoe.

At the time of the First World War, Britain had the greatest fleet in the world. They needed it too. Island Britain had an empire that stretched from the Arctic to Antarctic Circles. Their warships protected the fleets of cargo ships which carried goods and raw materials to and from British colonies. During wartime, the warships also prevented cargo ships from delivering goods to Britain's enemies. Most crucial of all, the British fleet ensured that supplies and troops from England could sail safely across the Channel to the Western Front in northern France. Only Germany had a fleet powerful enough to threaten the British. As the head of state of an up-and-coming superpower, Kaiser Wilhelm II had wanted to build a rival navy to complement Germany's growing importance in the world. But Wilhelm's policy was a double-edged sword. His insistence on building a powerful navy had soured previously good Anglo-German relations, and had been one of the main reasons Britain joined France and Russia against Germany when war broke out.

Today, it is difficult to imagine the hold battleships had on the imagination of people at the start of the 20th century. In the early 21st century, such weapons are largely obsolete; aircraft carriers, warplanes with their formidable arsenal of bombs and missiles, and the intangible threat of terrorism are the stuff of modern warfare. But, at the start of the First World War, the battleship was considered the superweapon of its day. The largest and most heavily armed battleships were known as dreadnoughts – after *HMS Dreadnought*, the first of their kind, launched in 1906. *Dreadnought* weighed a formidable 17,900 tons and packed a mighty punch with ten 12-inch* (30cm) guns. By the time war broke out many of these dreadnought battleships had even bigger guns – 13.5-inch (34cm) monsters, that could fire a shell weighing 640kg

*The guns on warships were referred to by the width (in inches) of the shells they fired. A 12-inch gun fired a shell that was 12 inches wide.

(1,400lb) over 21km (13 miles). These guns were housed in pairs in large turrets, usually at the front and rear of the ship. Such weaponry gave the battleship its ferocious bite. Each gun turret had a crew of around 70 men, split into teams who performed the complex task of bringing up shells and propulsive charges from the ship's magazine, and then loading, aiming and accurately dispatching them. Working in such a turret could be exceptionally dangerous. If an enemy shell hit the turret, the entire mechanism would be engulfed in a massive explosion, killing everyone inside it.

HMS Dreadnought overshadowed every other warship afloat. Not only was it very powerfully armed, it was fast and shielded by a thick metal protective covering. This ship carried a crew of over a thousand men, and was nearly 215m (700ft) from bow (front) to stern (rear). The arrival of *HMS Dreadnought* began a ruinously expensive arms race between Britain and Germany. By the time war broke out, Britain had built 28 such ships, and Germany 16.

The revolutionary dreadnoughts were also joined by another new kind of warship, the battlecruiser. The first of their kind was *HMS Invincible*, launched in April 1907.

Battlecruisers were smaller but almost as heavily armed as dreadnoughts, with eight 12-inch (30cm) guns. They were faster than battleships, having a top speed of around 25 knots, compared to a battleship's 21. But this speed was gained at the expense of lighter protection.

When war began in August 1914, a full-scale confrontation between the British and German fleets seemed inevitable – in fact, both countries had built up their massive navies to face such a task. The German fleet may have been smaller than the British fleet, but its ships were better designed. The Germans also made very effective use of their U-boats, sinking so many cargo ships bound for Britain that the country was often in danger of starvation. But, throughout the war, the British never lost control of the sea. The Royal Navy placed a blockade around German waters, preventing vital goods from getting in. This caused great difficulty for Germany's war industries, and ensured that there was never enough food for her home population.

Barely six months into the war, the German battlecruiser *Blücher* was sunk in the North Sea, with great loss of life. The disaster led to the sacking of the German navy commander-in-chief, Admiral Ingenohl. But it also encouraged his successor, Admiral Hugo von Pohl, to be extremely cautious. Then, in February 1916, suffering from ill health, von Pohl resigned. He was replaced by Admiral Reinhard Scheer, a far more aggressive and daring commander-in-chief.

For the first two years of the war, each navy had tested the strength of its opponents, tentatively pushing and probing, engaging in small-scale skirmishes, with only the occasional battle. But, as the carnage of the Western Front continued with no visible benefit to either side, pressure mounted on the German navy's High Command to force the British into a do-or-die battle that could tip the balance of the war Germany's way.

Scheer decided that the German fleet would try to lure the British into the North Sea for a grand confrontation. Such a move would be called a "high-risk strategy" today. If Scheer succeeded, the war would be as good as won. With its fleet destroyed, Britain would be unable to prevent a German naval blockade around her coastal waters. Food supplies would quickly run out, and the country would starve. British troops and supplies would no longer be able to travel safely across the Channel. The great British politician Winston Churchill once described Admiral Jellicoe as the only man who could lose the war in an afternoon. In the early summer of 1916, Jellicoe had the chance to do just that.

Scheer's plan was simple enough. He would send a battlecruiser squadron into the North Sea, under the command of Admiral Franz von Hipper. Then he would follow at a distance with his High Seas Fleet. The British, it was hoped, would send out their own battlecruisers to intercept Hipper's ships. These would almost certainly come from the base at Rosyth, which was the nearest to the outgoing German ships. When the British were sighted on the horizon, Hipper would change course, and lead the enemy back to Scheer's main battle fleet. Here, outnumbered, they would be destroyed.

The plan also assumed that the main British naval force – the aptly named Grand Fleet – would take to sea too, from the more northerly base of Scapa Flow. Here, Scheer meant for lurking U-boats to pick them off as they sailed to intercept him; and he intended to use zeppelins to keep watch on the British navy and radio in information on the movements of their ships.

But, like many simple plans, there were unforeseen hitches...

On May 31, 1916, Scheer put his plan in motion. From bases on the northern coast of Germany, the High Seas Fleet took to sea. Admiral von Hipper set out ahead with five battlecruisers and another 35 smaller ships, to try to lure the British navy into battle. Scheer followed on, in the battleship Friedrich der Grosse, accompanied by 60 other battleships, battlecruisers, cruisers and destroyers, and sundry smaller boats. By one o'clock that afternoon, the two German squadrons were way out in the North Sea, 80km (50 miles) apart.

As they had intended, von Hipper's squadron was soon sighted by the British reconnaissance ships that patrolled the coast off Germany. British intelligence had also picked up and decoded German radio signals which indicated that there was a build up of German ships in the North Sea. As foreseen by Scheer, Admiral Jellicoe immediately ordered his Rosyth battlecruiser squadron, under Admiral Beatty, to take to sea.

But, unknown to Sheer, Jellicoe was already at sea with his Grand Fleet, patrolling an area of the North Sea known as the "Long Forties", 180km (110 miles) east of Aberdeen. Jellicoe ordered the Grand Fleet to head south and follow Beatty. Between them, the two British admirals had 149 ships under their command.

The stage was set for an epic confrontation. To this day, no greater naval battle has ever taken place. The opposing admirals, perched high in command posts above the decks of their ships, began a game that was a strange combination of hide-and-seek and chess. At stake were the lives of 100,000 sailors, the fate of nearly 250 ships and, quite possibly, the outcome of the First World War. Jellicoe, particularly, was hoping for a victory to match Trafalgar. There, in 1805, the Royal Navy under Admiral Nelson had destroyed the French and Spanish fleets, and left Britain in undisputed control of the sea for the next century.

Right from the start, Scheer's scheme did not go to plan. The U-boats stationed outside the bases on the Scottish coast failed to attack the British ships as they emerged to patrol the

North Sea. A technical problem meant that wireless orders permitting them to engage their enemy were never received.

Scheer's novel use of zeppelins as reconnaissance aircraft was also a failure, due to bad weather and poor visibility. The zeppelins could see almost nothing through cloud or foggy haze. This was a major drawback. Today, thanks to radar and satellite surveillance, navy commanders can detect an approaching enemy long before his ships or aircraft are even over the horizon. In 1916, navy ships and guns were immeasurably more sophisticated and powerful than those used by Nelson at Trafalgar; but their communication and detection technology was much the same. Scheer and Jellicoe might have had guns which could fire a heavy shell 22km (14 miles), but they still looked for their enemy with a telescope and naked eye. Also, due to the danger of wireless communications being intercepted by the enemy, in battle they still preferred to communicate with their ships using signal flags and semaphore.*

Early that afternoon, neither admiral knew the size of the enemy fleet fast approaching them. The British thought only

*A method of ship-to-ship communication whereby particular hand positions, indicated by a sailor carrying two flags, stand for letters of the alphabet.

Hipper's squadron was at sea. And Scheer had no idea he was soon to face the entire Grand Fleet.

Beatty's fleet first sighted von Hipper's ships at around two o'clock, when they were about 121km (75 miles) off the Danish coast of Jutland. Thereafter, the epic confrontation that followed would be known as the Battle of Jutland.

The first shots were fired about 15 minutes later, between small scout ships, which sailed ahead of the main fleets. The day was quite hazy, and the sun was now well behind the German ships, giving them a much better view of their approaching enemy.

Beatty sailed forward to engage von Hipper's forces. By then, it was around half past three. Beatty knew the Grand Fleet was coming up behind him, but he would be on his own for several crucial hours before Jellicoe caught up with him. Hipper, in turn, knew he had to lure Beatty's ships into the jaws of the High Seas fleet behind him. As they had done in the days of Nelson and Trafalgar, both fleets sailed "in line" – that is, one after the other, in tight formation.

At ten to four, the battlecruisers began firing at each other. The odds seemed to be on Beatty's side. He had six

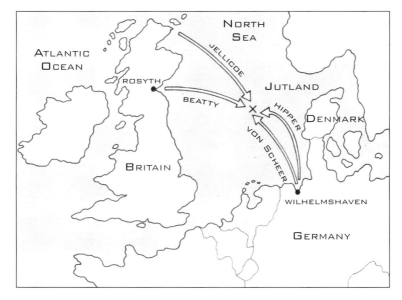

The scene of the Battle of Jutland

battlecruisers, where Hipper had five. Almost immediately, firing between the opposing forces was so constant that each squadron seemed to be navigating its way through a thick forest of towering shell splashes. Bizarrely, in the No Man's Land between the fleets, a small sailing boat sat motionless. Its sails hung limp in the still air as deadly shells whistled and screamed, arcing high over the heads of the hapless sailors on board.

The superiority of the German guns and ships soon became obvious. Just after four o'clock, just 12 minutes into the fighting, the British battlecruiser *Indefatigable* became the first major casualty of the day. The German ship *Von Der Tann* had landed three shells on her almost simultaneously. *Indefatigable* disappeared in a vast cloud of black smoke, twice the height of her mast, and fell out of line, as she was hit by two more shells from *Von Der Tann*. Inside *Indefatigable* something terrible was happening. Searing flames were gnawing at her ammunition supplies. Thirty seconds after the second shells hit home, the entire ship exploded, sending huge fragments of metal high into the air. She rolled over and sank moments later. Only two men on board survived, rescued by a German torpedo boat.

Among several other British ships, Beatty's own battlecruiser *Lion* was hit, when a shell penetrated the central turret, blowing half the roof into the air and killing the entire gun crew. The roar of the guns, and the whistle of the shells as they approached, was enough to distract anyone from what was happening to other ships around them. Aboard the *Lion*, Beatty barely noticed the loss of *Indefatigable*. He had enough troubles of his own. Six shells from von Hipper's flagship, the battlecruiser *Lützow*, hit his ship within four minutes, and fires raged on deck and below. Half an hour later, another explosion caused by slow-burning fires shot up as high as the masthead. But the *Lion*, and Beatty, survived to fight on.

The other British ships fighting alongside had to contend with similar problems. Twenty minutes later, the battlecruiser *Queen Mary* blew up too, breaking in half and sinking within 90 seconds. When the ammunition supplies exploded, the huge gun-turret roofs were blown 30m (100 feet) into the air. Only eight men survived from the entire ship. One of them was gunner Ernest Francis.

When the *Queen Mary* began to sink, he called out to his comrades around him: "Come on you chaps, who's coming for a swim?"

Someone replied, "She'll float for a long time yet."

But Francis knew in his bones he had to get away. Diving into the freezing, oily water, he began to swim as fast as he could away from his ship. Within a minute there was a huge explosion, and chunks of metal filled the air around him. Only diving deep beneath the waves saved him from being killed by

HMS Queen Mary *disappears in a cloud of smoke during the Battle of Jutland. Only eight men survived, from a crew of over 1,200. The ship sank in a minute and a half.*

flying fragments. When he reached the surface, gasping for breath, he was immediately dragged under again by the downward suction of the ship as it sank. Beneath the water, he felt utterly helpless and resigned to death.

"What's the use of your struggling?" he said to himself. "You're done."

But something made him strike out for the surface. Just as he was about to lose consciousness, he broke through the waves. Ahead was a piece of floating debris, and Francis wrapped his wrist around a rope trailing from it before he became unconscious. Eventually he was rescued, but not before an earlier ship had picked up the few other survivors, leaving him for dead.

Beatty had seen the destruction of the *Queen Mary* at close hand. In the strange and rather callous manner of the British upper class at war, he remarked on the loss of the *Queen Mary* and *Indefatigable*, and over 2,000 lives: "There seems to be something wrong with our bloody ships today."

There was something wrong with the British ships: they were badly designed. German warships had solid bulkheads (the partitions inside a vessel) passable only by going to the upper deck and then down into the next section. British ships had bulkheads with doors that permitted passage between them. This was far more convenient, of course, but a serious weakness when a massive explosion ripped through a ship. The British also had a much more careless attitude to their ammunition. German shells were kept locked away in blast-proof containers until they were ready to be fired. British gunners piled their shells next to their guns. So they were far easier to set off accidentally if the ship was hit.

But Beatty's *sang froid* in the midst of the partial destruction of his own ship was admirable too. Unlike army generals who direct land battles from headquarters behind the front line, when fighting starts at sea, an admiral has just as much chance of being killed by an enemy shell as the most humble seaman.

Moments after the *Queen Mary* sank, Scheer's German High Seas Fleet was spotted steaming over the horizon to join von Hipper's battlecruiser squadron. Jellicoe and his Grand Fleet were still 20km (12 miles) away. Beatty's composure was being tested to the limit. Facing both Scheer's and Hipper's forces, and two battlecruisers down, Beatty gave the signal for a 180° turn. Scheer's plan, to use Hipper's forces to entice the British into the jaws of the High Seas Fleet, was now being turned on its head. As the German ships pursued the fleeing British, Beatty was now luring them into the massed fire power of the British Grand Fleet.

Shortly after five o'clock that afternoon, Scheer's fleet had come close enough to Beatty's retreating ships to begin attacking the stragglers. But, an hour later, Jellicoe's fleet of 24 battleships was steaming over the horizon. No matter how good the German ships were, they were now heavily outnumbered. Scheer was in serious trouble, and he sent out an order for his ships to head north.

Jellicoe was puzzled. From his position high on his flagship *Iron Duke*, he could observe the enemy turning away from him; but he was suspicious. Was Scheer trying to lead them into a trap, hoping perhaps that the British would blunder into a minefield, or into the path of waiting submarines? There was too much at stake. So Jellicoe decided not to follow. Instead, his ships were ordered to head south, where Jellicoe guessed they might once again make contact with the German fleet.

Meanwhile, von Hipper's ship *Lützow* had been badly damaged and he was forced to abandon her, transferring to the battlecruiser *Seydlitz*, and then to the *Moltke*. But the *Lützow* still managed to sink another British ship. The unlucky vessel was the very first battlecruiser, *Invincible* – the third major victim of the day. At half past six, a shell hit one of her gun turrets, causing a huge explosion which broke the ship in two. Of the 1,032 men on board, only six survived. For a while, both the bow and stern of this huge, 17,000-ton battlecruiser stood motionless in the water, like two church spires in a sunken village. Then the stern began a relentless descent to the bottom of the sea. The bow stayed upright until the next day, when it too sank. Those trapped inside must have spent an agonizing night, wondering what on earth was happening to them in their topsy-turvy world. Expecting to be swallowed by the sea when the ship went vertical in the water, their inevitable death was drawn out for a miserable few hours more.

As the evening wore on, Jellicoe's intuition that the German ships would head south proved correct. Soon after seven, the two fleets sighted each other again. Scheer made several moves to try to place his fleet at an advantage to the British. Both sides were following a tactic known as *crossing the T*. The idea was to line up your fleet of warships at a right angle to your opponent's, as they approached you in a straight line, so your fleet made the top of the "T" and the enemy fleet made the descending stroke. In that way, a commander could fire all the guns aboard his ships, both bow and stern, while his enemy would only be able to use his front guns.

But Scheer failed to outwit his enemy and, disastrously, found his ships scattered at an angle to the approaching British fleet. Worse still, the sun was now behind the British, and it was only possible to see them by the flash of their guns. At this point in the battle it was British shells that were falling with greater accuracy, while Scheer's ships were faltering.

It was at this moment that Scheer made the most ruthless decision of the day. To avoid his entire fleet being reduced to wreckage by the much larger British force, Scheer ordered Admiral Hipper to take his squadron of four battlecruisers and sail straight at the British fleet. His signal read: "Battlecruisers at the enemy! Give it everything!" There was a cruel logic to his decision. Hipper's fleet was made up of older and less powerful warships; Scheer would be saving his best ships to fight another day. This action has subsequently become known as the *death ride*. Scheer intended the British fleet to concentrate their fire on von Hipper's force, allowing the rest of his High Seas Fleet to turn away and escape.

Von Hipper's ships – *Derfflinger*, *Seydlitz*, *Moltke* and *Von der Tann* – had been in the thick of the action since the battle began. All had sustained serious damage. As they headed out into the fading light, each ship's captain was convinced he would not live to see the coming night. But, in warfare, nothing is predictable.

Ahead of them, Beatty and Jellicoe's ships seemed to stretch in a curve as far as they could see. Every one of these British ships began to fire directly on the four approaching German battlecruisers. Leading these warships was the *Derfflinger*. Its chief gunnery officer, Georg von Hase, recorded:

> *"[We] now came under a particularly deadly fire... steaming at full speed into this inferno, offering a splendid target to the enemy while they were still hard to make*

out... Salvo after salvo fell around us, hit after hit struck our ship."

Both the main rear turrets of the *Derfflinger* suffered direct hits, exploding with horrific consequences for those inside. But, thanks to good design, the rest of the ship survived. The other German battlecruisers suffered similar blows but, although they took many hits from British shells, these formidable ships were not blown to pieces.

Von Hipper was a brave commander, but he had no intention of committing suicide. Once he was sure the rest of the German fleet had escaped, his ships turned away to rejoin the rear of Scheer's departing squadrons. Again Jellicoe was suspicious. Rather than following von Hipper's ships directly, he turned south and raced to catch them via a more indirect route. Just as the sun was sinking on the horizon, von Hipper's slower squadron was caught again by the British. This time, they were not so lucky. *Lützow* sustained more damage and would sink later that night, and *Seydlitz* and *Derfflinger* were badly damaged.

In the dark the two opposing navies continued to exchange fire, but the main action was over. The German battleship *Pommern* was one of the final victims of the battle. Four torpedoes from British destroyers caught her close to home, and all 866 men on board were killed.

Dawn broke around three o'clock on the morning of June 1. Jellicoe had hoped to resume contact with the German fleet at first light, but his lookouts strained their eyes over an empty sea. The German ships were in sight of their home port, and the battle was over.

The two greatest navies in the world had taken part in the one great sea battle of the First World War. In fact, it was to be the last great sea battle in history. Thereafter, battleships would never again meet in such numbers. As the century wore on, there would be naval weapons even deadlier than the great guns that battleships carried – insidious submarines, phalanxes of dive bombers and, more recently, fast and accurate guided missiles. All of these technological advances made battleships too vulnerable to be useful weapons.

Scheer's gamble had failed, but the events of the day had shown that he had had every right to be confident. Germany's ships were better than Britain's, and they had proved this by sinking more of their enemy's fleet. The British lost 14 ships and 6,274 men; the Germans, 11 ships and 1,545 men. On the day after the battle, it looked like a German victory. But, in the end, the might of the Royal Navy had prevailed. Britain still controlled the sea. Like the other grand battles of 1916 at Verdun and the Somme, a clash of huge opposing forces had taken place, and nothing had changed. Jellicoe had not lost the war in an afternoon after all. He hadn't won it either; but he *had* ensured that Germany would not win it.

After the battle, the tactics employed by Jellicoe and Beatty were dissected and discussed in clinical detail. Communication between the British ships had been very poor and Jellicoe, in particular, was criticized for not attacking the German fleet with more enthusiasm. But, with hindsight, the British still came out of it less badly than the Germans. It only took them a day to recover from the battle, before Jellicoe was able to announce that his fleet was once again ready for whatever threat it might face. The German High Seas Fleet, on the other hand, never put to sea again.

The outcome of the Battle of Jutland had far-reaching consequences. As the High Seas Fleet had proved unable to undermine British control of the seas, the German High

Command decided to adopt a policy of unrestricted U-boat warfare instead. This meant their submarines were given permission to attack any ship, including neutral ones, that they came across in British waters. This change of tactics led to the sinking of American ships, which in turn became one of the main reasons the United States entered the war against Germany – a move which assured her defeat.

The great German High Seas Fleet remained in port for the rest of the war. Boredom and poor rations led to mutinies and, at the end of the war, revolutionary insurrection. After the armistice of November 1918, the fleet was ordered to sail to Scapa Flow while peace terms were discussed in Paris. Shortly before the peace treaty was signed in the summer of 1919, it was suggested that the High Seas Fleet should be split up and its ships given to the victorious nations. But this was too much to bear for the skeleton crews of German sailors left aboard the ships, and so they scuttled – deliberately sank – their navy in Scapa Flow. Eventually, most of these vast, magnificent warships were raised from the sea bottom and towed away for scrap. But some still remain to this day, where they are a constant source of fascination for divers.

THE FIRST DAY OF THE SOMME

JULY 1, 1916

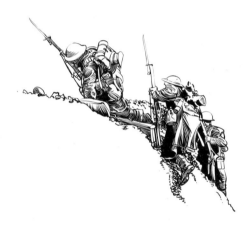

MOVING IMAGES WERE FIRST captured on film in the early 1890s. By the time the First World War broke out in 1914, movie cameras were an accustomed sight at any momentous event. Although the war is best remembered through photographs, much of it was also captured on black and white movie film. There are dramatic shots of artillery bombardments and full-scale infantry attacks, and chilling footage of the aftermath of close-quarter trench fighting. But one of the most haunting scenes of the war to be caught on film was not very spectacular at all. It shows a platoon of British soldiers resting before they "go over the top" on the morning of Saturday July 1, 1916 – the first day of the Battle of the Somme.

The time is about 7:25am, five minutes before the start of the attack. Filmed in a sunken road on the edge of the British front line, the men stare uneasily into the camera, faces tense with anxiety. They had been assured by their commanders that the forthcoming battle would be a walkover, but few, it seemed, believed this. Some share a final cigarette, one or two crack grim jokes, their mouths smiling or laughing, but their eyes full of fear. They all look immaculate – freshly shaven and well turned-out. For many, it would be their first time in battle. For most, it would be the last five or ten minutes of their lives. In the final moments before battle, they fix their bayonets to the ends of their rifles, and then they are gone. Within a few minutes, most were killed – caught out in the open by murderously effective machine-gun fire from the German trenches.

Bayonets fixed, British soldiers charge towards the German front lines, in this propaganda film made to commemorate the first days of the Battle of the Somme.

For a great number of the men embroiled in the Somme offensive, their journey to oblivion began in the first days following the outbreak of war. The soldiers who took part in this great battle were mainly volunteers who had joined up at the beginning. They had been dubbed *Kitchener's Army*, after the British war secretary, Lord Kitchener, who had appeared on recruitment posters asking for volunteers.

A million men flocked to join – many enticed by the promise that they could serve alongside their friends in what became known as *Pals battalions*. The idea was a good one in theory. Battalions within a regiment would be made up of men from the same town, or village, or workplace. They trained and worked together; and when the time came, they would fight together too.

The smoky, industrial town of Accrington, Lancashire, was one such community. It provided a Pals battalion for the East Lancashire Regiment. When war broke out, the town had hit hard times. A strike at the local textile machinery factory had ended in stalemate. A local cotton mill had also laid off 500 men and women. Undoubtedly, many men rushed to join up for the benefit of a soldier's pay as much as for any patriotic motive. The pay was, after all, twice what workers got in the mill or factory. Those not tempted by financial advantage faced more subtle pressures. One recruitment poster declared: "Will you fight for your King and Country, or will you skulk in the safety your fathers won and your brothers are struggling to maintain?" Another poster carried a more personal message, with a young man being shamed by his girlfriend's father: "Look here... if you're old enough to walk out with my daughter, you are old enough to fight for her and your Country."

Whatever these other reasons for joining, many men also did so out of plain, honest patriotism – an unquestioning feeling of duty and love of country. Accrington was a poor town, and a good number of those who flocked to enlist were malnourished and small in stature. Many failed their medical examination and were rejected as recruits, much to their disappointment and even humiliation. But such was the outcry in the region, these standards were dropped. Instead of requiring recruits who were at least 18, over 5ft 6in (168cm) tall and with a chest measurement of 35in (89cm), the rules were relaxed to 5ft 3in tall and 34in in the chest. Age was never a problem, as it was easy enough for 16 year olds to pass themselves off as older; and this was rarely checked. Local worthies who had huffed and puffed that the army top brass in London had "dared to think Lancashire patriotism could be measured in inches" were mollified.

When it was time to go, the new recruits lined up in the market square and marched down to the grimy granite railway station, watched by the whole town. They milled onto overcrowded platforms and waited for the steam train that would whisk them away from their familiar world. Seeing photographs of these men smiling bravely for the camera, their lower legs wrapped in puttees – tightly woven khaki cotton bands – which was part of the uniform at the time), it is plain that they had no idea what they were letting themselves in for.

As 1915 drew to a close, the British and French high commands became convinced that the way to end the war would be one "big push" – a massive attack, on a broad front, that would be enough to break the German lines and form a gap for the cavalry to rush through. Such a tactic, if successful, would reinstate a "war of movement" instead of the dreadful stalemate of the trenches. The spot chosen for the big push was the Somme, a chalky part of northern France near the Belgian border, named after the river that runs through it. The Somme had no particular strategic value. It was picked merely because this was the area of the Western Front where the British and French lines met – the most convenient spot for a combined attack.

But, as the new year began, the Germans had their own plans. Intending to "bleed the French army white" – wearing them down by constant attack – the German chief-of-staff, General von Falkenhayn, launched a dreadful battle of attrition on the French fortress of Verdun. Beginning in February 1916, Falkenhayn succeeded all too well, though at dreadful cost to his own army. The French army never really recovered from Verdun, and was certainly in no position to offer more than token support to the British when their own big push began in the summer.

In these circumstances, British commander-in-chief, Field Marshal Haig, and the Fourth Army commander, General Rawlinson, who commanded British troops in that section of the Front, began the final plan for the Battle of the Somme. They had a formidable army at their disposal. In August 1914, a British force of four infantry divisions and one cavalry division had been sent to defend Belgium. Now, nearly two years later, Haig had overall command of four armies, made up of 58 divisions.

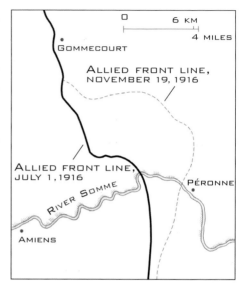

The front line on the Somme

Most of these men were Kitchener's Army recruits who had joined in 1914. Now they were trained and ready to fight, they were keen to show what they could do.

Right from the start, there was something painfully unimaginative about the tactics Haig and Rawlinson proposed, although Haig was convinced God had helped him with his battle plans. The date for opening the attack was July 1, at 7:30 in the morning, after a five-day bombardment by

1,350 artillery guns. It was all too obvious to the enemy. The five-day bombardment indicated a forthcoming attack in that sector as clearly as a skywriting biplane.

Those who had rushed to join up, in the first flush of enthusiasm for the war, were about to find out the true nature of 20th-century warfare. On the evening before the attack, the soldiers destined to take part in the first day of the battle were taken to front-line trenches. With extraordinary thoughtlessness, some squads of men were marched past open mass graves, freshly dug in anticipation of the heavy casualties to come. Then, as close to the enemy as most of them had ever been, they tried to settle into their uncomfortable final positions, and to ready themselves for the next morning. Sleep, with the artillery bombardment reaching a cacophonous peak, was quite impossible.

On the day before the beginning of the offensive, the commanding officers had briefed their men on the task ahead. They had been told that the trenches they were to attack would be virtually undefended – the five-day bombardment would have seen to that, and would also have cut the barbed wire in front of the German trenches to pieces. So confident were the generals that their men would have no problems taking the German front line that troops were sent into battle with 30kg (66lbs) or more of equipment – equivalent in weight to two heavy suitcases. This was because they were expected to occupy the German front lines and repel any counterattacks.

The Somme was not a good place to launch an attack. The major reason for its chosen location – the joining point of the British and French front lines – had been reduced to a minor consideration after Verdun. Now, only five French divisions were going to take part in the battle, along with 14 British ones. But, all along the front, the Germans occupied higher ground, forcing the British to advance uphill. The chalk ground had also made it easier for the Germans to dig 12m (40ft) underground, constructing heavily fortified positions that were mostly immune to the massive bombardment.

The five days of shelling was not as impressive as it sounded, either. The one and a half million shells fired had been produced in haste, and quality control had slipped considerably. Many were duds which never exploded. And, rather than making the attack easier, the bombardment churned up the ground in front of the German trenches, making it much more difficult to pass through.

The British artillery bombardment ended at 7:30 that morning. Then, several huge explosions rocked the German trenches. Explosives had been placed in mines dug at intervals under German positions along the 28km (18 miles) of the front designated for the attack. Following this mountainous explosion of earth, a strange silence settled over the battlefield. After the constant roar of the last five days, it seemed quite unnatural. The German soldiers knew immediately that something was about to happen. They quickly emerged from their deep bunkers and set up their machine guns.

All along the battlefront, whistles blew: the signal to attack. Troops climbed up wooden ladders placed along the outer edge of the front-line trenches. They arranged themselves into the neat lines they had learned to form in training, and waded into No Man's Land in successive waves. Some battalions had tin discs pinned to their backs, to glint in the sun. The idea was to show the artillery where they were, so they wouldn't get hit by shells falling short. It was a bright summer morning, already so hot the men could feel the heat of the sun on the backs of their necks.

It was Rawlinson's plan of action that called for the soldiers to advance in straight lines to a precise timetable. Other tactics had been discussed. Haig had suggested sending advance parties to check that the wire had been destroyed. But Rawlinson rejected such ideas. He thought his inexperienced troops were incapable of following anything but the simplest plan. There was to be no flexibility or initiative, just momentum. He intended a vast, sprawling tide of men to sweep the Germans from their positions.

The first wave advanced. As they approached the German lines, those leading the attack saw to their horror that the barbed wire had not been destroyed at all. The British artillery shells had just blown the barbed wire into the air, and it had settled back again where it had previously been. There were gaps in the wire, but these had been deliberately left by the Germans to herd attacking enemy troops into "killing zones" where German machine-gun fire was concentrated at its heaviest.

According to Allied thinking, any Germans who survived the bombardment were supposed to have become disoriented and overwhelmed by the sheer size of the force sent against them. But, instead, they just got on with the grisly business of butchering their attackers. They set up their machine guns – alarmingly effective weapons that could fire 600 bullets a minute – and mowed down the approaching British troops like swathes of corn before the scythe.

In one famous incident, a captain in the Eighth Battalion, East Surrey Regiment, gave the signal to attack by climbing onto the rim of his trench and kicking a football in the direction of the enemy lines. No doubt he was trying to allay the fears of his men with a show of devil-may-care bravado. But he was killed almost instantly, somewhat undermining the effect he was trying to create.

One of the soldiers sent in to attack that day was Henry Williamson, who survived the battle and went on to become a writer – *Tarka the Otter* being among his most famous works. He also wrote about his experiences in the war, and described the horror of taking part in the attack with haunting vividness: "I see men arising and walking forward and I go forward with them, in a glassy delirium," he recorded. All around him, his fellow soldiers fell to the ground – some almost gently, others rolling and screaming with fear. Williamson pressed on through ground he described as resembling, "a huge ruined honeycomb." He watched, miraculously unscathed, as his comrades were shot to pieces. Three other waves came up behind him to meet the same pitiful fate. Londoner Arthur Wagstaff, who also went over the top at 7:30 that Saturday morning, recalled the opening minutes more simply: "We looked along the line and we realized there were very few of us left."

In accordance with the plan, the attack went on all morning, with four waves of men going out to the same grim fate. The British army was probably the most rigid and inflexible fighting force of the war. Junior officers in the heat of battle were expected to obey their orders to the letter, even if they found themselves in almost impossible circumstances. Communications between the officers at the Front and the generals at the rear of the battle were poor too, dependent as they were on telephone lines, which would often be broken by shellfire, and runners, who carried messages from the Front to the rear, and were often killed. Soldiers and their officers had been briefed to go forward at any cost, and this they did, despite the obvious futility of doing so. Field Marshal Haig and General Rawlinson might as well have been marching their men straight over a cliff.

By early afternoon, news of the slaughter trickled back to army headquarters, and further attacks that day were called off. The casualty figures were the worst for any single day in the history of the British army, and the worst for any day, in any army, of the entire war.

Back at the casualty clearing stations to the rear of the front, men who had returned from No Man's Land milled around in confusion, searching for a familiar face. Then came the ritual of the roll call, which established who had returned from the attack and who had not.

"So many of our friends were missing, and obviously had been killed or wounded," remembered Tommy Gay, of the Royal Scots Fusiliers, interviewed for a TV documentary shortly before he died in 1999. "All those bullets," he recalled. "All those bullets, and not one with my name on... I was the luckiest man in the world."

Of the 120,000 men who took part in the first morning's fighting, half were casualties. There were 20,000 killed, and another 40,000 wounded. That night, a slow trickle of men who had been injured in No Man's Land, and who had spent the day hiding in shell craters under the hot sun, managed to return to their trenches under cover of darkness.

The way the attack was reported in the British press sheds an interesting light on the way news was managed during the war. One newspaper painted a picture of the opening day of the battle as a great victory, and described the disaster as a good day for England. "A slow, continuous and methodical push, sparing in lives" was how another described it. No doubt such reports offered reassurance to anxious families at home, but they made the soldiers who had taken part in such attacks deeply angry.

Some battalions had come through with few casualties, but others had suffered terribly. The Second Battalion, Middlesex Regiment, for example, had started the day with 24 officers, and 650 men. At roll call that evening, only a single officer and 50 men remained. The Accrington Pals, who were among the first to attack the German line that morning, lost 584 men out of 720

– killed, wounded or simply vanished – in the first half hour of the battle. Despite the total lack of reliable news from the front, their families at home in Lancashire began to suspect something terrible had happened to their men. The regular flow of letters from France suddenly stopped. A week after the battle started, a train full of wounded soldiers from the Somme briefly stopped at Accrington station on the way to an army hospital further north. One man on the train called out to a group of women on the platform, "Where are we?" When they told him, he said, "Accrington... The Accrington Pals! They've been wiped out!" News spread quickly, and an awful atmosphere, like dull, heavy air before a thunderstorm, hung over the town. Then, letters from wounded men assuring their families that they were still alive began to arrive. The letters came in such numbers, it was obvious that something really big had happened. Those who received no such letter were left in a dreadful limbo – should they hope for the best or fear the worst?

Aware that its readers were desperate for information, the local paper the *Accrington Observer* knew the story could wait no longer. But it concealed the real news in heroic hyperbole, typical of the style of the day. "What is certain is the Pals Battalion has won for itself a glorious page in the record of dauntless courage and imperishable valour," said the *Observer*, before it went on to admit, "the dead and wounded are more numerous than we would fain [willingly] have hoped."

Then, agonizingly slowly, over the next six weeks, official War Office letters began to arrive at homes throughout the town, confirming the deaths of those killed on the first day of the Somme. For the whole summer, the *Observer* was filled with row upon row of photos of those who had died. The town was devastated, as the fatal flaw in the idea of the Pals battalions made itself apparent. When men in battle were slaughtered on such a scale, entire towns would be thrown into mourning.

There was to be something even worse about the Somme than 60,000 casualties in a single morning. Despite the losses, Haig and Rawlinson remained convinced their failure lay in not sending in enough men – they thought the big push had not been big enough. So, for the next five months, the volunteers of Kitchener's Army were poured into a hideous grinding machine to be destroyed in their thousands, caught in barbed wire and lashed by machine-gun bullets.

The first day of the Somme

There were a few successes amid the carnage. A night attack on July 14 caught the Germans by surprise, and 8km (5 miles) of front-line German trenches were overrun. Next morning, this breakthrough was followed up by a cavalry charge – the standard tactic used in 19th-century warfare when the enemy's front line had been pierced. The cavalry men did not look quite as dashing as they once did; their red jackets had been replaced by dreary khaki. Bugles still blew and lances glittered in the hot, summer sun. Like all cavalry charges, it was a magnificent sight. But it ended in a hail of machine-gun bullets, flailing hooves and twitching bodies.

Australian troops made their debut on the Western Front, and fought with great courage. Three weeks into the battle, they captured the village of Pozières. But they paid a terrible price for their victory. So many were killed, one soldier described it as, "the heaviest, bloodiest, rottenest stunt that ever Australians were caught up in."

On September 15, 1916, tanks were employed for the first time in history. The British pinned great hopes on these new weapons; "machine gun destroyers" they called them. Indeed, for a German machine gunner in his trench, there was nothing quite so terrifying as facing a huge tank, metal tracks clanking and grinding as it lumbered forward to crush his defensive barbed wire, with bullets bouncing off its heavy steel flank. The tank would eventually prove to be one of the most effective weapons of the century – but not at the Battle of the Somme. Most broke down before they could even reach the front line.

After 140 days, when the battle finally ground to a halt in November 1916, over a million men had been killed or wounded. In all, there were 420,000 British casualties, 200,000 French and 450,000 German. The defenders, mainly men of the German Second Army, suffered so many casualties because their own general, Fritz von Below, had decreed that any ground gained by the British or French had to be recaptured at all cost. "I forbid the voluntary evacuation of trenches," he said. "The will to stand firm must be impressed on every man in the Army... The enemy should have to carve his way over heaps of corpses."

Having been mown down in their thousands attacking front-line German trenches, the Allied soldiers exacted a grim revenge, as the enemy exposed themselves to similar carnage in an effort to win back lost ground. "You've given it to us, now we're going to give it to you... Our machine gunners had a whale of a time," recalled one British soldier.

Any positive military advantage from this whirlwind of destruction was almost unnoticeable. In some areas along the 28km (18-mile) Front, the front line had been redrawn by 8km (5 miles) here or there. But, like so many other battles of the First World War, death on such an industrial scale had not served any useful purpose. Soldiers in the British army would never show such misplaced enthusiasm for battle again. From then on, ordinary soldiers would refer to the campaign on the Somme with a bitter and heartfelt loathing.

To this day, the horror, naiveté and carnage of the early hours of that Saturday morning still shocks anyone who studies the war. For those who took part and survived, it would be the defining moment of their lives. One survivor, Sergeant J.E. Yates of the West Yorkshire Regiment, recalled the effects the first day of battle had on him:

"Almost imperceptibly, the first day merged into the second, when we held grimly to a battered trench and watched each other

grow old under the day-long storm of shelling. For hours, sweating, praying, swearing we worked on the heaps of chalk and mangled bodies. Men did astonishing things at which one did not wonder till after... At dawn next morning we were back in a green wood. I found myself leaning on a rifle and staring stupidly at the filthy exhausted men who slept round me. It did not occur to me to lie down until someone pushed me into a bed of ferns. There were flowers among the ferns, and my last thought was a dull wonder that there could still be flowers in the world."

Eye of the Morning

1914-1917

F AME AND ESPIONAGE seem an unlikely combination. Who would have thought that beautiful Margaretha Zelle, the Dutch-born dancer who had enchanted all of Europe in the early years of the 20th century, would make a suitable spy? In fact, who would have thought she would be remembered as one of the most famous spies of all time?

Margaretha Zelle a.k.a. Mata Hari in full 'exotic dancer' regalia.
The Dutch beauty made several ruinous mistakes in her life. Agreeing
to spy for both the French and the Germans was the most disastrous.

At the height of her fame as a dancer, she toured the capitals of Europe, from London to Rome, Vienna to Berlin. In Paris, such was her popularity that police had been called out to control the crowds that flocked to see her. She had a string of famous lovers, including the German kaiser's son, Crown Prince Wilhelm. But Margaretha's fame was not like fame is now. In the days before television, and newspapers and magazines obsessed with celebrity life, her face faded soon enough in the memory of most men and women in the street.

Margaretha's life was anything but ordinary. Born in 1876 to a wealthy Dutch hat maker and his Javanese wife, she was spoiled as only a privileged, unusually beautiful child can be. But her mother died when she was only 14, and Margaretha was sent off to a convent. At 19, she married a Dutch army officer named Rudolph MacLeod. The couple went to live in Java (now part of Indonesia) which was then a Dutch colony.

Married life was far from easy for Margaretha. MacLeod was a brutal man who drank heavily, and was often unfaithful. He also tried to hoodwink acquaintances by setting them up in compromising situations with his wife, and then blackmailing them.

A son was born to the couple in 1896, followed by a daughter. The son was poisoned by a servant whom MacLeod had mistreated, and died. Shortly after this tragic event Margaretha divorced her husband and returned to Holland with her daughter.

Margaretha, now approaching 30, was alone and penniless, and had no obvious way of making a living. But what she did have was a supple body and a vague memory of some Javanese dances learned during her time in the colony. And she was still stunningly beautiful.

Leaving her daughter with relatives, she set about completely reinventing herself. Margaretha Zelle left for Paris, and arrived there as exotic oriental dancer Mata Hari, which means "Eye of the Morning" in Javanese. She soon found work in a prestigious night club, and became the talk of the city. Margaretha was also an accomplished ballet dancer, and appeared in acclaimed ballet productions. Nine years of celebrity followed, and famous or wealthy lovers who showered her with money and jewels.

But in 1914 the First World War began, and Margaretha's merry-go-round life came to an abrupt end. She was in

Berlin at the time, and returned home to Holland as soon as she could.

Life was so much drearier in wartime. Margaretha was now almost 40, and for the first time in her life she was bored. After two years of wartime in neutral Holland, stuck at home with nothing to do, she was desperate for excitement.

So she was in a particularly receptive state of mind when an unusual visitor knocked on her door one night in May, 1916. He was Karl Kramer, Press Attaché to the German Consulate in Holland, and he had a particularly unusual request. He sat down with her at the dining table. When he was certain they were alone, he began to speak.

"In all your years of fame," Kramer explained delicately, "you have known some of the most powerful men in Europe. Would you consider returning to Paris now to mingle again with these influential gentlemen? And, while you're doing this, might you be able to keep me informed of anything interesting they might say?"

Margaretha looked curious but non-committal.

Kramer went on, "We could pay you well for this information – say 24,000 francs."

Margaretha allowed herself to show a glimmer of interest.

"Possibly, Herr Kramer, possibly. 24,000 francs might do well enough."

But, inside, Margaretha was absolutely thrilled. She was missing the money and excitement of her previous life quite acutely. What could be more glamorous than being a spy?

Kramer returned to her house a few days later, carrying a small leather case. Inside was 24,000 francs and three small bottles. Two held a pale, transparent liquid, the other a bright, blue-green substance.

Kramer explained, "This, my dear Madame Zelle, is invisible ink. Now watch this very carefully. First you dampen the sheet of paper with the fluid in the first bottle, then you write down any useful information for me with the liquid in the second bottle. Then you dab the blue-green liquid over the top and let it dry..."

Margaretha looked on with great interest. Kramer felt like a magician performing a magic trick.

"...and then, you can write a more innocent letter over the top, telling me about the ballet you went to last night, or your dear little poodle or whatever. Then, when I get it, I sprinkle yet more chemicals on top, and the message underneath comes through quite clearly."

Kramer almost added, "Make sure you do it right though. If you're caught, you could be shot." But somehow, he felt, this would be an unwelcome dose of reality in Margaretha's world. He did give her a code name, however – she was to be known to him as *H21*.

Margaretha returned to Paris only with some difficulty. At this time, the border between France and neutral Holland was being guarded very carefully, and the border police were only letting people with special passes travel between the two countries. But Margaretha showed her worth at once. She knew many important people in France, and several letters from politicians and high-ranking army officers to the French Consulate in Amsterdam soon persuaded officials to provide her with the necessary pass.

Margaretha didn't take her spying career very seriously. To her it was just a game which allowed her to spend 24,000 francs. Some invisible ink reports filtered back to Kramer, but most of the time, Margaretha just enjoyed renewing old acquaintances and visiting the haunts of her glory days.

Actually, she was having the time of her life.

But while she didn't take her spying very seriously, the French and British secret services did. They had received reports that she might be a German spy, and were watching her closely. But nothing she did gave them any cause to believe their suspicions were justified.

In Paris, Margaretha met a young Russian officer named Vladimir de Masloff and soon they were passionately in love. Then Vladimir, who was fighting alongside the French, was wounded on the Western Front. Margaretha was desperate to see him, but he had been sent to a hospital near the front, which was forbidden to civilians. Margaretha went at once to the French War Ministry, intent on getting a permit to visit her lover. When she got there she marched through the first door she came to. Before her sat an official at a large, important looking desk, and she began to explain why she had come.

What Margaretha didn't know was that the War Ministry building also housed the French Security Service. By a strange quirk of fate, she found herself sitting opposite Captain Georges Ladoux, head of French counterintelligence – the agency set up to investigate foreign spies.

He knew all about Margaretha Zelle, and was quite aware that she might be a spy. Now here she was, sitting before him, telling him she wanted to visit a forbidden area. It was too good to be true. He played her along, and told her she would get her pass at once. When she had gone he immediately notified two of his agents, telling them to follow her and watch her like a hawk.

Of course, Margaretha had wanted her permit only with the intention of visiting Vladimir. Ladoux's agents had nothing suspicious to report. So, after her return, Ladoux called her into his office. Like Karl Kramer, he too knew that she had friends in very high places, and he tentatively inquired if she might be able to travel to Germany and do a little spying for the French.

As far as Margaretha was concerned, this was all money for nothing. Fate was offering her another wonderful slice of good fortune. But, cool as ever, she looked him straight in the eye and asked him for one million francs.

Ladoux struggled to keep a straight face. That was more than he would pay a dozen of their best agents put together. He was frank with her.

"Madame Zelle," he said, "you are virtually unknown to us. We don't know if we can trust you, and even if we decide we can,

I can pay you no more than 25,000 francs for your services."

Margaretha shrugged. It could be worse. Then she made an error so fatal she could have been signing her own death warrant. Eager to show Ladoux she would be value for money, she boasted:

"I know a man who can organize everything for me in Germany. His name is Kramer."

Ladoux knew him too. If Margaretha Zelle was familiar with him, then in all likelihood she was a German spy after all. Clearly, there was more to her than met the eye. He asked her to go back to Holland and await instructions.

Margaretha returned home by sea, but en route her boat was stopped in the English Channel by a British ship. The British were searching for a dangerous German agent named Clara Benedict, and they had with them a photograph of the woman they were seeking. Unfortunately for Margaretha, she bore a close likeness to Clara, and she was arrested immediately and taken to England.

Two weeks of interrogation followed. After a great deal of shouting and unpleasantness, Margaretha convinced the British that she was the famous Mata Hari, and not Clara

Benedict. But even then, she was not released. Her interrogator, Sir Basil Thomas, told her:

"I would be delighted to set you free, but something rather curious has happened. We have been in touch with our people in Holland, and they tell us that Madame Zelle, or Mata Hari, is suspected of being a German agent."

Margaretha's double dealings were catching up with her. She thought wildly, then burst out:

"I am not a German agent. I work for Captain Ladoux in Paris."

Thomas contacted Ladoux at once. "Never heard of her," came the baffling reply. Ladoux obviously did not want to admit to asking Margaretha to spy for the French.

Eventually, the British let Margaretha go. Thomas had her placed on a boat bound for neutral Spain, warning her that she was way out of her depth and playing a very dangerous game. But Spain was the worst place they could have sent her. Madrid was teeming with spies of all nationalities. Once again, Margaretha was penniless, only this time she was in a foreign country. She decided to buckle down and get some serious spying done.

Uncertain of whether to work for the French or the Germans, she decided to spy for both sides – after all, she reasoned, they had been stupid enough to let her do so before. To the French she gave reports of German agents landing by submarine on the coast of Morocco. To the Germans she passed on news of forthcoming attacks by French and British troops.

But all of her information was second hand, and no more than what each side was certain the other side already knew. The French and German secret services were just testing her, almost certain that she was working for both sides. Eventually the Germans lost patience. They had wasted 24,000 francs, and now they had had enough. They deliberately leaked information to the French, to confirm that she had been working for them.

Margaretha was summoned to Paris. No sooner had she arrived than she was immediately arrested and sent to Captain Bouchardon of the French Secret Service to be interviewed at length. He had been expecting a legendary beauty, and was surprised to see Mata Hari looking tired and gaunt.

Tired she may have been, but Margaretha was not going

to give up without a fight. As they talked she denied everything, trying frantically to offer explanations of her dealings with the German secret service. She even tried to pass off Kramer's 24,000 franc payment as compensation for some valuable furs she had left in Berlin.

Bouchardon looked at Margaretha Zelle and sighed. He remembered her as a fabulous, exotic dancer in pre-war Paris. How much had changed. Clearly, she was no longer the exotic beauty who had enchanted an entire continent, but she was still a striking woman, and Bouchardon was not immune to her charms.

Everything about Margaretha told Bouchardon that she was a bumbling amateur. Whatever information she had given to the Germans was almost certainly worthless, and she had been working for the French too. In another time they would have let her go home to Holland, with a stern warning never to come back to Paris. But the war was going badly for France. Millions of men had been killed and people were demanding scapegoats. Spies, it was said, were everywhere. An example had to be made. So it was decided that Margaretha was to be tried as a spy – a crime that carried the death penalty.

On July 24, 1917, Margaretha Zelle stood before a closed military court. She was on trial for her life. Her lawyer, an old lover who could not believe that she had been a traitor to France, hoped to call influential friends from her past as character witnesses to defend her. But the tide had turned against her. Nobody wanted to be publicly associated with a woman who was now perceived as a dangerous German spy.

The trial went badly from the start, although Margaretha defended herself bravely. As she had done with Bouchard, she tried to pass off evidence of German payments to her as compensation for lost belongings, or gifts from lovers. It all looked increasingly implausible. Yet equally implausibly, the prosecution described her as one of the greatest spies of the century, and alleged that she was responsible for the deaths of tens of thousands of soldiers. Margaretha listened to the accusations unbowed. But when the prosecution also revealed her secret German code name, H21, her resistance and composure collapsed. She began to panic and her whole body started to tremble.

It was all over in less than two days. Margaretha was found guilty of spying against the French and sentenced to death. In deep shock, she could not bring herself to believe her wonderful life had turned out so badly.

"It's not possible, it's not possible," she repeated over and over.

Margaretha watched the summer fade to autumn from her cell window. Appeals were lodged and rejected, and now a date had been set for her execution – October 15. She was to be taken to Vincennes, a chateau on the edge of Paris, and shot by firing squad.

She slept well the night before, and was woken by Captain Bouchardon at 4:00am. In her cell were two nuns, there to keep her company.

"It's not possible," she said again to them. Then, "Don't worry, sisters. I know how to die. You'll see a good death."

She had decided she would leave the world as she had lived – with as much splendour as she could manage. She put on an expensive dress, some beautiful shoes, a fine shawl, a hat and long gloves. She seemed quite calm.

"Why do you have this custom of executing people at dawn?" she said to the nuns. "In India and elsewhere it takes place at noon. I'd much rather go to Vincennes about three o'clock, after a good lunch."

And so she continued for the final two hours of her life. She stepped out of the car that took her to Vincennes with as much dignity as she could manage, and walked confidently before the firing squad. She refused a blindfold and would not be tied to the stake set up for her execution.

It was over mercifully quickly. Twelve shots rang out and she slumped to the ground. As the morning mist lifted, the body that had once entranced a continent was loaded into a coffin and taken away.

Mata Hari continues to be an object of great fascination in the world of espionage. Plenty of photographs still exist showing the dancer in her sultry prime, and ensuring that she is still remembered over eighty years after her untimely death. Her stage name has become an all-purpose description for an attractive female spy. The Dutch Mata Hari Foundation, an organization set up to prove her innocence of the charges made against her, still hope that she will one day receive an official pardon.

Her story has been the subject of several films and, until the creation of James Bond, she was the classic symbol of glamorous espionage. Greta Garbo played her in a 1931 film called *Mata Hari*. Like many films, the truth is buried among the drama on the screen, which focuses on her love affair with Vladimir de Masloff. In the film, she sends news to her lover that she is dying in a hospital, rather than about to be shot. Another film of her life was made in 1985, this time starring Sylvia Kristel.

In the late 1990s, Margaretha was in the news again, for a very bizarre reason. After her execution her head was preserved in a private museum, but it was stolen, and has so far not been recovered.

The allure of Mata Hari stretches into the 21st century, and recently a computer software package for seeking out hard-to-find Internet information was named after her.

THE QUIET REBELLION
MAY-JUNE 1917

DURING THE FIRST WORLD WAR, trench soldiers on both sides faced a kind of warfare that no one before or since has had to fight. Every day promised soldiers a gruesome death or injury from sniper fire and artillery bombardment. Once or twice a year, there would be a "big push" that tended to kill at least half the men they knew. And, along with the danger, there was the barren panorama of No Man's Land and the unending hardship of the trenches.

Ice and snow, rain and mud, baking heat – whatever the weather, a trench was no place for men to be. Rats gnawed at their dead companions, they were perpetually plagued with lice, and any sort of plumbing system for the daily effluent of hundreds of thousands of front-line troops was clearly out of the question. In this tortured landscape, with the hideous stench of excrement and rotting corpses, the war went on, and on, and on... until those fighting believed it would go on forever. "O Jesus, make it stop!" was the heartfelt plea ending British front-line officer Siegfried Sassoon's 1918 poem *Attack*.

But not all soldiers were prepared to carry on fighting. The British and American armies avoided any major outbreaks of rebellion, but every other major fighting nation had its share. Naval mutinies in Germany occurred in 1917 and at the end of the war. Some Austro-Hungarian troops fighting on the Eastern Front mutinied as early as 1915. Most critical of all, Russian soldiers deserted and mutinied in droves, and brought on the revolutions of 1917 which led to Russia's withdrawal from the war.

THE QUIET REBELLION

The French army mutinied too, in the spring and early summer of 1917. It was a decisive moment that could have cost France the war. Fortunately, the German generals didn't believe the reports they received from spies and prisoners of war about the mutiny. By the time they realized it was really happening, the mutiny was over.

The word "mutiny" conjures up images of drunken violence and a descent into anarchy. It is a word to make an officer's blood run cold. For, without order and obedience, one man cannot tell other men to carry out actions that will undoubtedly result in death and injury. Mutiny renders an army ineffective more surely than a curtain of machine-gun fire or an artillery barrage. It can lead to utter defeat in a matter of days, so it is usually punished with great severity. In ancient Rome, mutinous army legions that had returned to military discipline were subject to "decimation" – one man in ten was plucked from the ranks and executed. Who could ever have guessed that this ancient, barbaric remedy would be employed again in the 20th century, to restore order to one of Europe's greatest armies?

The French mutinies of 1917 had their roots in German general Erich von Falkenhayn's decision to fight the war by taking French lives rather than French territory. In February 1916, he chose the French fortress of Verdun to do this. In a horrendous 10-month battle, the French and Germans fought for possession of this stronghold. Much of the fighting took place in dank, concrete forts awash with blood, and steeped in the stark terror of men in hand-to-hand combat. When the battle ended in December that year, 350,000 French soldiers and 330,000 German soldiers had been killed or injured. There was nothing to show for all this slaughter. No territory had been won or lost. Each side had lost an almost equal number of troops. Falkenhayn was dismissed from his post. But his declared aim of "bleeding the French army white" had had more of an effect than he realized.

The French people were immensely proud of their army's success in defending Verdun, and the soldier's terse battle cry, "Ils ne passeront pas." ("They shall not pass.") became a slogan of national self-esteem. The two generals held most responsible for fending off the Germans, Philippe Pétain and Robert Nivelle, became national heroes. But, after Verdun, many French soldiers who had fought there felt they had nothing left to give.

Another major French offensive was planned in the early spring of 1917. Nivelle, still basking in his success, promised the troops a quick victory at Chemin des Dames, on the River Aisne. This, he told his men, would be the battle that would win the war. Morale was high, especially as the French soldiers were told they would be trying out a new tactic sure to save lives. They would head over to the German trenches under the protection of a "creeping barrage" – a hail of shells which would fall in front of them, gradually advancing like a protective wall of fire. Tanks would be used too – a new type of weapon which promised to crush defensive barbed wire and destroy the deadly machine-gun nests, which could sweep away scores of men with a single burst of fire.

A million men took part in the attack on April 16. It failed pitifully, and the same senseless slaughter ensued. The tanks broke down and the artillery bombardment failed to destroy the enemy strongpoints. The weather didn't help; the French soldiers often had to advance in driving rain. After 10 days, 34,000 men had been killed, with 20,000 missing, almost certainly dead too. Another 90,000 had been wounded. But still the attacks continued.

Not all the soldiers had believed Nivelle's promises of an easy victory and decisive breakthrough. In fact, some companies of men had marched to the front line bleating like sheep, believing they were lambs to the slaughter. It was a warning sign that was carelessly ignored. Chemin des Dames became the place where the morale of the French army finally broke.

Nivelle's career was over. Already seriously ill with tuberculosis, he would not live to see the end of the war. His replacement was the other hero of Verdun, Pétain. He moved from his post of chief of the French general staff, to become commander-in-chief of the French northern and northeast armies. Pétain had only been in his new job for three days when he received reports of mutinies among front-line soldiers.

The first occurred in the 2nd Battalion of the 18th Infantry Regiment. Out of 600 men, only 200 had survived the Chemin des Dames offensive. After a brief respite behind the

French front lines, they were once again ordered back to the trenches. It was the early evening of April 29, 1917. Many of the men were drunk on the cheap red wine that was supplied free, and frequently, to French troops. Almost all refused to return, gathering in large groups and shouting "Down with the war!" But, by early the next morning, the men had sobered up, and marched back to the front line.

As they marched, the officers of the battalion decided this insurrection should be immediately punished. At random, a dozen men were pulled from the ranks and charged with mutiny. Five of them were shot. Another had an amazing escape. As he was being led to the firing squad by a group of guards, a German artillery bombardment fell around them. He ran into nearby woods and was never seen again.

Four days later, another mutiny broke out. This was far more serious as it involved the entire Second Division – thousands of men, almost all drunk and refusing to carry their weapons or go back to the trenches. But, when the drink wore off, most of the men gave in and marched to the Front. The few who still refused to go were quickly arrested, and no one else in the division was singled out for punishment.

It was just the beginning. In early May, this drunken rebellion spread throughout the army. It was an odd sort of mutiny, though. There were no reports of officers being attacked or killed, and no political demands. When officers spoke to the men who had been elected by their comrades to represent them, they were told the soldiers would continue to defend

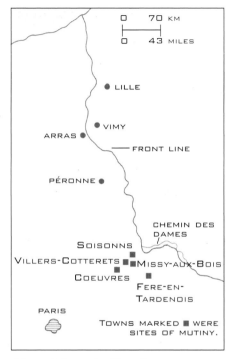

Map of the 1917 French mutinies

their trenches. It was the attacks against the Germans they were no longer prepared to take part in.

While large-scale mutiny swept the ranks of the French army, extraordinary events were taking place in Russia, where a similarly widespread mutiny had led to the overthrow of the Tsarist government, deeply alarming the other Allies. The

French authorities were lucky there were no equivalents of Lenin or Trotsky among their troops; if there had been, the history of France, and Europe, over the course of the 20th century might have been very different. The French rebellion had no obvious leaders and was not being directed by anyone. But, despite this, the mutiny spread so fast that by June, 54 divisions – over half the entire French army on the Western Front – were affected. Some 30,000 men just left their front-line posts and tried to walk home.

The causes of the mutiny were both simple and complicated. In essence, the ordinary French soldier had lost faith in his generals. He was not prepared to lay down his life for a way of fighting he no longer believed in. But there were other causes too, and these were serious enough to make anyone wonder why the mutiny had not happened before.

Compared to their British counterparts, the French soldiers had had to put up with harsher conditions and military discipline. Their pay was miserly. The food they had to eat was often cold and of very poor quality – an especially troubling state of affairs for such a nation of gourmets. The British army, by comparison, made great efforts to keep its trench soldiers supplied with hot food of reasonable quality. British soldiers from the other side of the Channel also spent more time away from the trenches, and with their families, than French soldiers. This was especially painful for the French, as many were fighting less than a day's train journey away from their homes; but they were rarely offered leave. Although all sides suffered horrendous casualties, of the Allies, the French lost the most men. One in four Frenchmen between the ages of 18 and 30 would die in the war – a million and a half in all, with millions more wounded and maimed for life.

In the French High Command, the mutiny caused a sense of panic. France had already suffered so much – so many men had been sacrificed to keep the German army from overrunning their country. How awful it would be if the French lost the war because their troops had just given up and gone home.

Pétain, as commander-in-chief of the mutinous divisions, was the man who had to sort it all out. Fortunately for France, he chose to address his soldiers' complaints, rather than simply to suppress the revolt with great brutality. He had three major problems. First, he had to take immediate steps to introduce reforms to make life more bearable for his men, most of whom were conscripts fighting for the duration of the war, rather than career soldiers. Second, in order to uphold discipline in the army, he had to punish those responsible – a difficult task when the mutiny really did seem to be spontaneous and lacking in "ring leaders". Third, and most important of all, he had to keep the mutiny secret from the Germans. If they knew what was going on, they could break through the French lines and be in Paris within a week. Then the war would be lost for sure.

Several older generals were immediately replaced. The quality of food fed to front-line troops was improved. A system of home leave was introduced, and rest camps behind the front lines were made more habitable. The arrival of Pétain, although it happened just before the mutinies occurred, was a stroke of luck. This veteran French general, already 60 years old in 1917, had a reputation for being careful with the lives of his men. Almost alone among the officers of the French High Command, ordinary soldiers trusted him not to throw away their lives in useless offensives.

Nonetheless, punishment for the mutiny was random and transparently unfair. For example, in early June, a battalion of 700 men under the command of General Emile Taufflieb was marching back to the Front when they all disappeared into a forest at the side of the road. Earlier in the day, word had swept through the troops that there was a vast cave nearby in which they could all hide. Taufflieb, showing commendable bravery, went into the cave and talked to the mutineers. He told them to return to the front by daybreak, or they would all be slaughtered. The men came out. But once they were back under army command, 20 were pulled from the ranks and shot. Taufflieb had neglected to mention this would happen. But, in other divisions, once order had been restored, the momentary mutiny was swiftly forgotten and no one was punished.

In all, perhaps 24,000 men were arrested and put before military courts. Of these, 554 judged to be leaders of the revolt were sentenced to death. But only 45 were shot; the rest were sent to the penal colony of French Guiana – a miserable fate for conscripted soldiers who had fought bravely until they could take no more. Those executed were shot before their comrades, who were then made to file past the dead men. Many more French soldiers were shot at random and without trial, but the number of those deaths is difficult to estimate.

The mutiny was dealt with carefully. But, beneath the concern, there was an iron fist determined that such widespread disobedience would never be allowed to happen again. Among the rebellious divisions was a regiment of Russian soldiers, sent to the Western Front as a goodwill gesture by the ailing Tsarist regime before it was overthrown. These soldiers had endured even worse conditions and even more incompetent leadership than their French and British allies. They were all too ready to follow their rebellious French comrades and mutiny. Their fate was pitiful. The French authorities had had to deal with their own soldiers with some leniency – there were too many to punish, and harsh discipline might have provoked worse rebellions, and even revolution. The Russians, though, were expendable. The regiment was surrounded and blown to pieces by French artillery.

The mutiny had lasted for six weeks. The French army had escaped a crushing defeat by the skin of its teeth. But the soldiers who had rebelled had sent a clear message to their generals. From now on, there would be no more mass attacks; French soldiers would only take part in small-scale assaults on the German lines. And so the horrific bloodletting of the previous three years came to an end. For the rest of the war, the lion's share of the fighting against the Central Powers would be left to Britain and the Commonwealth, and fresh and enthusiastic American troops, who had entered the war just in time to save the Allies from an almost certain defeat.

Behind the front lines, the government reacted by tightening censorship in the French newspapers and imprisoning those who had campaigned for an end to the war. These days, such people would be called peace campaigners. In 1917, they were called anti-war agitators.

Even now, the mutiny is still a shameful and touchy subject in France. On its 80th anniversary in 1997, the French prime minister, Lionel Jospin, suggested the mutineers needed to be understood and forgiven. This provoked a stern denunciation from the French president, Jacques Chirac. The act of expressing sympathy for those war-weary men was still considered an outrage. But, nowadays, most people would agree that the mutineers deserved pity rather than condemnation. They were, said French politician François Hollande recently, "simply men who got lost in a hell of fire and blood."

THE CELLAR HOUSE OF PERVYSE

1914-1918

Elizabeth "Elsie" Knocker and Mairi Chisholm were not used to such deprivation. Elsie, a young widow of 24, and Mairi, only 18, were sleeping on straw surrounded by a bunch of filthy, ragged soldiers. Three months earlier, theirs had been a world of grand houses, servants, fine china plates and strictly observed etiquette. But the world had turned. Now they were volunteer nurses attached to the Belgian army, in headlong retreat before the German army, and taking shelter in a derelict cellar in the Belgian village of Oudecappelle.

Elsie found sleep impossible. Rats scurried around her head, and the men snored horribly. She got up slowly, and gingerly picked her way through the outstretched limbs of the sleeping soldiers, out into the cold, bright moonlight. Hours before, this landscape had been subjected to an artillery barrage, which had left many houses in ruins. But now all was silent. The air was still dusty from the bombardment, but felt like a crystal mountain breeze after the fetid atmosphere of the cellar. As she stood breathing in great lungfuls, she heard a sound behind her. There, stumbling through the rubble, was Mairi, come to join her.

Close by, an artillery bombardment started up, sending shells over to the German lines and shaking the ground beneath their feet. A biting wind blew in from the sea, and the two women hugged each other tight for warmth. To the east, a thin band of light on the horizon cast a sickly glow on the ruined village.

In the first light of dawn, they decided they were in this horrible jam for the long term, and they had better get used to it. Taking a pair of surgical scissors, Mairi cut away Elsie's dark, silky hair, leaving her with a short, two-inch crop. Elsie did the same for Mairi's long, fair hair. Then they gathered up the shorn locks and threw them into the canal that ran close to their shelter. In Edwardian times, at the start of the 20th century, a woman's long hair was her "crowning glory" – an absolutely central part of her beauty. So it was a gesture of infinite significance to cut it off. Elsie later recalled: "With that bundle of hair went all our nervousness, all our fear of rats, our dislike of dirty food, and our ideas of home comforts. We became soldiers from that hour."

Soon after, they posed together for a photograph. Standing stiffly in their khaki overalls, high riding boots and nurse's hats, their determination is clear. Elsie, tall and fragile, stares sternly at the camera. She looks sad, large dark eyes peering from her gaunt face, wisps of black hair curling around the edge of her hat. Mairi called her "Gypsy" because of her dark looks. Elsie was a sensitive woman, but that didn't stop her from expressing strong opinions, and she did not suffer fools gladly. The photo shows Mairi as shorter and stockier, a hint of a smile playing around her mouth. She looks very young, but formidably determined. She was, noted a friend, the kind of woman who cannot bear to sit down in an untidy room. They made a good team. But how did these two young women come to find themselves in such circumstances?

At the beginning of the 20th century, there were strict conventions about what was right and proper for a woman to do. Most men had deep prejudices about women's capabilities. Many women accepted that they should live within these narrow boundaries. But these were changing times, and the war would make a considerable difference to women's lives.

In the years before the war, a mass political movement of feminists, including the Suffragettes, had campaigned for the right for women to vote – as the vote was then only available to men. When war broke out, the movement suspended its activities and threw its support behind the government and the country. Voluntary women's organizations were formed, especially to help sick and wounded soldiers both behind the front line in France and as they slowly recovered. Huge numbers of women came forward to volunteer to work as

Baroness de T'Serclaes (née Elsie Knocker) (left) and Mairi Chisholm (right) near the Western Front. Defying social convention, they spent most of the war nursing injured soldiers right on the front line.

nurses and ambulance drivers, and to set up soup kitchens and field canteens to feed troops. There was a strict ban on allowing women in the front line, though.

Things were changing at home, too. Men in the Territorial Army (part-time soldiers) and those who had rushed to join up at the start of the war left their jobs to go to fight. When casualties mounted and the army could no longer rely on volunteers to replace their missing numbers, conscription was introduced. This created hitherto undreamed of employment opportunities for women, who flocked into previously male-only occupations to fill the gaps in the workforce. At first, the sight of women bus drivers or conductors was considered faintly shocking. But, by the time the war was over, thousands of women throughout Europe were working. Many of these jobs were in factories such as munitions works, producing shells and bullets. Women even worked in the coal mines. But the old attitudes still died hard. Throughout the war, women continued to face absurd prejudices. Even in 1917, the British newspaper *The Daily Telegraph* was running headlines asking such questions as: "Are women capable of driving at night?"

What Elsie Knocker and Mairi Chisholm did in Belgium would be remarkable even today. When the war broke out, Elsie, a trained nurse, went at once to London to offer her services to the authorities. Arriving in the capital, she was caught up in a wave of frantic planning and excitement. Committees were set up to get women volunteers to the war zone as quickly as possible, as nurses and ambulance drivers. But all these plans were curtly rejected by both the War Office (the government department responsible for the army) and the British Red Cross. To be fair, some of the schemes were hare-brained, such as the one that envisaged nurses on horseback being sent out to scour the battlefields for wounded soldiers. Ideas like this belonged firmly to the previous century. They had no place in the shell craters and barbed wire of the No Man's Land between the trenches. But few people in the summer of 1914 had any idea what the war would actually be like. Most were convinced it would be a great adventure.

Elsie was determined not to wait for a bunch of men to tell her what to do. She had heard of a volunteer organization called the Flying Ambulance Corps, which was going straight out to Belgium. When she presented her credentials, they snapped her up. She was not only a trained nurse, but an expert driver and a mechanic too – unusual skills for a woman in 1914. At this time, only the rich could afford cars, so many women from wealthy backgrounds put their motoring skills to use driving ambulances.

The corps had been founded by a Scottish doctor, Hector Munro, whom Elsie described affectionately, but sharply, as "an eccentric Scottish specialist, one whose primary object seemed to be leadership of the feminist crusade, for he was far keener on women's rights than most of the women he recruited." According to Elsie, "he was a likeable man and a brilliant impresario, but wonderfully vague in matters of detail, and in appearance the very essence of an absent-minded professor."

Perhaps it was because of Munro's transparent eccentricity, but the services of his Flying Ambulance Corps were rejected, not only by the War Office and the British Red Cross, but the French and American Red Cross too. But the Belgian Red Cross wasn't so fussy – perhaps because their country was in the thick of the German invasion.

Along with Munro, two other doctors, a couple of drivers and an army chaplain, Elsie and a handful of women volunteer nurses set off across the Channel for Belgium. Among the nurses was Mairi Chisholm, whom Elsie had known before the war. They had met again in London while doing volunteer dispatch riding for the Women's Emergency Corps, another new organization set up at the start of the war. Mairi was an enthusiastic and fearless motorcyclist. She rode down to London as soon as war broke out, to offer her help. She had no knowledge of nursing, but was confident she could pick up what she needed to know on the job.

Because they were not part of any government-approved organization, the members of Munro's ambulance corps had to finance their own expedition. The women bought their own clothes, including heavy khaki overcoats, high lace-up boots and riding breeches. Elsie had inherited some money when her husband died, which paid her expenses. Mairi came from a wealthy background, but went to Belgium in the teeth of fierce parental disapproval. She had to sell her motorbike to pay for her clothing and travel costs. They might have been forgiven if they had felt indignant about having to pay their own way –

after all, they were offering to risk their lives to aid the Allies in the war. But they were determined to put the best possible spin on everything. As Elsie said: "We preferred to be financially independent. It gave us greater freedom of movement, and spared us some of the annoyances of red tape."

The Flying Ambulance Corps set up in Ghent, a little way behind the Belgian front line, and made themselves immensely useful. They cared for wounded soldiers, and carried cocoa and soup out to the front-line soldiers. Their work was often hair-raisingly dangerous. On one occasion, Elsie and Mairi rescued a wounded Belgian officer in a village that was being overrun by German soldiers. As they attended to him and other wounded men, hand-to-hand fighting was taking place a mere block away.

But Elsie quickly spotted a major problem with their work. Many wounded soldiers died while being transported to medical posts safely behind the front lines. Wouldn't it be better, she thought, if they could receive medical attention right next to the actual fighting? Mairi agreed. So, after two months behind the front, they set out to find a suitable spot nearer the trenches. By this time, almost all of Belgium had been overrun by the German army, and only a small triangle of territory near the Channel coast remained in Belgian hands. Right behind the front line was a small village called Pervyse – and here they made their base.

The route to Pervyse was littered with enough portents to convince even the least superstitious visitor to turn around and go back. It was lucky that Elsie and Marie were too sensible to believe in omens. As they drove through mud and past shell holes, the side of the road was marked by the bloated bodies of dead cows, sheep and horses, all killed in murderous artillery bombardments or caught in the crossfire of combat. Some of these carcasses had been left to rot, others stripped of meat by soldiers desperate for a meal. Then, at less regular intervals, but frequent enough to remind them of the terrible danger they were placing themselves in, there were burned-out vehicles. Some still had the charred, mangled remains of their passengers inside them.

Pervyse was as grim as the route that led to it. Many of its stone houses had been destroyed by shells, and all the trees around the village had withered. The church was peppered with holes and the graveyard had been churned up, with long-dead bodies poking through the broken ground. As if this was not enough to despoil the scene, the low-lying land had been flooded during the German advance. Dank seawater had mixed with the freshwater of the canals and rivers, and dead freshwater fish killed by the salt lay rotting on the surface.

It was here, in late November of 1914, that they found a derelict house, and set up a medical post in its cellar. The room was a mere 3m x 2.5m (12ft by 10ft) and without any facilities. The house had been quite handsome in its time, but now the roof was in tatters and every window pane was smashed. A stove was found in a nearby house and dragged over to the cellar. Straw was spread on the floor to sleep on. Water was brought in from wherever it could be found. Not only did they need it to drink and cook with, but it was also essential to use for boiling water to sterilize surgical implements. There was barely more than "a teaspoon" left for them to wash.

With them in this first outpost were two men supplied by the Belgian army. One was a driver (although both women could drive); the other was a cook. All four slept in the straw of their cellar, surviving as best they could on food they would never have dreamed of eating a few months before. Most of it was soup. It was either terribly thin – "one tomato and 15 pints of water," as Mairi tartly observed – or thick and swimming in fat, which floated unappetizingly on the surface.

Positioned directly behind the front line, they were in constant danger from artillery fire and stray bullets. There was also the ever-present possibility that the German army would break through the Belgian trenches and overrun the town. But such was the static nature of the fighting that the two women were able to remain in this village, just behind the front line, for almost the entire war.

When they first arrived, the village had only been partially destroyed by the fighting. But, as the war progressed, the whole place fell into dereliction. A big convent was totally destroyed, and the church was razed to the ground. One part of the village by a road junction became known as *Suicide Corner*, because shell fire was particularly intense there.

Sometimes, during lulls in artillery barrages, the women would venture into No Man's Land, to search for wounded soldiers in the churned-up mud. If they found anyone, they would carry the man on their shoulders back to the medical post. Such work was extraordinarily dangerous, because they were plainly visible to the German trenches and could easily have been shot at by German soldiers.

After a few months, the cellar became unbearably cramped, so the two moved their medical post to another house in the village. But this too was semi-derelict, with half the roof missing. While they were away from the house, German artillery destroyed it, so another spot was found nearby. This medical post proved the best yet, and they were able to stay there for the rest of their time at the front. Over the months, and with help from Belgian soldiers, the two women took considerable steps to protect themselves and their patients. A fortified concrete blockhouse was built in the house, and they worked inside it. The outside of the house was covered in sandbags to protect them from the blast of shells exploding nearby.

Running the medical post cost money, of course, and Mairi and Elsie had to fund their activities by occasional visits back to Britain to collect money for their work. Although the

Belgian authorities did not offer to finance them, the army supplied soldiers to help with the driving and the care of wounded men. But, more often than not, such helpers were unfit for front-line combat, so were of limited use.

As Elsie and Mairi were the only two women on the Western Front to work so close to the trenches, they became quite well-known. Newspapers referred to them as "the Heroines of Pervyse" and, in February 1915, King Albert of the Belgians visited Pervyse to present them personally with the Belgian Order of Leopold – a medal given in recognition of their bravery.

Most days were a dizzy succession of catastrophes and tragedies. Although many casualties were men injured by shells or bullets, others were soldiers who were suffering from illnesses caused by living in the open trenches: frostbite, "trenchfoot" (a form of frostbite) and bronchitis. When there was a lull in the fighting, and the stream of casualties coming to their door slowed, Elsie and Mairi would forage for cabbages and potatoes in the nearby fields, to make soup for the soldiers. Occasionally they would return with shrapnel holes in their clothing but, amazingly, both escaped injury. On one occasion, Elsie was watching a Belgian doctor approaching the medical post. Suddenly, a shell fell from the sky and he vanished in a flash of dirty brown earth. How they kept going for so long is a mystery. They were up at six o'clock every morning, to make hot chocolate or coffee for the men in the nearby trenches and, when they were not cooking, they were nursing.

Once their patients had been given first aid, it was Mairi's and Elsie's responsibility to drive them to a hospital well behind the front lines. This was extremely difficult and dangerous. The roads on the 24km (15 mile) journey were often deep in mud and littered with shell craters. The ambulance often came under heavy fire too, even at night when most of the driving was undertaken. Frequently, the vehicle would slide off the road to become stuck in a ditch or hole, and Mairi would have to ask passing soldiers to help her push it out.

Driving at night in such conditions, with no lights, took special skill and was extremely stressful. Whenever the ambulance skidded off the road, the badly injured men would tumble around in the back of the vehicle, often screaming in agony. Sometimes, Mairi would make two or three such journeys a night, and return to her bed with "eyes on stalks, bloodshot and strained... I never felt so googly [exhausted] and utterly played out in my life," she later wrote.

As the war progressed, the village lay in ruins, although Mairi felt it had a strange kind of beauty in the moonlight. All around them were the horrors of war. Corpses floated in vast pools of stagnant water, and occasionally the arms or legs of men torn to pieces by shell fire were found just lying in the road. By the end of the war, little remained of the village except rubble and gable ends.

But, in these dreadful circumstances, Elsie Knocker fell in love. She met a Belgian pilot named Baron Harold de T'Serclaes. In early 1916, they married and Mrs. Knocker became the Baroness de T'Serclaes. At first, Mairi thought the relationship would take her friend away, but Elsie continued to work closely with her at their medical post.

In 1917, the two were summoned to rescue a British pilot who had crashed in No Man's Land. He was badly injured and in need of urgent medical attention. Risking their lives, they managed to arrange a truce with German soldiers, and brought the pilot safely back. For this they were awarded the British Military Medal – another decoration recognizing their immense courage.

In an effort to raise funds for their project, the two women gave their letters and diaries to a friend, who wrote an account of their adventures called *The Cellar House of Pervyse*. On the final page, a pink insert pleads with the purchaser to send money to fund the medical post. The book's gushing and mawkish style is very much of the era; their wounded Belgian patients, for example, are invariably referred to as "dear little soldiers". Yet between the lines the reader gets a glimpse of the daily horror facing both these extraordinary young women. Here, Elsie has to deal with a soldier who has had half his head blown off by a shell:

> *"Suddenly a little soldier came to our open door and told me, with tears in his eyes, that a comrade had been terribly badly injured... I saw at once that the poor brave little soldier was past my aid. I said to his comrades 'Il est*

mort.' [He is dead.] They turned to me with an
incredible look, as if I had spoken from inexperience, but
I have seen so many – the number runs into thousands –
that I could make no mistake. Poor comrades! They
looked so sad and heartbroken... Here was a laughing,
cheerful healthy man, one short quarter of an hour ago,
and now still and silent, and past all pain."

It was a miracle Elsie and Mairi managed to survive unscathed for as long as they did. But, after three and a half years, their luck ran out. During the late winter of 1918, a cloud of mustard and arsenic gas was sent over to the Belgian trenches from the German lines, and it enveloped Pervyse. Both women were badly affected, especially Elsie. She was evacuated to England, where she stayed for the last six months of the war. Mairi returned to the post to work alone, but she was gassed again a few weeks before the war ended. Gas rarely killed its victims outright. Instead, those worst affected died a lingering death in the decades after the war, their corrupted lungs fighting a long, losing battle against the corrosive chemicals they had inhaled.

Others often suffered its effects for the rest of their lives.

Both women made a determined recovery and survived the war. But, like many wartime romances, Elsie's marriage to the baron did not last. They separated in 1919. When war broke out again in 1939, she joined the Women's Auxiliary Air Force (WAAF), and devoted much of her life to fundraising for the RAF Benevolent Fund. She died in 1974. Mairi Chisholm also joined the WAAF, and later became a pioneer racing driver. Following her injury from gas, she suffered from fragile health for the rest of her life, but this did not stop her from living to the ripe old age of 85.

NIGHTMARE AT BELLEAU WOOD
1918

THE YEAR BEFORE the Americans entered the war, the United States had a small army of barely 100,000 men. US president Woodrow Wilson had mixed feelings about committing his country to the conflict. Many American citizens were European immigrants, who had fled to the New World partly to avoid wars like the one currently tearing their old countries apart. Also, a sizable proportion of America's immigrants were from Germany, further complicating any decision about which side to support.

In January 1917, Germany's military commanders decided to allow their U-boats to sink any ship found in British waters. Inevitably, this led to the loss of American cargo ships and the occasional passenger liner, too. This shifted public opinion in America from wary neutrality to a more anti-German outlook. Wilson guessed the time was right; so in April 1917, the United States finally joined the war on the side of the Allies.

Once the Americans had joined the conflict, they set about preparing to prove themselves on the world stage with all the enthusiasm of the bright, upcoming and immensely prosperous nation they had recently become. By the time the war ended in November 1918, there were four million US citizens in the armed forces, and three and three-quarter million of them had been transported over to Europe. They came packed like sardines, in liners hurriedly transformed into troopships. Here, men slept in steel and wire bunk beds placed four on top of each other. The journey was so bad that many soldiers later remarked the trenches that awaited them were more comfortable.

The Germans knew America joining the Allies would make their own victory far more unlikely. Yet in 1917 the war was going Germany's way. Russia, in the throes of revolution, was desperate to make peace, which would end fighting on the Eastern Front. Germany prepared to turn its full attention to the Western Front, intending to sweep away the exhausted French and British armies with the full force of its previously divided army.

At the beginning of 1918, American troopships with newly trained soldiers began to arrive in France, but there were still only a few thousand American troops in Europe. It took time, after all, to raise and prepare a fighting force almost from scratch, and to transport huge numbers of men across the Atlantic. The German generals knew that to win in the West, they would have to strike hard before the Americans arrived in unstoppable numbers. At the end of March, in a carefully planned attack known as the Ludendorff Offensive, German troops broke through the Allied front lines. Part of their success was due to a new tactic. They made surprise attacks to discover their enemy's weak spots, then broke through in strength when they found them.

Throughout the spring, the German armies made a series of extraordinary advances, causing panic among British and French forces. In April, British commander-in-chief Field Marshal Haig issued the desperate order: "With our backs to the wall, and believing in the justice of our cause, each one of us must fight to the end."

Haig feared the loss of the French and Belgian Channel ports, from which troops and supplies were easily transported from Britain to its army on the Western Front. The threat to the French was even more drastic. By early June, the German army had reached the River Marne and the town of Château-Thierry, barely 70km (40 miles) from Paris. As roads became clogged with French civilians fleeing from the fighting, exhausted and demoralized troops melted away, unable to find the will to fight the tidal wave of German troops that welled up before them.

In these desperate circumstances, the British and French generals turned to the American Expeditionary Force (AEF) –

the first wave of American troops to arrive in Europe – to save the situation. The AEF was under the command of General John J. Pershing. He was well aware that his British and French allies had all but lost the will to wage the war. So the burden of winning was now mainly on the shoulders of his fresh and enthusiastic troops. Yet, so far, Pershing had found commanding his army in Europe to be an unexpectedly frustrating experience. Rather than welcoming the Americans as equal partners, the British and French generals had persistently talked down to Pershing and his staff. They assumed the Americans were naïve and inexperienced – which of course they were. In particular, the Europeans believed that American soldiers would not really have the courage and motivation to fight. One of Pershing's staff remembers the American commander-in-chief banging his fists on the table in a rage and shouting, "I am certainly going to jump down the throat of the next person who asks me 'Will the Americans really fight?' "

The fault for this lack of understanding and trust between the three sides did not entirely lie with the Europeans. Throughout the war, British and French generals had fought together as allies. The Americans, on President Wilson's insistence, did not wish to be considered allies, preferring the term *co-belligerents*. They intended to fight alongside the French and British, but not with them. But this situation changed for the better during the Ludendorff Offensive. Drastic, combined action was called for. For the duration of the crisis, all the Allied forces were placed under the control of the veteran French commander, Marshal Ferdinand Foch.

It was in May 1918 that American soldiers first engaged the German army in heavy fighting, at the small village of Cantigny, near the River Somme. Over a third of the American forces there were killed or injured in three days of intense combat – more than enough to prove they were capable of fighting with as much determination as anyone.

At the end of May, Pershing was asked to send soldiers to plug a weak spot in the Allied lines at the town of Château-Thierry. As the German army approached, French troops had fled along with a desperate stream of terrified civilians, clogging the roads away from the town. The nearest American soldiers, the 2nd and 3rd Divisions, were 160 km (100 miles) away. The Americans had to make an exhausting overnight journey, and were expected to begin fighting as soon as they got there. As they approached their destination, the roads became thicker with fleeing French troops and civilians. "You're too late," they kept shouting at the Americans, which can hardly have helped to boost their confidence.

When they arrived in the almost deserted town on June 1, the Americans found a small number of African troops defending it – left behind by their French colonial masters to fight and die in a seemingly impossible situation. Now, they were joined by 17,000 American troops, from both the army and the marines. When the Germans arrived, the battle for the town was intense, but the Americans held on. Fighting turned instead to the nearby town of Lucy-le-Bocage, close to Belleau Wood – a dense, almost impenetrable area of forest and rock around a mile long, and half a mile deep. Belleau Wood had no particular value in itself, but German troops had set up defensive positions there over June 2 and 3. It was proving to be a particularly effective base from which to harass the Americans, so army commanders decided that the Germans had to be driven out – especially as machine-gun fire from positions cleverly hidden in the thick undergrowth was causing high casualties.

It had already been a hard battle for the Americans. The whole time they had been in Château-Thierry it had not stopped raining. Artillery fire had fallen on them constantly, and German planes frequently swooped down from the sky to strafe them. It was difficult to shake off the feeling that they were facing a foe far superior in strength and experience.

In many ways, the German troops were much better. They had the most vital advantage any soldier can have – experience. But the Americans were out to prove themselves. They were fresh, well-armed and determined to win. When a French senior officer suggested to Colonel Wendell C. Neville, commander of the 5th Marines, that his men should withdraw, Neville spat: "Retreat? ...we just got here."

His marines had had a particularly difficult journey to the Château-Thierry battlefront and, for many of them, it would be their first time in combat. They had been dropped at Meaux station, 30km (20 miles) from the fighting, and had then had to march for two hours uphill. All around them, French artillery batteries fired a continuous barrage over to the German lines, and the ground shook constantly. Neville's men were exhausted, drenched from the rain, and had not been able to wash or shave for days.

Eventually, they arrived at a rendezvous point and were transferred to trucks which carried them towards Château-Thierry. Once there, they were sent to the nearby town of Lucy-le-Bocage, right next to Belleau Wood. Above the woods they spotted German observation balloons, which they nicknamed "sausages" because of their elongated shape. This was not good news. Certain they had been spotted, they awaited their enemy's attentions.

One marine private, William Francis, noted his thoughts about the place in his diary: "The Germans are shelling us pretty hard and the town is practically destroyed... A building on our right is burning, and as the flames light up the ground around us I can see dead marines lying in the narrow road..." Then his battalion was ordered into Belleau Wood itself:

At three o' clock [a.m.] we started again for the front trenches. We must reach the front lines before daylight. The woods we are going through is [sic] very dense, it

*seems impossible to make our way through, the limbs of
the trees are hitting us in the face and the men are cursing
like the devil... After a miserable night of hiking we
reached the front-line trenches... The Germans are
shelling us very hard; a shell hit close by caving in our
dug-out. A friend by the name of Burke was just killed, a
piece of shrapnel taking his head off."*

The trenches his fellow soldiers found themselves in were
barely waist-high. After their exhausting day, men had to try to
sleep while crouching ankle-deep in water.

Over the next couple of days, the Germans launched
night attacks on the newly arrived Americans. Francis
recorded that they were attacked throughout the hours of
darkness. On one occasion, a soldier threw a grenade at the
approaching Germans, only to have it bounce off a tree and
land back in his trench: "... we saw it just in time to hit the
bottom of our trench and keep from getting killed. I could
hardly keep from laughing for the boy on the other side of me
started cursing because he came near to getting killed by one
of our own men."

On June 6, marines were involved in a particularly costly assault on the woods, when they were ordered to charge against well-defended German positions over an open field. Pinned down by heavy fire during this attack, marine veteran Sergeant Dan Daly had inspired his men with the winning phrase: "Come on ya sons of ****, ya wanna live for ever?" A journalist had been on hand to capture the moment. Daly's immortality in Marine Corps folk law was assured. Such gung-ho bravery in the face of daunting odds was exactly what the marines were supposed to be all about. Daly survived the attack, and the war, although he was wounded in the fighting at Belleau Wood.

What followed was the worst single day's fighting in Marine Corps history, with 1,087 men killed or wounded. But the marines gained a foothold in the woods, and captured the small town of Bouresches on its edge.

Fighting for possession of Belleau Wood took on a grisly, claustrophobic quality. Inside this confined battleground, trees were close together and it was constantly dark. Thick underbrush often covered the ground left between the trees, and there were huge boulders there too, complete with their own little nooks and crannies.

The entire battle was fought in an atmosphere of great confusion. So dense were the woods, it was possible for enemies to pass within a few feet of each other and not see their opponents. In such a place, edgy soldiers had to exercise great care not to shoot their own comrades. As both German and American troops poured into this enclosed place, the ground between the trees became thick with fallen bodies. The personal debris of these dead soldiers – their knapsacks, letters from home and tattered uniforms – all blew around in the wind, pathetic remnants of their young lives, and dark omens for those who were still alive. Hand grenades, machine guns, gas and explosive shells all stripped the leaves from the trees.

When enemies met, it was often in that most dreaded form of fighting, hand-to-hand combat. Men fought with knuckle-dusters, bayonets and a hideous device the marines called a "toad-sticker" – a long, triangular blade attached to a knuckle handle. One marine private, who had been in the thick of hand-to-hand fighting for a terrifying 15 minutes before their surviving German opponents fled, wrote of the awful psychological strain such combat caused. After the fighting, he noted in a letter home, "most of us just sat down and cried."

Having to hold onto such a tightly confined space was an unnerving experience. Shells fell constantly on the American positions, and machine-gun and rifle fire continually sprayed through the trees, raining down chunks of rock, earth and splintered wood on the soldiers. The Germans also fired trench mortars at them – tube-like projectiles 1.3m (4ft) long, packed with high explosives, that the Americans called aerial torpedoes. They would sail up in the air, stop leisurely at the apex of their short, high arc, and then come crashing down with an explosion that shook all the ground around.

Gas shells also landed in the woods, leaving pockets of highly noxious fumes lurking low on the ground. Usually, the gas dispersed enough to be harmless, but it could catch sleeping or resting marines lying in shallow fox-holes, and leave them choking and retching. On one occasion, in the middle of a gas attack, Gunnery Sergeant Frederick Stockham gave his gas mask to a wounded marine. Stockham died a wretched death a few days later, his lungs destroyed by the gas, but he was posthumously awarded a Medal of Honor in 1939.

When the woods were shelled at night, violent flashes of blue flame would silhouette the splintered tree trunks and branches. Sometimes, said one marine officer, the flashes would come so fast, "it looked as if a great ragged searchlight was playing up and down in the dark." The shell blasts would hammer on the eardrums of the soldiers in the woods, until their ears sang in a constant, disorienting hum. But, more often than not, the shell fire proved ineffective. The blast of the shells was muffled by the density of the trees and vegetation.

With visibility so poor, soldiers on the edge of the woods followed the course of the battles within by listening to a ghastly procession of noises. From time to time, there would be a rapid ripple of machine-gun fire. This could only mean marines were attacking a machine-gun nest, and men were surely dying as they rushed at it. Then there would be an ominous pause, as the machine gunners were killed by bayonets and trench knives – the silent weapons of hand-to-hand fighting.

NIGHTMARE AT BELLEAU WOOD

American troops in the thick of fighting during the summer of 1918. Their arrival on the battlefields of the Western Front had a decisive effect on the outcome of the war.

By June 11, two-thirds of the woods had been captured by the Americans, who were now close to physical exhaustion. But the Germans counter-attacked in force, and intense fighting continued. As corpses piled up inside the woods, marines picked their way past the bodies of their enemy. Sometimes among the dead would be a living soldier, who would rise up behind them to shoot them in the back. The woods were full of snipers, both high in the trees and hidden in the undergrowth. These courageous men, hand-picked for a job that promised almost certain death, were an ever-present hazard when the machine-gunning and shelling died down, and the woods took on a sinister silence.

As if this were not enough, it was easy to get lost in such thick woods. There were few landmarks, and a man could lose all sense of direction. Soldiers had to carry compasses to make sure they returned to their own lines, rather than the enemy's.

On June 23, the Americans withdrew their troops and bombarded the forest for a full 14 hours. Then the soldiers entered again in force, and fought for another two days to try to rid Belleau Wood of German troops. Fighting was so heavy that 200 ambulances were needed to ferry away the wounded.

Eventually, on June 26, Belleau Wood finally fell into American hands. It had taken an agonizing 26 days.

Belleau Wood was one of the most significant battles of the war. If the Americans had not halted the German advance, the Germans could have carried on to Paris. US army general Robert L. Bullard was in no doubt as to the value of these men's achievement: "Had [the marines] arrived a few hours later I think that would have been the beginning of the end – France could not have stood the loss of Paris." The fighting at Belleau Wood was so intense, it also put an end to the speculation about whether American soldiers would really have the heart to fight.

But, for this victory, the marines paid a terrible price. On average, one in three men who took part in the battle was killed or wounded. One company lost 230 of its 250 men.

When the fighting ended, Marine Colonel Frederick May Wise, commander of the second battalion of the 5th Marines, reviewed his men: "At the battle's end... I lined the men up and looked over them. It was enough to break your heart. I had left Courcelles [their previous French position] on May

31 with 965 men and 26 officers – the best battalion I ever saw anywhere. I had taken them, raw recruits for the most. Ten months I had trained them. I had seen them grow into marines. Now before me stood 350 men and six officers; 615 men and 19 officers were gone."

Belleau Wood showed that the American military meant serious business. The Americans would fight a hard war, and casualties would be high, despite the short time they were engaged on the Western Front. By the time the war ended, over 126,000 American troops had lost their lives and 250,000 were wounded.

The American marines were immensely proud of their victory at Belleau Wood. The name is now given to a marine aircraft and troop carrier currently in service in the United States Navy. But, nearly 90 years later, the battle is still a source of controversy and resentment. Some American military historians feel marines should never have been sent into the woods. After all, similar fighting, especially between British and German troops in heavily wooded areas around the Somme and Ypres, had resulted in similarly high casualties. Perhaps American commanders should not have agreed to requests from their French counterparts to clear and hold this dreadful battleground.

Today, the forest looks as beautiful as any deep wood, and is a popular spot for family picnics. When the sun shines, dappled light plays through the branches, giving a luminous glow to the green moss growing up the trees and a fleeting warmth to the dank, brown carpet of leaves covering the ground. But, for decades after the fighting there, bodies and unexploded shells continued to be discovered in the forest, and only in their nightmares would visitors venture into the darker depths of Belleau Wood.

FROM GREAT WAR TO
FIRST WORLD WAR

1918

BARELY A YEAR AFTER the conflict ended, journalist Charles A'Court Repington of the London *Times*, coined the term "The *First* World War". Like many others, he had realized that "the war that will end war" would actually become the major cause of another world war in the future. Even when the warring nations were conducting peace negotiations in Paris in 1919, their leaders knew the peace they were making was not going to last. The French supreme commander, Marshal Ferdinand Foch, dismissed the proceedings as a 20-year cease-fire. British Prime Minister Lloyd George privately remarked: "We shall have to do the whole thing again in 25 years at three times the cost." He was nearly right – the Second World War broke out 20 years later and claimed four times as many lives, rather than three. So the most terrible war in human history had a fitting conclusion – it bred another that would be even worse.

The decision reached in Paris to "make Germany pay" was especially shortsighted. Germany was forced to make payments of billions of dollars, known as *reparations*, to the victorious nations. The American delegates, wisely, never agreed to this idea. But France, in particular, insisted on prompt payment.

As the war ended, Germany was hovering on the brink of a communist revolution. Then it suffered the shame of defeat, lost territory and an economy ruined by war and reparations. The German population was outraged. They had won the war in the east, and the war in the west had ended before Allied soldiers invaded Germany. How could it possibly be claimed that they had lost the war? Their bewilderment was especially intense because German newspapers had not reported the full extent of the German army collapse. In the 1930s, a former front-line soldier by the name of Adolf Hitler capitalized on this source of resentment. His Nazi party came to power in 1933 and set in train the events that caused the Second World War.

Men had fought in the war for many reasons. For some, it was duty, patriotism or the belief that they were fighting for a better world. For others, it was the simple fact that they would be imprisoned or shot, and a disgrace to their families, if they didn't. Men who survived the war expected some reward for their efforts. Most were disappointed.

The war left Russia with a Bolshevik government which inflicted famine, murderous purges and severe repression on its population for the next 70 years. France had won, but it was hardly worth the price. It never recovered its position in the world as a great power. The war left Britain and the British empire with over 942,000 dead and an economy close to breakdown. Only America had done well, emerging as the world's strongest and richest nation.

In another twist of fate, just as the conflict ended, a colossal influenza epidemic swept through the world. Weakened by the stress and deprivation of four years of war, 10 million people died. Among them were William Leefe Robinson, who had shot down the first zeppelin over London, and the now world-famous Austrian painters, Gustav Klimt and Egon Schiele.

Those who survived the war would suffer its consequences for the rest of their lives. Soldiers with lungs ruined by gas, or missing three or even four limbs, slowly faded away in nursing homes. Throughout Europe, asylums were full of men suffering from "shell-shock". Today, this is a psychological condition known and recognized in combat soldiers as post-traumatic stress disorder. But, in 1918, military tradition and society as a whole were only a couple of years on from believing that such men should be shot for cowardice. There are still men and women alive today whose fathers were shot during the war because they suffered mental breakdown brought on by the strain of fighting in the trenches.

Even those who survived with no obvious physical or psychological damage were tormented by what they had seen and done. One in eight men who fought in the war were killed. Most were under 30, and many still in their teens. Hundreds of thousands of women around the same age were unable to marry, because there simply weren't enough men to go around. "When I think I could have been a happy grandmother today if it hadn't been for that terrible war," said one elderly single woman near the end of her life, reflecting a view that must have been held by thousands of others.

The war is now part of our history, and it is still, just about, part of living memory. In 1998, at the 80th anniversary of the armistice, there were 160 men still alive in Britain who had fought in the Great War. Perhaps similar numbers existed in Germany, France, Russia and America. By the time this book is published, almost all of them will have died. The war is still a frequent topic of novels, films and television documentaries. It is difficult to find anything positive to say about it. But perhaps those of that luckless generation born at the end of the 19th century would take comfort from the fact that the slaughter they endured still haunts us today as a stark reminder of the horror of war.

A small cemetery close to the Western Front, in the years between the wars. Hope that the conflict would be 'the war to end all war' withered in the bitter peace that followed the Treaty of Versailles.

"As dirty a business as the world has ever seen..."

1939-1945

MORE THAN HALF A CENTURY now separates us from the Second World War. The number of films, TV documentaries and books still produced on the subject show that it continues to exert a powerful fascination. Today the numbers of those who actually fought in the war is rapidly dwindling, but many people have grandparents or other relations who remember it all too well as children. The conflict is not some distant history – it is still within graspable, living memory.

The stories in this book touch on many different aspects of the war. There are epic naval encounters between titanic warships, and monumental battles between armies of hundreds of thousands of men. But there are also single-handed duels between opposing snipers, and other tales of lonely individuals facing almost certain death.

For those who survived the war it would remain the most intense and vivid experience of their lives. Many of those who died were in their late teens or early twenties – and many of them would still be alive today had the war not come to scythe them away.

The Second World War was fought between two great power blocs. On one side was the Axis – an alliance of Germany, Italy and Japan, who were also joined by Hungary, Romania and Bulgaria. On the other side were the Allies – principally Britain and her empire, Soviet Russia and the United States. These gargantuan forces faced off against each other in four major areas of fighting: Western Europe, Eastern

"As dirty a business as the world has ever seen..."

Europe and the U.S.S.R, North Africa, and the Eastern Pacific and South East Asia (see maps on pages 194 and 196).

The cause of any war is usually too complex to reduce to a simple explanation. But, in essence, the Second World War was caused by the desire of the Axis powers to gain empires and the unwillingness of the Allies to let them. Nazi dictator Adolf Hitler dreamed of *lebensraum* (living space) in Eastern Europe and Russia, for his German master race. Mussolini wanted to create a new Roman empire for Italy. Japan's military rulers sought to take over the Asian and Pacific territories fading European powers had seized for their own empires in previous centuries.

The war began with the German invasion of Poland on September 1, 1939. Here Polish cavalry charged against German tanks with predictably disastrous results. It ended on September 2, 1945, six years and a day later, when Japan finally surrendered, following the destruction of two of her cities by atomic bombs. At first Germany and her allies made spectacular advances, and almost all of Europe fell under their control. This was largely due to the effective fighting strength of the German army and their *Blitzkrieg* (lightning war)

"As dirty a business as the world has ever seen..."

German tanks rumble through the cobbled streets of the Czech capital Prague, in the spring of 1939. Aside from the mostly-willing Austrians, the Czechs were the first nation to fall under Nazi control.

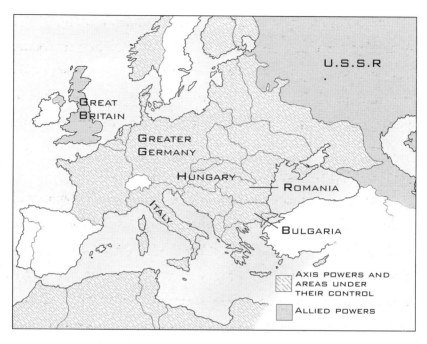

Map showing the two sides in Europe, October/November 1942

tactics. Here, tanks, aircraft and other powered vehicles, were used to make fast and highly effective work of opposing armies. In the first two years of the war, only Britain held out, protected from an invasion by its air force, navy and the English Channel. The Battle of Britain – the first significant aerial battle in history – was Hitler's first defeat.

"AS DIRTY A BUSINESS AS THE WORLD HAS EVER SEEN..."

With Britain isolated at the edge of the continent, Hitler turned to his chief ambition, the conquest of Soviet Russia. The invasion on June 22, 1941, was the greatest in history. By the autumn of that year, German troops were at the gates of Leningrad and Moscow. But a suicidal resistance by Red Army troops, and the onset of the ferocious Russian winter, prevented Hitler from snatching his greatest prize.

On the other side of the world, Germany's ally Japan had been establishing her own empire on the Asian Pacific seaboard (see map). On December 7, she attacked the United States at Pearl Harbor. So began a devastating campaign, which saw her armies sweep through the Philippines and Malaya, then down to Java and Burma, to threaten both Australia and India. When Japan attacked the United States, Hitler also declared war on the Americans, despite the fact that he had still to defeat the British and the Russians. British prime minister Winston Churchill was ecstatic. "So we had won the war after all. Our history would not come to an end," he reflected that night. "Hitler's fate was sealed... As for the Japanese, they would be ground to a powder. All the rest was merely the proper application of overwhelming force."

"AS DIRTY A BUSINESS AS THE WORLD HAS EVER SEEN..."

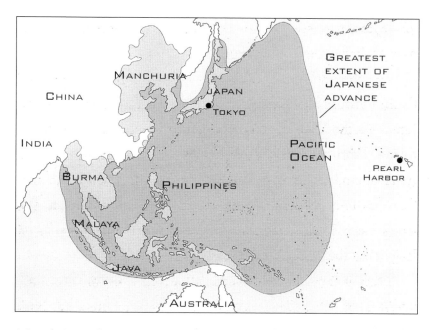

Map showing the greatest extent of the Japanese advance

He was absolutely right. Germany and Japan had decided to wage war against the most powerful nation on Earth. America responded to their challenge by diverting her vast industrial strength to winning the war. In three and a half years, her dockyards built 1,200 new warships. By 1944, her factories were producing one new warplane every five minutes. Quite aside from this mammoth expenditure,

"As dirty a business as the world has ever seen..."

$2 billion was still found to fund the development of the world's first atomic weapons.

In the summer of 1942, American, British and Commonwealth troops began to claw back territory seized by Japan in the first six months of the Pacific war. In North Africa, a British victory against German and Italian troops at El Alamein, in October 1942, scotched any possibility that German and Japanese troops would link up in India. The victory also allowed for the American and British invasion of Italy from the south, which took place in July 1943.

During 1942, the Soviets began to recover from the invasion of 1941. Their armies were better equipped, both from their own factories and substantial American and British arms imports, and their soldiers had become a formidable fighting force. When Russian troops destroyed the German 6th Army at Stalingrad over the winter of 1942 to 1943, the war in the east turned into a slow retreat that ended with the Soviet occupation of the German capital, Berlin.

On June 6, 1944, American, British and Canadian troops took part in the D-Day landings in Normandy. Now Hitler's armies had to fight on three fronts – Eastern Europe, Western

"As dirty a business as the world has ever seen..."

Europe and Italy. Within a year the war in Europe was over. Hitler committed suicide on April 30, 1945, and on May 8 Germany surrendered. Japan lasted through to the summer, until the devastating atomic bomb attacks on Hiroshima and Nagasaki.

Novelist John Steinbeck's description of the war: "As dirty a business as the world has ever seen..." seems a fair epitaph. At least fifty-five million people died as a direct result of it.

THE FIRST AND FINAL VOYAGE OF THE *BISMARCK*

THE WAR AT SEA, MAY 1941

IN EARLY MAY OF 1941, the crew of the *Bismarck* had been feverishly preparing for an inspection by none other than the German *führer* (leader), Adolf Hitler. Now he was here among them. Decks had been scrubbed, rails polished, uniforms pressed and the ship's barber had worked his way through as many of the 2,100 men as time and his blistered fingers allowed. The visit to Germany's greatest battleship was going well. The crew, whose average age was all of 21, were immensely proud of their new vessel. As Hitler passed their assembled ranks, they stood there, faces stiff with pride and overawed to be in the presence of their leader. Not everyone on parade was impressed with Hitler, though. As he walked by anti-aircraft gunner Alois Haberditz, the Nazi leader looked straight through him. Haberditz shuddered. Hitler had eyes as cold and pitiless as a shark.

The Führer, who had an almost schoolboy fascination with battleships, was taken on a tour of the ship. He seemed particularly interested in the *Bismarck's* gunnery control system – a state-of-the-art computer mechanism which took in the ship's speed and course and that of its enemy, wind direction and shell flight time. This produced changes of correction of aim at what was – by the standards of the time – lightning speed. Hitler also noted with pride the two huge swastikas – the emblem of his Nazi party – painted at either end of the ship, which served to identify it to their own aircraft.

Germany had a small navy, but her warships were the most advanced in the world, and the *Bismarck* was the pride of her fleet. A truly gargantuan war machine, over a sixth of a mile long, and bristling with huge guns, she was unquestionably the fastest and best armed and protected battleship of her day.

Among the officials with Hitler on this tour of inspection were *Bismarck's* two most senior officers. The Captain was Ernst Lindemann, a stiff, rather frail looking 45-year-old, who was never seen without a cigarette. In his official portrait, Lindemann stares out at the world with piercing, intelligent eyes, his blond hair slicked back on his head, with two enormous ears. But his stern and slightly comical look was misleading. His crew held him in both high regard and affection – some even referred to him respectfully as *our father*. He emanated both approachability and confidence, and being appointed captain of the *Bismarck* was the greatest break in his naval career.

Also sent to sea with Lindemann was the fleet commander, Admiral Günther Lütjens, together with 50 of his staff. Lütjens was a starkly handsome 51-year-old, bearing a passing resemblance to American film actor Lee Marvin. Lütjens, like Lindemann and many officers in the German navy, was not a great supporter of Hitler, and had tried to protect Jewish officers under his command. Right from the start of the war he had believed Germany would be defeated. Perhaps that was why he was such a forbidding man to be around, and it was said that he almost never smiled or laughed. Although he was a fine and experienced commander, he did not have Lindemann's leadership skills, as subsequent events would show. Lütjens knew the British feared his powerful ship, and that they would do everything in their considerable power to destroy it. He, more than any man aboard the *Bismarck*, did not expect to return from this posting alive.

At this stage of the war, Britain was the only major European power still undefeated by the Nazis. Hitler, and Germany's commander-in-chief of the navy, Grand Admiral Erich Raeder, intended to use the navy to starve their isolated island opponent into defeat. Britain's survival, after all, depended on cargo ships from her colonies and North America. So far this tactic was working. In early 1941, the battleships *Scharnhorst* and *Gneisenau* had ventured out into the North Atlantic on raiding missions and sunk 22 merchant ships between them. Now, in May of this year, the *Bismarck* was preparing to do the same. The expedition was code-named *Rheinübung*, or *Operation Rhine*, and sailing out with the *Bismarck* was another modern ship, the *Prinz Eugen*. This raid would be different. On previous missions German warships had been told to avoid battle with the British Navy at all cost, and concentrate solely on destroying merchant ships. But now, so confident were the officers of the German High Command in their new warships, they had given permission for them to fight back if they came under attack.

Most of the crew, in their invincible youth and invincible battleship, had no idea of the horrors that awaited them. But a few more experienced ones had been aboard sinking ships, and were old enough to know that the British Navy was actually quite a formidable foe. Even Grand Admiral Raeder had admitted to confidants that the surface vessels in his navy (as opposed to his lethally effective submarine fleet) could do no more than take part in hit and run raids. They were heavily outnumbered by the British, who had always depended on their powerful fleet to keep control of their sprawling overseas empire and protect their trade. When Raeder heard that war had broken out with Britain, he greeted the news with resignation. "Our surface forces can do no more than show that they can die gallantly," he declared.

Almost from the start of their mission, *Bismarck* and *Prinz Eugen* were shadowed by British planes and ships – all carefully keeping out of range of their powerful guns. When news reached the British Admiralty that the two German ships had left Korsfjord, in Norway, to venture out into the shipping lanes of the North Atlantic, immediate action was taken. The Royal Navy ordered two of their own most powerful warships – *Hood* and *Prince of Wales* – to intercept them, and these ships slipped away from their Orkney base at Scapa Flow in the early hours of May 22. In overall command of this force was Vice-Admiral Lancelot Holland, who sailed aboard the *Hood*. A grey-haired, distinguished-looking man, he had the air of a venerable BBC commentator wheeled out to present a royal funeral. Within a day, another great battleship, *King George V*, the aircraft carrier *Victorious*, and four cruisers, had also set off to join him.

The *Hood* was quite possibly the most famous battle cruiser in the world. Built in 1918, she was a handsome and formidably-armed vessel, a sixth of a mile from bow to stern. *Hood* had become a symbol of British naval power, and had a fearsome reputation. During training exercises, the crew of the *Bismarck* had frequently run through attack and resistance tactics, with *Hood* as their imaginary enemy. Now they were about to fight her for real.

Bismarck and *Prinz Eugen* took a course up past the north of Iceland, and through the Denmark Straits, which separate Iceland from Greenland. Here they sailed close by the huge sheath of ice which forms around the coastal waters of Greenland for most of the year. On the journey up, the two deck swastikas were hurriedly covered over with a fresh coat of paint. The only aircraft out here would be British ones – and such insignia would clearly indicate that the *Bismarck* was an enemy ship. It was in these chilly waters that the *Hood* and the *Prince of Wales* raced to intercept them.

This far north, during spring and summer, night falls for a few hours or not at all. In late May, dawn came before 2:00am, casting a pale grey light over a heaving sea, dotted by patches of fog and brief flurries of snow. Men stationed in lookout posts aboard the ships longed to scuttle back to the cozy fug of their cramped quarters, as a biting wind gnawed at their bones, and icy spray whipped over the bows to sting their numb faces. This desolate spot near the frozen top of the world was one of the most dismal places on Earth.

Aboard the German ships, crews were expecting an imminent attack. But they had no real idea how close the British actually were. The cruiser *Suffolk* had sighted them just after 11:00 in the evening on May 23. Alerted, Vice-Admiral Holland closed in at once. By 5:00 the next morning, he was expecting to sight his enemy at any minute. Sure enough, two ships were spotted at 5:30am, black dots 27km (17 miles) away on their northwest horizon.

On *Bismarck* and *Prinz Eugen*, the crews had spent an anxious night. There had been several false alarms as hydrophone (sound detection) operators thought they had picked up the incoming rumble of British engines. But it was a radio message from German headquarters, who had been monitoring British transmissions, that told them their enemy was almost upon them. Just after the message arrived, lookouts spotted two smoke trails from the funnels of the approaching British, on the southeast horizon. Even then, the Germans were not sure this was an attack. Perhaps they were still being shadowed by smaller vessels, who were just keeping tabs on them.

But by 5:50am it was obvious to Lütjens that the approaching ships meant to attack him. He sent a terse radio message to his headquarters: "Am engaging two heavy ships." Then he prepared himself for the battle to come.

In all four ships, in an oft-rehearsed procedure, one ton of high-explosive shells were hauled up to the huge gun turrets by a complex system of pulleys and rails from magazines deep inside the hull. In *Bismarck* and *Hood*, these monstrous projectiles were 38 or 41cm (15 or 16 inches) across, and were loaded into guns 6m (20ft) long and weighing 100 tons each.

Holland gave the order to open fire at 21km (13 miles), and almost at once all four ships began exchanging broadsides. At these distances shells would take up to half a minute to reach their target. It was just before 6:00am. So loud was the roar of their huge guns they could be heard in Reykjavik, the capital of Iceland. But when battle began it soon became apparent that the *Hood*'s reputation had been undeserved.

Built just after the First World War, she had been given heavy steel protection along her vertical surfaces – when current warship designs assumed enemy shells would travel in low and hit her sides. Twenty years later, such assumptions no longer applied. By 1940 warships aimed their shells in high, arc-like trajectories, where they plunged down on top of decks and turrets. Here were *Hood*'s weakest spots. And the *Bismarck*'s second and third salvo had an astonishing effect on the British ship. Men aboard *Bismarck* and *Prinz Eugen* watched in astonishment as their much-feared opponent exploded like a giant firework, lifting the entire front half up out of the water, and breaking the battleship in two. A huge, strangely silent sheet of flame shot high in the air, as intense as a blow torch and so bright it could be seen over 50km (30 miles) away. *Hood* turned over and sank. In less than five minutes, in the bleakest of battlegrounds, Vice-Admiral Holland and all but three of his 1,421 crew died.

Prince of Wales veered sharply to avoid hitting the *Hood*. She was in deep trouble herself. Seven shells from *Prinz Eugen* and *Bismarck* had hit her, including one at the bridge which had killed everyone there but the Captain, John Leach, and two of his officers. Several of her main gun turrets had also jammed. Sensing another catastrophe, and with no chance of destroying either German ship, Leach ordered a speedy retreat.

Aboard the *Bismarck* and *Prinz Eugen* there was an atmosphere of euphoria. The crews had been led to believe they were aboard the most powerful warships on the planet, and events had proved this to be true. Hadn't they? Yet the atmosphere on *Bismarck*'s bridge was strained. Lütjens and Lindemann had exchanged sharp words about the wisdom of going after the *Prince of Wales*. Even though she was an easy target, Lütjens had decided to stick to his original mission – sinking enemy merchant ships. He was not prepared to take any unnecessary risks.

And there was bad news too. Although *Prinz Eugen* had escaped unscathed, *Bismarck* had taken two shells from the *Prince of Wales*. Men had been killed and the ship's medical bay was filling up with burned and scalded casualties. Most serious of all, a shell had sailed clean through the front of the ship close to the bow. It had not exploded, but had left a man-sized hole, just above the water line. As the *Bismarck* lurched up and down through the choppy ocean, the sea flooded in and drained out, gradually filling the surrounding compartments with 2,000 tons of water. Fuel lines had been broken, leaving 1,000 tons of fuel in the forward tanks cut off from the engine room, and the ship was seeping a sickly brown trail of oil. Part of the ship's engine had also been damaged.

News of the *Hood*'s destruction caused a sensation across the world. British prime minister Winston Churchill would recall it as the single worst moment of the war. The British Admiralty issued a famous order: "SINK THE *BISMARCK*", and four battleships, two battle cruisers, two aircraft carriers, 13 cruisers, and 21 destroyers were dispatched to avenge the *Hood*. The man given the responsibility of hunting down the *Bismarck* was Admiral John Tovey, commander of the British home fleet. A small, dapper man, whose sharp, determined features gave him something of the look of a bull terrier, Tovey had considerable forces at his disposal, including his own flagship *King George V*.

The first and final voyage of the Bismarck

Tovey's first task was to ensure the *Bismarck* did not vanish from sight. The North Atlantic, after all, stretched for more than a million nautical square miles. Although she was still being shadowed by smaller British vessels, it would be easy enough to lose her.

On the morning of *Bismarck*'s first extraordinary day in action, the rain and drizzle eventually gave way to an occasional hint of sunshine, but the sea was still heaving. Lütjens and Lindemann had been considering their options. Their ship was losing fuel and taking in water. Although it still had full firepower, it now lacked speed – an essential attribute for its hit and run mission. Lütjens ordered the *Prinz Eugen* to break away from *Bismarck* and continue alone. He would take his own ship back to the port of St. Nazaire, France, for repairs. At their current speed, they should make the 2,700km (1,700 mile) journey in just under four days.

Meanwhile, the British made their first counterattack with *Swordfish* torpedo bombers from the aircraft carrier *Victorious*. These quaint biplanes looked like relics from the First World War, and they lumbered dangerously slowly through the sky. *Bismarck* fought off the *Swordfish* with ease – her AA (anti-aircraft) guns putting up a protective sheet of flame that prevented the planes from launching their torpedoes accurately. There was one hit, but it caused minimal damage. But, far to the south, another British aircraft carrier was hurrying up to intercept the *Bismarck*. The *Ark Royal*, and her *Swordfish* crews would soon prove to be far more deadly.

Sunday May 25 was Lütjens birthday. He had always believed he would die on this mission, and had resigned himself to the fact that this would be his last ever birthday. That midday he made a speech to his men – talking to them over the ship's PA system – and something of his dark mood rubbed off on a crew still exuberant from their brush with the *Hood* and *Prince of Wales*.

"The *Hood* was the pride of England," he told them. "The enemy will now attempt to concentrate his forces and set them on to us… The German nation is with you. We will fight till our gun barrels glow red and the last shell has left the breech. For us soldiers it is now 'victory or death'."

It was not a diplomatic choice of words – but even admirals are human, and Lütjens knew all too well what was coming. But he was too pessimistic. During the night of May 25 *Bismarck* had outrun her British pursuers, and when dawn came they had lost sight of her. But Lütjens did not know this. Later that day he sent a long, despondent message to German High Command. This was picked up by British radio trackers, who concentrated an aerial search in the area where they detected the signal. But even then, luck was still with Lütjens. Tovey's fleet miscalculated his position – and assumed *Bismarck* was heading back to Norway, rather than France. They altered their own pursuit course accordingly.

It would be a whole 31 hours before the British found the *Bismarck*. Around 10:30 on the morning of May 26, observant members of the crew noticed an RAF *Catalina* flying boat circling just outside the range of their AA guns. By now the ailing battleship was approaching the Bay of Biscay. The port of St. Nazaire was a mere day or so away, as was the imminent prospect of both U-boat and air escort. *Bismarck*'s position was duly reported by the *Catalina*, and Tovey's fleet altered course.

To the south, the carrier *Ark Royal* was closing in fast, its huge bulk heaving alarmingly in the rough sea. Amid torrents of seawater that sprayed the flight deck, ground crews prepared the ponderous *Swordfish* bombers, loading heavy torpedoes to their undersides. In the middle of the afternoon, 15 *Swordfish* lumbered into the air. They did not expect to sink the *Bismarck*, but they hoped, at the very least, to cause enough damage to slow her down, so that pursuing British warships could catch up and attack. Slipping through low cloud, fog and driving rain, they pounced, flying just above the churning waves to unleash their torpedoes toward their target. If the crews of the *Swordfish* were surprised by the complete lack of defensive fire from the ship below, it did not cause them to pause and consider their target. All the torpedoes missed – which was fortunate for the *Swordfish* crews, because the ship they had actually attacked was the British cruiser *Sheffield*.

Amid huge humiliation and embarrassment, a second wave of 15 *Swordfish* was sent off into the slow falling dusk. This time, they found the *Bismarck*, still 1,000km (620 miles) from St. Nazaire. They moved so slowly they seemed to be hanging in the air. But they flew in so low, their wheels almost brushing the waves, that *Bismarck*'s guns could only fire above them. This time two torpedoes hit home. One caused only minor damage. The other went off underneath the stern,

THE FIRST AND FINAL VOYAGE OF THE BISMARCK

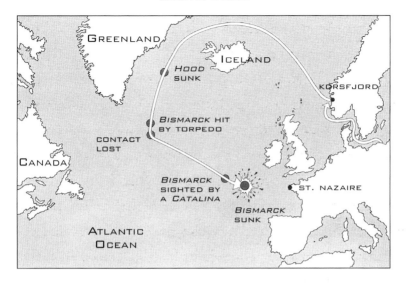

The last voyage of the Bismarck, *May 1941*

with a huge watery explosion that shot like a whiplash through the length of the ship. It buckled deck plates and bulkheads, and threw men to the floor or against metal partitions and instruments, with breathtaking violence. Above the site of the explosion, water surged into the ship with a vengeance, flooding the entire steering compartment. The sea burst through once waterproof compartments. It gushed down cable pipes that ran the length of the ship, to spurt out unexpectedly, far away from the site of the damage.

Aboard the *Ark Royal,* senior commanders listened to the wildly excited reports of their young pilots, and tried to sift fact from fiction to determine exactly what damage had been done. One pilot's account seemed to indicate something extremely significant. After the attack, the *Bismarck* had been seen to make two huge circles on her course, then slow down almost to a halt. Clearly, her steering had been badly damaged. In fact, the rudder had jammed at 15° to port.

Aboard the stricken vessel desperate measures were called for. The *Bismarck* carried three seaplanes. Plans were made to remove the hangar door where they were stored, and weld it to the side of the stern, to counteract the effect of the rudder. But bad weather made such a scheme impossible.

Following the *Swordfish* attack, Lütjens sent another grim signal home: "Ship no longer steering." German naval authorities reacted by ordering U-boats to head for the *Bismarck*'s position as soon as possible. But U-boats are not the swiftest of vessels, and there were none nearby. Informed of the *Bismarck*'s grim predicament, Hitler had a radio signal sent to Lütjens: "All of Germany is with you. What can still be done will be done. The performance of your duty will strengthen our people in their struggle for their existence." It was not a message that offered any hope of survival.

Bismarck's crew passed a long, dreadful night – each man wondering whether he would live to see another dusk. Many had nightmares, and men woke screaming or sobbing. When word spread that the rudder had been put out of action, the older members of the crew took this to be a death sentence. Later in the night, permission was given for the crew to help themselves to anything they wanted – food, drink – a tacit admission that the ship was doomed. But Lindemann had assured them U-boats and aircraft were heading out to protect them, and some of the younger sailors still held out hope that they would survive after all.

During the night, Lindemann ordered the engines to stop. When the chief engineer requested they be started again, Lindemann replied, "Ach, do as you like." After five nights with virtually no sleep, and all the stress and worry of commanding a ship in a now impossible situation, he was a man at the end of his tether.

The first and final voyage of the Bismarck

To keep the crew from brooding overmuch about the battle to come, records of popular songs were played over the ship's PA system. But such obvious psychological tactics failed – the songs reminded the men too much of girlfriends or wives and families back home. Lindemann had also come up with the ruse of getting men with no immediate job to do to construct a dummy funnel of wood and canvas. The idea was to change the *Bismarck*'s silhouette, so that enemy ships or aircraft would think it was another battleship, and leave it alone. This was some considerable task, and men were kept busy painting the canvas and building the scaffolding structure right through the day.

At first light on May 27, the day *Bismarck* had hoped to reach the safety of a French port, Tovey and his fleet closed in to finish the job. Along with his own flagship *King George V*, was the huge battleship *Rodney*, the cruisers *Norfolk* and *Dorsetshire*, and several others.

Aboard the *Bismarck*, exhausted lookouts saw two massive ships heading straight for them. Tovey intended the sight of *King George V* and *Rodney* boldly closing in to unnerve the German crew, and it worked. The battle that followed, which started with a salvo from *Rodney* at 8:47am, was unspeakably grisly. As they homed in, the British ships took carefully timed evasive action, darting one way then another, to avoid the *Bismarck*'s powerful guns.

This time luck was with the British, and few of the *Bismarck*'s shells found their mark. By 8:59am *King George V* and *Rodney* were both firing steadily. Four salvos a minute were falling around the *Bismarck*, which was now completely obscured by smoke and spray from the huge towering columns of water sent into the air by near misses.

At 9:02am a shell from *Rodney* hit *Bismarck* near the bow, and the entire front end of the ship was momentarily swallowed by a blinding sheet of flame. This one shot, ten or so minutes into the battle, was the most crucial of the day. After that, *Bismarck*'s two front turrets fired no more. In one, the huge guns pointed down to the deck, in the other, one barrel pointed up, and the other down. In that one explosion, perhaps half the ship's crew had been killed. Only one man from the entire front section survived the battle.

Bismarck may have been the most technologically advanced battleship in the world, but she was completely outgunned. For a further hour, hundreds of shells fell on her. On deck or below, men were blown to pieces or burned to death, as her interior turned into a blazing deathtrap. As the British ships drew closer, *Bismarck*'s exceptionally effective construction merely made her destruction even more prolonged. As the shelling continued, fierce fires blazed all over her deck and superstructure, and *Bismarck* began to list to port.

By 10:00am the British ships were close enough to see streams of men leaping into the sea, to save themselves from the flames and still-exploding shells. When it was obvious that the crew were abandoning their ship, Tovey ordered the shelling to stop. Burkard Freiherr von Mullenheim-Rechberg, fire-control officer for the *Bismarck*'s after guns, emerged from his battle station and surveyed the damage. "The anti-aircraft guns and searchlights that once surrounded the after station had disappeared without a trace. Where there had been guns, shields, instruments, there was empty space. The superstructure (upper) decks were littered with scrap metal. There were holes in the stack (funnel), but it was still standing…"

THE FIRST AND FINAL VOYAGE OF THE
BISMARCK

Survivors from the Bismarck *are pulled aboard a British warship. Moments after this picture was taken, the rescuers hurried off, fearing a U-Boat attack, leaving many of these men to die in the freezing water.*

Von Mullenheim-Rechberg could see that the ship was slowly capsizing. Amid the carnage and rubble, men were running around, desperately searching for ways to save themselves. Such was the destruction on the decks that not a single lifeboat, life raft or float remained. Amid the smoke and ruin, von Mullenheim-Rechberg saw doctors busy attending to the wounded, giving them pain-killing morphine jabs to ease their agony.

Many men were trapped inside the ship, as fires cut off escape routes, and shells buckled hatches which now no longer opened. Some were able to escape by climbing up shell hoists, wiring shafts or any other kind of duct large enough to take a man. Many others gave up hope and sat where they could, waiting for the ship to go down. But still the *Bismarck* stayed afloat.

During the morning, Tovey was expecting both submarine and air attack by German forces, and was anxious to leave the area as quickly as possible. He ordered any ship with torpedoes left to fire them at the *Bismarck*, to send her to the bottom of the sea. The *Dorsetshire* fired three from close range, and all struck home. Finally, at 10:39am, the *Bismarck* turned over and sank. To this day it is unclear whether or not she sank because of these torpedoes, or because her crew deliberately flooded her, to keep their ship from falling into British hands.

Men in the water near the bow witnessed one final extraordinary scene. Although Lütjens had been killed by shellfire early in the battle, Captain Lindemann had survived. Now he was sighted with a junior officer, standing near the front of the ship, with seawater fast approaching its sinking bows. From his gestures he appeared to be urging this man to save himself. But the man refused and stayed next to Lindemann. Then, as the deck slowly turned over into the sea, Lindemann stopped and raised his hand to his cap in a final salute, then disappeared. Afterwards, one survivor recalled: "I always thought such things happened only in books, but I saw it with my own eyes."

By now the *Dorsetshire* and the destroyer *Maori* were the only remaining ships at the scene. Close to where the *Bismarck* had gone down, British sailors could see hundreds of tiny heads floating in the water. *Bismarck*'s crew had been told that the British shot their prisoners – a sly piece of Nazi propaganda designed to ensure German military forces would always be reluctant to surrender. But as the freezing survivors swam toward the British ships, they discovered this was not the case. Men were hurriedly bundled aboard. But in a cruel twist of fate, a lookout from the *Dorsetshire* spotted a whiff of smoke a couple of miles away which was thought to be a German U-Boat. The British ships were immediately ordered to move off. Although over a hundred men were rescued, 300 were left in the water. As the day wore on, these exhausted men who had seen their hopes of survival raised then crushed, slowly succumbed to the intense cold of the ocean. Only five lived to tell the tale. Three were picked up by a U-boat, and two by a German weather ship. When other German ships arrived on the scene they found only rubble, lifebelts and a few floating bodies.

Bismarck turned completely upside down on her descent to the ocean floor 5km (3 miles) below, and her four huge gun turrets fell from their housings. By the time she hit the slopes of a vast underwater volcano 20 minutes later, she had righted herself, and set off a huge landslide which carried her further down the slope. There she lies today, where she was recently discovered by the marine archaeologist Robert Ballard. In 1989, his underwater cameras showed that the hull remains intact. Shells, barnacles and sundry other small sea creatures line the wooden planks of the deck. And as the fresh paint applied a few days before she sank gradually dissolved in the seawater, the swastikas on *Bismarck*'s bow and stern have made a sinister reappearance.

THE VENLO SNATCH

1939

IT WAS OCTOBER 21, 1939, and the Second World War had just begun. In Zutphen, a town in neutral Holland, rain drummed down on the roof of a large Buick limousine. Behind the wheel Sigismund Best adjusted his monocle and squinted through the window of his car. Suddenly another car drew up. A man jumped out. Best leaned over to open the door and the man climbed in beside him. The Buick roared into life and rolled through the streets, wipers flailing.

Best looked like the typical English gentleman. Tall, with an aristocratic manner, he wore spats and a tweed suit. His hair was carefully oiled; he even wore a monocle. But this was deceptive. Best was in fact half Indian. He was also a spy. He lived in Holland with his Dutch wife, and ran a small business importing bicycles, but really he was a member of Z Branch – an independent group of agents which formed part of Britain's Special Intelligence Service – SIS.

Best's credentials were impressive. He spoke four languages, and during the First World War he had run a successful network of spies behind enemy lines. Currently, he was trying to make contact with dissatisfied Germans willing to fight against Hitler and the Nazis. As far as he could tell, things were going very well indeed.

Best had been contacted some weeks earlier by one of his agents, a refugee who had fled from persecution in Germany. The man knew many high ranking officers within the German army and he had assured Best that there was a great deal of resentment against Hitler, resentment which had built up to a strong resistance movement. Best had probed deeper and had been given the name of an officer involved with the resistance movement – Hauptmann Schaemell. This was the man now sitting in the car with him.

Best spoke German well, and the two men drove through the Dutch countryside chatting together in German about classical music. At the town of Arnhem, they picked up two of Best's colleagues, an English officer named Major Stevens, and a Dutch officer named Captain Klop. Although Holland was neutral at the time, Klop was assisting the British. He wanted to keep his nationality a secret, so he was pretending to be Canadian and was using the name Coppens. This was a convincing alias. Klop had spent several years living in Canada, and the country was an ally of Britain's.

Best drove on. Schaemell, he reflected, seemed like a good catch. As they drove, the German reeled off a list of officers who were eager to see Hitler's downfall and named an important general who was prepared to lead the resistance. Schaemell promised to bring the general to their next meeting, which they set for October 30.

What Best didn't know was that the Germans were one step ahead of him. The refugee who had introduced him to

Schaemell was in fact a German spy named Franz Fischer. The resistance movement Best was hearing all about did not exist. Schaemell himself didn't exist either. He was really Walter Schellenberg – a 29 year-old ex-lawyer who was now head of German foreign intelligence. Instead of spying for Best, he wanted to annihilate him.

Schellenberg's plan was simple. Over the coming weeks, he intended to lull the British and Dutch agents into a false sense of security, by pretending to be a willing collaborator. Then he would lure them into meetings, which would enable him to penetrate the SIS and find out about their operations.

First, however, Schellenberg had to convince Best that he was genuinely working against the Nazis. When he returned to Holland from Germany on October 30, he brought with him two army friends. One of the men was silver-haired, with an old-fashioned elegance which made him look as if he might be a disgruntled aristocrat seeking to overthrow the Nazis. It was a plausible disguise – many upper class Germans did regard Hitler as a common upstart.

They crossed the border and drove to Arnhem, where Best had agreed to meet them. But Best was not there. They waited. After three-quarters of an hour, they were about to give up when they saw two figures approaching their car. But these were not the British agents they were expecting. They were Dutch police officers, and they got into Schellenberg's car and curtly ordered him to drive to the police station.

This was not at all what Schellenberg had been planning. He was meant to be hoodwinking them, and now it looked like they had caught him instead. The head of German foreign intelligence was quite some prize.

There at the station Schellenberg and his army friends were given a thorough going over. Their clothes and luggage were searched from top to bottom, and this was nearly their undoing. In the wash-bag of one of Schellenberg's accomplices, open on the table ready for inspection, was a small packet of aspirins. Unfortunately for the Germans, these were not any old aspirins. They were a type issued to the SS (*Schutzstaffel*), the elite Nazi military corps, and bore the official label *SS Sanitaetschauptamt*, the main medical office of the SS. When Schellenberg spotted the pills, he turned white with alarm.

Thinking quickly, he looked around the room. Fortunately for him, the police officers searching their luggage were preoccupied with another bag. So Schellenberg swiftly snatched the aspirins and swallowed the lot – wrapper and all. The bitter taste was still in his mouth when there was a knock at the door. It was Klop, alias Coppens, Best's fellow agent. Schellenberg could only fear the worst.

But Klop had come to rescue them. He apologized profusely for the trouble they had been put to. It was all an unfortunate misunderstanding, he assured them. But Schellenberg was no fool. He knew exactly what had been going on. The British and Dutch still suspected them, and this whole exercise had been a test to see if they could expose the Germans. If the police had found anything suspicious, such as the SS aspirins, then they would have been arrested.

Schellenberg himself had an even luckier escape. The paper and silver foil of the aspirin wrapper prevented his stomach from absorbing the drug, which could have seriously damaged his body.

From then on, everything went smoothly for the Germans. They were driven to the SIS headquarters in the Hague, and wined and dined like visiting royalty. The next day, Schellenberg and his friends were given a radio set and a call sign. They were told to keep in contact by radio, and that a future meeting would soon be arranged. They all shook hands and were driven back to the German border.

Over the next few weeks Schellenberg was in daily radio contact with Best's group. Two more meetings were held, and he now felt confident that they had accepted him as completely genuine.

But then a major fly landed in Schellenberg's ointment, and flies didn't come much bigger than Heinrich Himmler, head of the SS. There had been an assassination attempt on Hitler – a bomb had exploded shortly after he had left a Nazi party celebration in Munich. Hitler was convinced the SIS was behind the plot, and wanted Best and his men captured immediately.

Schellenberg protested strongly. This would ruin his carefully thought-out scheme.

"The British are completely fooled," he pleaded. "Just think of all the information I'll be able to wheedle out of them."

But Himmler was curt.

"Now you listen to me. There's no but, there's only the Führer's order, which you will carry out."

So that was that.

With no option, Schellenberg devised a plan. He had already arranged his next meeting with the British – at Venlo, a small town on the Dutch-German frontier. He now contacted Alfred Naujocks of the SS, and arranged for a squad of twelve SS men to accompany him. Schellenberg met the men for a hurried briefing, and they sped off to the border.

Naujocks, a thuggish character, was known as "the man who started the Second World War". Two months earlier, he and a hand-picked squad of men dressed as Polish soldiers, had staged a fake raid on a German radio station on the German-Polish border. This gave the Nazis the opportunity to claim they had been attacked by the Poles, and an excuse to offer their own people, and the world, for invading Poland, which they wanted to turn into a German colony.

Curiously, Naujocks was not impressed with Schellenberg, and later described him as a, "namby-pamby, pasty-faced little man." He wondered how he would cope with the unquestionably dangerous business they were about to undertake.

The rendezvous with Best was at two o'clock, at the Café Backus, which was situated in a strange no-man's land between the German and Dutch frontier posts. Schellenberg was very uneasy and ordered a brandy to steady his nerves.

Finally, at 3:20pm, nearly one and a half hours late, Best's Buick came into sight. It turned into an alley by the café. Best and Klop got out, and Stevens stayed in the car. Schellenberg walked over as if to greet them, but as he did so shots rang out and a car roared down the street. It was the SS who had been lurking on the other side of the border. They had driven straight over the barrier firing as they went. It broke all the rules of neutrality – Holland was not at war and German soldiers had no right to cross the frontier.

There was instant chaos. Klop drew a pistol and fired at Schellenberg who flung himself to one side. The SS car pulled up at the end of the alley. There were soldiers hanging from its doors and two machine gunners perched on its front fender. Klop ducked and shifted his aim. He fired, then let loose another shot, narrowly missing Naujocks in the front seat of the car. He jumped out and returned fire from behind the open door, while his men scattered for cover, their guns blazing.

Naujocks ran up to Schellenberg and shouted in his face.

"Get out of this! God knows how you haven't been hit!"

Schellenberg ducked around the corner to avoid the shots and ran head-on into an SS soldier. Unfortunately this man had not been to the briefing and did not recognize Schellenberg. He assumed he was Best, as both men wore a monocle. The soldier grabbed him and stuck a pistol in his face.

"Don't be stupid," said Schellenberg, "put that gun away!"

There was a struggle and the SS man pulled the trigger of his gun. Schellenberg grabbed his hand and felt a bullet skim past his head. At that moment Naujocks ran up and told the soldier he'd got the wrong man – for the second time that day he'd probably saved the "namby-pamby" man's life.

Schellenberg peered around the corner and saw Klop making a break for it. He had been hit and was now trying to get away across the street, the spent shells pumping from his pistol as he fired. But it was no use. A burst of machine gun fire brought him to his knees, and he crumpled into a heap. As he fell, SS men swarmed over to drag Best and Stevens into their car. A couple of them stopped to pick up Klop too, bundling him into their car like a sack of potatoes, but he was already dead. The German cars sped off to their side of the border, with a roar of over-revved engines, burning rubber marks into the asphalt road.

In the moment after they left, a strange silence hung over the scene. Passers-by and border guards emerged from doorways and blockhouses, and stood open-mouthed and motionless. Engine exhaust, burning rubber and the acrid tang of spent bullet cartridges hung in the air. A few pools of red blood stained the road, glistening sickly in the fading autumn afternoon.

The operation had been a huge success for Schellenberg. He had learned much about the methods of the SIS, and had obliterated Z Branch in Holland. A major threat to the Nazis had been put out of operation – and the war was barely two months old.

The Venlo incident was easily the British secret service's most embarrassing blunder of the entire war, and it had huge repercussions. Hitler used the event to justify the German invasion of Holland in 1940, claiming it proved that the Dutch were not really neutral after all. Furthermore, when Germans who were genuinely opposed to Hitler tried to make contact with British intelligence agents later in the war, they were treated with such suspicion that nothing ever came of their approaches.

Following their capture, Best and Stevens were interrogated at length by the Germans, and gave much away. Stevens was even carrying a list of all the British agents in Holland when he fell into the German trap.

Both men were sent to Sachsenhausen concentration camp where they remained for the rest of the war. They were freed when the camp was liberated by American soldiers in April 1945. Stevens died in 1965 and Best in 1978.

Schellenberg rose to become the head of Nazi foreign intelligence. After the war he settled in Italy, and died in 1952. Naujocks survived the war too, and died in 1960.

DEATH OF A SALESGIRL
1940-1945

I T WAS A STRANGE, sad little ceremony. On May 2, 1950, Tania Szabo, a seven-year-old girl, neatly dressed in her best frock and with a fetching bow in her hair, stood before the ambassador at the French Embassy in London. He crouched down low to kiss her cheek and pinned a medal on her frock – the *Croix de Guerre* – awarded for bravery. Tania was familiar with such ceremonies. She had already met the king, George

VI, who had given her a similar award – the *George Cross*. The medals weren't for Tania, of course. They were for her mother, Violette. As the ambassador knelt down, he noticed how strikingly like her mother Tania was. The little girl – once described as looking like "the prettiest doll in the shop" – had huge eyes and thick dark hair.

Violette, and Tania's father Etienne, had both died in the war. He had been killed in North Africa shortly after she was born, and had never met her. Violette had died in Germany when Tania was two and a half. Violette, the actual, real Violette, who had cuddled and comforted her, was a fading memory to Tania now. Only fragments and random recollections – the sound of her voice, the dark scent of her perfume – were left. Now Tania remembered her mother mostly from photographs, and her grandparents' stories. And what they told her was that her mother was a hero...

Violette Szabo was a British agent, sent to occupied France to fight against the Nazis. She worked for the SOE – Special Operations Executive – a secret service branch of the armed forces. One of Violette's contemporaries, Odette

The Franco-British spy Violette Szabo, in a shot that captures something of her 'porcelain' beauty. She was 23 when she was executed.

Sanson, once described her as, "the bravest of us all." She was a fine example of how the circumstances and fortunes of war can transform ordinary people into extraordinary heroes.

But perhaps Violette Szabo, a teenager working behind a perfume counter in a Brixton department store when war broke out, was never that ordinary. Many of the SOE agents were women who stood out in a crowd. Virginia Hall, was a towering, formidable American who had a wooden leg. Christina Granville was a willowy Pole with the face and figure of a catwalk supermodel. They were hardly the sort of people you wouldn't notice, and neither was Violette. Small – petite – and full of high spirits, one of her senior officers described her wistfully: "She was really beautiful, dark-haired and olive-skinned, with a kind of porcelain clarity…"

She was born Violette Bushell in 1921, to a French mother and English father. Her father set up his own taxi business in Britain and France, and Violette divided her life between both countries. Although the family home was in London, she grew up fluent in both languages, and comfortable with both cultures. Her father, who had met her mother in France during the First World War, was an excellent shot. He regularly horrified his family and friends by shooting apples off Violette's head. As the eldest daughter, Violette took to responsibility easily enough, helping her mother look after her three younger brothers and making herself useful around the house. Seeming much older than her actual age, she once took off to France after a family argument without even telling her parents. She seemed to have inherited her father's talent for shooting too – so much so that local fairgrounds banned her from their shooting galleries because she won too many prizes.

Bright and capable she may have been, but she was not especially academic. She left school at 14 to work as a hairdresser's assistant and then as a shop girl at Woolworths. When war broke out in 1939, Violette gave no thought to joining the armed services. But when France fell to the Nazis in 1940, London was flooded with French soldiers. Violette's mother thought it would be nice to invite one of them home, "to give them a proper French meal" – especially on Bastille Day, July 14, a French national day of celebration. Violette was sent off to a military parade to find a Frenchman to invite. She duly returned with a handsome Foreign Legion officer named

Etienne Szabo, whose bravery had already won him several medals. The Bushell family liked Etienne immensely, and within six weeks he and Violette had married.

Barely days after the ceremony, Etienne left England to fight in Abyssinia (now Ethiopia). Violette too decided to "do her bit" – as people said in those days. She joined the Auxiliary Territorial Service (ATS) – a branch of the army where women could do everything male soldiers were expected to do, except front line combat. Violette was assigned to an anti-aircraft battery, where she was well-liked and did whatever she was asked with great enthusiasm.

Etienne returned for a fleeting visit over a year later, in October 1941. During this time, Violette became pregnant, and had to leave the ATS. Tania was born in June 1942. Etienne heard about the safe arrival of his daughter while fighting the German army in North Africa. But, during this intense period of the war, he could not be spared for leave. He was killed at the Battle of El Alamein four months later.

News of his death filled Violette with an intense desire for vengeance. Soon after, out of the blue, she received an official army letter from a Mr. Potter, asking her to come to an interview at a hotel in central London. Although she did not yet know it, Violette had been contacted by the Special Operations Executive. The SOE had been set up with the intention of organizing opposition to the Nazis, especially in the territories they had conquered. Agents would be dropped by aircraft to rendezvous with local underground fighters, known as the Resistance. Factories, railway stations and military bases would be bombed. Troops would be ambushed, collaborators assassinated. Where possible, their job was also to stir up civil unrest against the Germans.

The SOE was a secret organization of course, so they could hardly place advertisements in newspapers asking for volunteers. Instead, they recruited more obliquely. Violette's army file noted that she was half-French and bilingual in English and French – qualities which would make her a useful agent.

At the hotel, Violette was directed into a bare room with two chairs and a table. Sitting across from her was Mr. Potter – who was actually Major Selwyn Jepson, a recruitment officer for the SOE. He spoke to her mostly in French, explaining that he was looking for people to do "dangerous work" in

France. Violette leapt at the chance so readily, Jepson was instantly wary. Impulsiveness was a character trait most unsuited to spying. He asked her to return in a week, to discuss the matter further.

When they met again Jepson did not mince his words. There was a one in four chance that she would be killed, he said. Violette was unperturbed by this, but did make detailed inquiries about her army pension, and financial support for her daughter should she die. At this meeting, Jepson's doubts about her receded. Her enthusiasm, he decided, was genuine, and driven by a desire to avenge her husband's death.

So Violette was recruited, and began to train intensively for her role. Although women were not expected to take part in front line combat, the military made an exception with SOE agents. First she was sent for a three week fitness course to toughen her up. She had always been good at sports, and cycled a lot as a teenager, so she was in good shape already. Then she went up to Scotland to learn how to fight – how to fire a machine gun, kill a guard silently and with her bare hands, destroy bridges and railway lines with explosives, lay an ambush, storm a house – all of which were not considered very ladylike pursuits, especially in the 1940s.

The final part of her training was the most secret of all. She was taught how the Nazis controlled their conquered populations with a mixture of intimidation and cooperation with collaborators. She learned how to assume the identity of another person – whatever alias she would be given on her mission – and how to parachute from an aircraft without breaking a leg. Despite the odd mishap, such as a bad sprain in parachute training, Violette proved a natural in all these activities. But she did struggle with her codes – essential for agents to transmit details of their activities home in secret. Her training complete, Violette was flown to France on her first mission. It was to be a particularly dangerous and difficult one. The German *Gestapo* (secret police) had made many arrests around Rouen, of a group of local Resistance members codenamed the "Salesman" circuit. Violette's job was to assess the strength of those who had evaded capture. Dealing with the French Resistance was never easy. They were divided among themselves, between supporters of the Free French movement in London, and those who were communist. They were also infiltrated by German spies. In the wake of the

Gestapo arrests, Violette would be arriving in an atmosphere fraught with fear and suspicion.

In April 1944, she was flown to France in a tiny *Lysander* aircraft, which could land and take off in a very small area. Flown over at the same time was a French SOE agent named Philippe Liewer, who had been a journalist before the war. They were dropped off in the countryside around Azay-le-Rideau, where they were met by a small party of Resistance fighters. Quickly hurried off to a safe house for the rest of the night, they went on to Paris the next day. Here Violette took a train to Rouen, to begin her mission. The journey itself was fraught, and full of opportunities for mistakes. German soldiers seemed to flock to Violette. She spent the whole trip refusing offers of assistance, of having her bag carried, of cigarettes… Violette fended off her admirers with a weary shrug – the way she thought a real French woman would act. She did not even want to speak to these soldiers – although her fluency in French was impeccable, she had the trace of an English accent. Perhaps the Germans would not have grasped her accent was imperfect, but the French anti-resistance militia, the *Milice*, who collaborated with the Germans, would not be fooled.

For three weeks she snooped around Rouen, trying to find out what had happened to the Resistance group there. She even visited the houses of known Resistance members. Not only did she have to remain undiscovered by the authorities, she had to convince those she came into contact with that she was a genuine British agent – not a spy sent by the Germans, or *Milice*, to winkle out more suspects. Violette had been thrown in at the deep end with a task requiring great tact and courage. Twice she was stopped by police, questioned, and released. She always remained calm, offering a convincing alias, and plausible reasons for being in Rouen. Neither did she let these narrow brushes with disaster deter her. She carried out her work with great skill, and established beyond doubt that the Salesman circuit had been well and truly broken.

Violette enjoyed being back in France – even under these dreadful circumstances. When her work in Rouen was finished, she took a train back to Paris where she had arranged to meet up with Philippe Liewer. From there they would go south to the countryside outside Chateauroux to be picked up by another *Lysander*. Violette had two days to herself in Paris. She roamed the streets, which she knew well from her youth, although wartime Paris was much drabber than the bustling city it once was. But there were still items to be had in the shops that could not be found in England. Violette picked up some perfume for herself and her mother. She also bought a beautiful dress for Tania, and some chic Parisian clothes for herself – three dresses and a sweater. Minor alterations were made to the fit, and Violette went to collect them on the morning she was due to return to England. After a final quick flit around the shops, she left.

On the night of April 30 she waited anxiously with Liewer for their planes to arrive – which could have been any time from 10:30pm to 1:30 the next morning. Each was to travel separately in a *Lysander*, with other French agents who were also being picked up. This arrangement tacitly acknowledged the danger of the flight back. If one plane was shot down and all aboard were killed, then at least the other would carry one agent who could tell the Special Operations Executive what had happened to the Salesman circuit. It was a well-justified fear. The pilot of Liewer's plane was killed on his next mission.

The pick-up was uneventful and Violette felt a surge of relief as the plane lurched off its bumpy runway to vanish into the dark. But outside Chateaudun the *Lysander* flew close to a German airfield. Immediately the sky was filled with searchlights, and anti-aircraft shells burst around the plane. Violette was terrified, and with good reason. The *Lysander* might have been able to land and take off on a matchbox, but it was a slow, lumbering aircraft, and was an easy target both for gunners on the ground and night fighter aircraft. The pilot twisted, turned, dived and banked to get away from the lights, and Violette was thrown violently around the aircraft cabin. But luck was with them and, as the plane flew on, the shell bursts grew fewer and more distant.

When they arrived at the RAF airfield of Tempsford, disaster struck again. The plane had had such a narrow escape over Chateaudun that the rubber on one of its wheels had been ripped to shreds. The landing was a near disaster. Violette was so disoriented she imagined they had crashed in France. When the pilot came to help her out of the plane she mistook him for a German come to arrest her. He was greeted with a bewildering tirade of angry French, but when Violette realized she was back in England, she flung her arms around him and gave him a kiss.

Now it was late spring, and an invasion of France from England was imminent. When the invasion came, Allied troops would land on the beaches of Normandy. It was also hoped that the French Resistance would rise up behind German lines to help them. Before and during the invasion, members of the SOE were dropped in France to organize such an uprising, and Violette was among them.

The invasion began at first light on June 6, 1944. The following night, Violette boarded a *B-24 Liberator* bomber at Tempsford, with Philippe Liewer and two other French agents. Whatever private fears they had about the parachute jump to come, and the mission ahead, they kept to themselves. The crew remember their four agents passing the time on the flight out by playing cards together. Before she jumped, Violette staggered around the lurching plane to kiss each member of the crew. When the *B-24* flew over the "drop zone" – the area where Resistance members had agreed to meet them – lights were lit on the ground to let the pilot know they were waiting. Then, with a wink to her fellow agents, Violette jumped just after 1:30am. She landed safely and right on target – outside the village of Sussac close to the town of Limoges.

Supplies for the Resistance, and the agents' personal possessions, were dropped in separate packages, and then hurriedly gathered up and bundled into waiting cars. All four agents were taken to a grocer's shop in Sussac and given a meal and a bed for the night. Violette felt exhausted – she had been up almost all night – but huge relief too. An agent dropping into France at night never really knew who would be waiting for them. Sometimes they would be betrayed, or messages would be intercepted, and German soldiers would be there to meet them.

For this mission, Philippe Liewer had been charged with the difficult job of directing Resistance forces around Limoges. Violette was there to help him. They had been briefed to expect a well-organized and professional team of fighting men and women. But the reality was very different. There were around 800 Resistance members under Liewer's command, but they were untrained, with no experience of fighting, and led by what he described as, "the most incapable people I have ever met." Liewer found that different groups in the area refused to cooperate with each other. Also, they seemed very reluctant to engage their enemy. Not one of the targets they had been asked to strike before the agents arrived had been attacked. When Liewer tried to organize any attacks, he had to spend hours arguing his case to local commanders.

Barely a couple of days into his mission, Liewer lost patience with the men he had been sent to command. But he had other options. There were Resistance groups in nearby areas, and he made steps to contact them. Violette was ordered to meet up with a Jacques Poirier, the leader of a group about 160km (100 miles) to the south. So on the morning of June 10 she and another Resistance fighter named Jacques Dufour set off in a large black Citröen. The plan was for Dufour to take her halfway, and then for Violette to cycle the remaining distance. If they were stopped and questioned, either by German soldiers, or the *Milice*, they agreed to say that Violette was an antique dealer visiting one of her shops in the south.

A bicycle was strapped to the roof of the car, but Violette also insisted on taking a couple of Sten guns – small, light machine guns. Why they took the guns will forever remain a mystery. The likelihood of being stopped and searched was high, and there was no convincing reason why an antique dealer and her driver would be carrying these British combat weapons.

On the way down south, they picked up another Resistance member named Jean Bariaud, who would keep Dufour company on his way back to Sussac. Not long after they picked up Bariaud, at around ten o'clock that morning, they drove through the village of Salon-la-Tour. Straight ahead of them was a German roadblock. Soldiers immediately ordered the car to stop. They were bound to be searched. Dufour waved back in a friendly manner as he neared the roadblock, but 30m (33 yards) from the block he stopped the car suddenly and all three passengers jumped out. According to eyewitness reports, Bariaud, who was unarmed, ran up the road, but Dufour and Violette started firing at the soldiers with their Sten guns. Using the car as cover, Dufour kept up steady small bursts of fire, and shouted over to Violette to head for a wheat field next to the road, and then to some woods which were a few hundred yards away. Under heavy fire, Violette dashed into the wheat, and then began firing too, so Dufour could follow.

The wheat field may have been thick, but it was easy enough for the soldiers to track the position of their fleeing foes. Military vehicles raced up to the field, and machine gun fire raked the wheat. Soldiers soon surrounded the field, and whenever they saw wheat stalks twitching they would aim a withering burst of fire. Dufour and Violette made exhaustingly slow progress – fearing that every movement would bring a hail of bullets, but they edged slowly toward the woods. They fought well, both firing off occasional short blasts, to keep the soldiers from charging into the field after them.

By now Violette was exhausted. Her clothes were badly ripped, and she was covered with scratches. She told Dufour she did not have the strength to run through the woods, but she would cover his escape, firing toward the German soldiers as he crawled into the wood. She knew she would either die in the coming fight, or be shot as a spy soon after it, and she was sacrificing her own life for her comrade. Dufour could see she was in no mood to argue. He escaped from the field, and found a perfect hiding place – a haystack next to a nearby farm.

Here Dufour lay, still and silent. After half an hour German troops arrived, and with them was Violette Szabo. Peering though the hay, he noticed she was limping, and had probably sprained an ankle in the chase. Dufour could hear them angrily questioning her about him. She laughed and told them: "You can run after him. He is far away by now." As she sat nearby, smoking a cigarette, the officer in charge of the soldiers told her she was the bravest woman he had ever met, and saluted as she was taken away.

The following day, Violette was driven to Limoges and, from there, to Fresnes prison on the outskirts of Paris. From here she was regularly taken for interrogation, to *Gestapo* headquarters at 84 avenue Foch in the middle of the city. Although she was questioned aggressively, and treated harshly, she was not tortured. Strangely, the *Gestapo* did not usually torture British agents, but were merciless with the French.

By early August 1944, the *Gestapo* decided they were not going to learn anything useful from Violette Szabo. On August 8 she left Paris for the last time, along with two other SOE agents, Denise Bloch and Lilian Rolfe. Their destination was the notorious Ravensbrück concentration camp for women, in northern Germany. The three SOE women were taken to the Paris Gare de l'Est station, where they were joined by several other captured British agents and put on a train under heavy guard. The men were taken to a special prison carriage and the women were chained together and sat in ordinary compartments with an armed escort. The train moved to the German border so slowly they were still in France the following afternoon. Just after 2:00pm they were attacked by Allied planes. Although many on board fled as soon as the attack began, including the German guards, the prisoners were left chained together or locked in their carriages. As bullets buzzed around their heads, and bombs exploded nearby, Violette and another woman crawled through the train corridors with water for the men in the prison carriage, who had not been given anything to drink for several hours. When the planes flew off, the guards returned, and the journey continued.

Ravensbrück was not a death camp, like Auschwitz or Treblinka, but it was almost as grim. Although some prisoners were executed there, most were sent to Ravensbrück to work, but harsh conditions meant many died. Originally built to house 6,000 women prisoners, it was enlarged during the war to take 24,000. When Violette arrived, there were 80,000, crammed behind its barbed wire and electric fences.

Here the day began at 3:00 every morning, when prisoners were roused by a siren from their lice-ridden straw bedding, where they slept two to a bunk. Roll call was at 3:45am and prisoners had to stand for hours to be counted, in all weathers and seasons, dressed only in their thin prison clothes. Then, names were called for work parties, and they were marched off for the day.

By the time Violette reached Ravensbrück, she had grown painfully thin, but her spirit was far from crushed. She met other captured Resistance workers and immediately began to make plans to escape. But before long, Violette and 500 other women were transferred to another camp, named Torgau, on the River Elbe. They were set to work in a munitions factory. Here too she planned an escape, and got as far as obtaining a key for one of the camp gates. But a woman Violette did not know well found out. She was not trusted by her fellow prisoners, so Violette threw the key away before it was discovered.

Conditions at Torgau were much better than at Ravensbrück, but some of the women objected to working in an arms factory, producing shells and bullets for the Nazis. They refused to work. It was a brave but pointless stand. Fritz Sühren, the camp commandant at Ravensbrück, was called in to deal with the mutiny. Half the women were sent to another factory, and half, including Violette, were sent to a camp at Königsberg in East Prussia. Here, as autumn turned to winter, they were set to work in the fields and forests, clearing trees and vegetation from ground that had frozen hard. Not only did they have to wear the thin summer clothes they had arrived in – Violette had a blue silk frock with short sleeves – they were fed an inadequate diet of soup made of water and unwashed potato peelings.

This was treatment designed to break the spirit of even the hardiest soul, and Violette grew increasingly depressed. But, even here, prisoners found comfort in friendship. When Violette returned from the fields, frozen to the bone and in deep despair, one of her friends at the camp, Marie Lecomte, would hug her to warm her up, and give her food she had saved from her own paltry ration. In the depths of winter, as further punishment, the women were refused fuel for their hut heater. As December wore on, Violette and her fellow prisoners grew increasingly skeletal. Many of the women on work parties dropped down dead, from exhaustion and cold.

In early 1945, the authorities at Königsberg received orders to transfer Violette back to Ravensbrück. This was not good news. When she found out, Violette went at once to her friend Marie and sobbed in her arms. Certain she would be killed, Violette wrote her family's address on a sheet of paper, and gave it to Marie. Then the two women made a pact: if either of them died, the other would look after their family. Just before Violette left, she kissed Marie seven times – one kiss for each member of the family she had left behind. She asked Marie to travel to London to tell them what had happened to her, and kiss them all from her.

Violette left Königsberg at 5:00 one morning, along with the two SOE agents who had been with her on the train from Paris – Denise Bloch and Lilian Rolfe. For some reason, the three women were given new clothing, and soap and a comb. Now Violette had a blouse, a skirt and a coat to fend off the cold, instead of her thin summer dress.

They arrived back in Ravensbrück to be placed immediately in solitary confinement. It was obvious that something was going to happen. Alone in her cell, Violette must have pondered the strange twists of fate that led her to Ravensbrück. If she had not chosen Etienne Szabo on that fateful day back in July 1940, the chain of events that had led her to captivity and imminent execution would never have begun.

The stay in Ravensbrück was brief. The war was coming to its inevitable end and Germany's Nazi elite were determined to extract maximum vengeance before power was wrested away from them. At *Gestapo* headquarters in Berlin, a list of names of British agents due for immediate execution had been drawn up. The list included Violette, Denise and Lilian. A few days after their return, on a bleak February early evening, the sound of marching feet was heard outside their cell doors. The doors clanged open, and each woman was ordered out. They were marched as a group to a block next to the crematorium, close to the inner wall of the camp. Here, waiting for them, was camp commandant Fritz Sühren, and a small party of other camp officials including the camp doctor, ready to carry out a grisly ritual.

Sühren read from a document informing the three women they were to be executed. Then, one by one, they were made to kneel down on a step between two camp buildings, and shot. As a method of execution it was, at least, mercifully brief. Denise and Lilian were too weak to stand without help, but Violette, still only 23, walked to her death with great courage. The last thing she saw was a bleak, narrow, dimly lit alley between two buildings, before a single bullet to the back of her neck ended her brief life. Immediately after the executions the three bodies were burned, and all traces of Violette, Denise and Lilian vanished from the face of the Earth.

When peace came to Europe, in the late spring of 1945, Violette's family waited for news of their daughter. They knew that she had been captured by the Germans, but had no inkling of her fate. But as the spring turned to summer, and it slowly became obvious that Violette was not among the survivors of liberated prisoner-of-war and concentration camps, they began to fear the worst. To put an end to the uncertainty, SOE dispatched some of their staff to discover what had happened to their missing agents. Camp officials at Ravensbrück were interrogated, and it was established that Violette Szabo had been executed in February 1945 – a mere three months before the end of the war.

Marie Lecomte, Violette's friend at Königsberg, survived the war. When she tried to get in touch with Violette's family via the British military authorities, she was discouraged from doing so. Perhaps they felt that hearing an account of the last desperate months of Violette's life would be too painful for the family. For years Marie was haunted by her failure. She ran a restaurant at Morlaix, and whenever British people visited, she would ask if they knew Violette's family. Then, in 1958, sorting though some old possessions, she discovered a newspaper cutting about Violette and her family, published a year or so after the war had ended. At the time she was given it, Marie had been extremely ill, and had not realized its significance. The newspaper was contacted, and Marie was put in touch with the Bushell family. She visited them, and was finally able to kiss each one, just as she had promised.

CRACKING ENIGMA

1941-1945

KAPITÄNLEUTNANT FRITZ-JULIUS LEMP peered through the periscope of submarine *U-110*. It was late in the morning of May 9, 1941, the last day of his life. Through the narrow lens, which surfaced just above the choppy sea south of Iceland, he could see a convoy of British ships bound for Nova Scotia.

Lemp's wartime service with the German submarine fleet

was brief and glorious. In 10 wartime patrols he had sunk 20 ships and damaged another four. Less than a year into the war, and all before he turned 27, he had been presented with the *Iron Cross* 1st and 2nd class, and the *Knight's Cross* – among the most prestigious awards available to German military men. This allowed him to be astonishingly insolent with his senior commanders. One instruction from navy headquarters sent to him on his U-boat received a curt two word dismissal: "S***. Lemp."

The medals, and the tolerance which greeted his outbursts, were a recognition of his calling. It was a wonder anyone, on any side of the war, volunteered to serve on submarines. It was an uncomfortable and highly dangerous life. But the reason they did volunteer was that submarines were devastatingly effective. In the course of the war, German U-boats sank 2,603 cargo ships and 175 of their warship escorts. But for such success they paid a terrible price. More than two out of three U-boats were sunk, taking about 26,000 submariners to the bottom of the sea.

U-boats kept in touch with their headquarters via radio signals. Here they would report their own positions and progress, and receive instructions on where to head next. Such reports were sent in code of course. It was a code that had incessantly perplexed the British. Their intelligence service had set up a special code-breaking department at Bletchley Park, Buckinghamshire, to try to crack it. If the British knew where the U-boats were, or where they were going, they could avoid them or hunt them down. For an island so dependent on food and material brought in by cargo ships, cracking the German navy code became one of the most vital tasks of the war.

On that May morning, Lemp was uneasy. He did not usually carry out daytime attacks, especially on convoys protected by warship escorts. It was far more difficult for such escorts to locate his submarine during a night attack. But his fear of losing contact with his quarry overrode such considerations. Just before noon, *U-110* unleashed three torpedoes. Two hit home, sending towering columns of spray into the air by the side of two unlucky ships. But when Lemp ordered a fourth torpedo to be fired, it failed to leave its launch tube.

This minor mishap soon added up to a major disaster for *U-110*. When a torpedo is fired, water is immediately pumped into the forward ballast tanks, to compensate for the missing weight and keep the submarine level under the water. So, even though the torpedo failed to leave its tube, water still poured into the front of the vessel, unbalancing the submarine. Inside *U-110* the crew fought to regain control. During the ensuing disorder, several British warships charged toward the U-boat. Only when Lemp had regained control of his submarine did he check his periscope. Seeing a warship bearing down on him, he immediately decided to dive deeper under the sea – the standard procedure for a submarine under attack. But it was too late. Inside the hull, the crew listened to the dull throbbing of approaching propeller blades. Then came two splashes as a couple of depths charges* were pitched overboard. With dry mouths and an awful tightness in the pit of their stomachs, the crew of *U-110* waited for the charges to float down toward them.

When the explosions came with a huge thunderous peal, the submarine rocked to and fro as if caught in a hurricane. The main lights went out, and for a few seconds there was a

*Heavy canisters loaded with high explosives

deathly total darkness. Then, blue emergency lighting flickered on. As their eyes adjusted to the dim light, terrified and disoriented men looked over to their captain for reassurance. Lemp had been under attack before, and he played his part to perfection. Leaning his short, stocky frame casually against his periscope mount, hat pushed to the back of his head, he looked like a suburban bus driver plodding though his usual dreary journey. Lemp's act had a serious purpose. If anyone on the submarine panicked and started yelling hysterically, the British ships would pick up the noise on their sound detection equipment, and home in on them rapidly.

Now, a deathly hush settled on the submarine, only disturbed by the occasional ominous creaking, and damage reports from other parts of the boat. Neither depth charge had hit the submarine directly, but the damage they caused was still considerable. The trim controls (which kept the submarine level underwater) had broken and the rudder no longer worked. The batteries had been contaminated with seawater and were now giving off poisonous chlorine gas. The depth gauges gave no reading, so it was impossible to tell whether the submarine was rising or falling in the sea. Worst of all, a steady hissing sound indicated that compressed air containers were leaking. Without this air, the submarine would not be able to blow water out of its ballast tanks and get to the surface. Now, even Lemp could not pretend that everything was going to be OK. "All we can do is wait," he told his men. "I want you all to think of home, or something beautiful."

These soothing words cannot have been much comfort. In the awful silence that followed, perhaps his crew thought of how their girlfriends or families would greet news of their deaths. More likely than not, in his mind's eye, each man imagined the submarine sinking slowly into the dark depths of the ocean. If that section of the sea was deep, steel plates on the hull would creak and groan until a fluttering in the ears told the crew the submarine's air pressure had been disturbed by water pouring inside the ship. Then the boat would be rent apart beneath their feet, and they would be engulfed by a torrent of black icy water. At such a depth, no one aboard had any chance of reaching the surface.

If that section of the sea was shallow, the submarine might simply sink to the bottom. Then, men would have to sit in the strange blue light, or pitch darkness, shivering in the damp cold, as their submarine gradually filled with water. The corrosive smell of chlorine gas would catch in their throats, and they would slowly suffocate in the foul-smelling air.

But just as the men were convinced they were going to die, *U-110* began to rock gently to and fro. A huge wave of relief swept through the men. This was a motion the crew all recognized – their submarine was bobbing on the surface. Lemp, still playing his bus driver part, announced, "Last stop! Everyone out!" In a well-rehearsed drill, the crew headed for their exit hatches and poured out on to the deck.

But their troubles were not yet over. As they filled their lungs with fresh sea air, three warships were fast bearing down on them, intending to ram the submarine before it could do more damage. Shells and bullets were whizzing past their ears. But none of the men had any intention of manning the guns on the deck of the *U-110*, or firing any more torpedoes. They had just stared death in the face, and were desperate to abandon their boat.

Men jumped overboard and drowned, others were killed by the shells and bullets that rained down on them. Amid the wild confusion, one of the ship's radio operators found Lemp and asked him whether he should destroy the ship's code books and coding machinery. Lemp shook his head, and gestured impatiently, "The ship's sinking." Below deck, the last few left aboard opened valves to flood their submarine, to make sure it really did sink. Then they too jumped into the frothy, freezing sea.

Aboard *HMS Bulldog*, steaming in to ram the *U-110*, its captain Commander Joe Baker-Cresswell had a sudden change of heart. When he could see that the members of the enemy crew were throwing themselves off their vessel, he ordered his ship to reverse its engines and it slowly came to a halt.

Other British ships, now certain that the *U-110* was no longer a threat, stopped firing. Then, the destroyer *Aubretia* pulled up nearby to rescue the crew. It had been her depth charges that had done so much damage. As Lemp and a fellow officer struggled to stay afloat, they noticed to their horror that the submarine was not going to sink after all. Clearly something had stopped the water from pouring in. Lemp shouted over that they should try to climb back on board to sink their boat. But, just then, a vast, rolling wave swept over them, and the U-boat was carried out of reach. The crew had missed their chance. Most of the men survived in the water long enough to be picked up. Lemp was not one of them.

From the bridge of *HMS Bulldog*, Baker-Cresswell surveyed the submarine with great interest. It was floating low in the water, but did not look as if it would sink immediately. Its crew had either been killed or were being rescued. It seemed likely to have been abandoned. So Baker-Cresswell decided to send in a small boarding party to investigate. This unenviable job went to 20-year-old sub-lieutenant David Balme. Together with eight volunteers, Balme clambered aboard a small boat, lowered from the *Bulldog*, and set off across the choppy sea. As they lurched closer to the *U-110*'s black hull, Balme grew increasingly tense. As the most senior officer in the boarding party, it was his responsibility to lead his men into the submarine. The only way in was through a hatch in the conning tower. There could be submariners inside, waiting to shoot anyone who entered. Even if no one was still on board, it was standard practice on an abandoned submarine to set off explosives on a timed fuse, or flood the boat, to prevent it from falling into enemy hands. Besides, if the crew had completely abandoned it, it was probably taking in water fast, and could sink at any moment.

So, expecting to die from either a bullet or an explosion, or in a torrent of water, Balme lurched off his boat and onto the slippery deck of the *U-110*. His men followed immediately after, but no sooner had the last man clambered aboard than a wave picked up their boat and smashed it into pieces on the deck of the submarine. This was not a good omen.

With his heart in his mouth, Balme climbed the conning tower to find an open hatch at the top. It stood before him, the gateway to his doom. Balme fought back his fears and told himself sternly: "Stop thinking… just do it." He took his pistol from its holster and peered gingerly down into the darkened interior. Immediately, a gust of warm air wafted up to meet him. It contrasted strangely with the icy Icelandic wind blowing off the sea, and would have been inviting had it not smelled so foul. All submarines have a distinct stench. Those not used to it find it almost unbearable. It is the stale dishcloth, rotten cabbage smell of 30 or more men confined for weeks on end in an enclosed, airless environment, unable to bathe properly or clean their clothes.

Balme sensed the impatience of the men behind him. They wouldn't be the first to be shot, but they were just as vulnerable as he was to explosives or a sinking submarine. "Just do it," chided a voice in his head. He swung down into the interior, expecting a bullet right through the buttocks. His boots clanged down the long steel ladder, but there was no one there to greet him. He reached the strange blue interior of the control room, and the others briskly followed. As their eyes grew used to the dim light, they blundered through the vessel, searching for any remaining crew.

But *U-110* was completely deserted. Quickly Balme's party began to search the boat for documents, knowing it could still sink or explode at any moment. Their courage was richly rewarded. Inside the radio operator's cabin was a sealed envelope containing codes and other useful documents, such as signal logs, code instruction procedures, and further code books. But there was also a curious machine that looked like a strange sort of typewriter. It had a keyboard, and one of the men pressed a letter on it. A light on a panel above the keyboard flickered on. The thing was still plugged in! It immediately dawned on Balme that it was a coding machine.

Four screws held it to the side of the cabin. These were quickly removed, and the device was carefully put to one side.

It became clear to Balme there must have been complete panic among the crew, to have left everything behind like this. As his search party worked on, the overpowering dread they first felt on entering the boat faded a little. An explosion never came, and neither did the bows of the ship suddenly lurch into the air, throwing them higgledy-piggledy down through the deck sections, just before the *U-110* slipped below the waves. But there were other things to worry about. The *Bulldog*, and other warships guarding the convoy, had gone off to chase other submarines. If the *U-110* sank in the meantime, they had no boat, and no immediate chance of rescue.

Finally, *Bulldog* returned to wait for the boarding party to finish their work. Shortly afterwards, Balme was sitting in the U-boat captain's cramped cabin. While he ate a sandwich which Baker-Cresswell had thoughtfully sent over, he reflected that life was looking up. When his men had finished their search, a boat was sent to collect them, then a tow rope was attached to *U-110*. The following morning, in rough seas, the submarine finally sank. Baker-Cresswell was distraught.

A captured submarine was quite a prize, and could even have been manned by a British crew and used again. But he needn't have worried.

News that *HMS Bulldog* had captured a coding machine from the *U-110* caused a sensation at the Admiralty – British naval headquarters. Signals were quickly sent out ordering Baker-Cresswell and his crew to maintain the strictest secrecy. When *Bulldog* reached the navy base of Scapa Flow in Scotland, two naval intelligence officers immediately came on board, eager to examine the items Balme's party had seized. What especially thrilled them was the code machine. "We've waited the whole war for one of these," said one. The documents also excited great interest. The next day, as the *Bulldog* sailed back to its Icelandic patrol, Baker-Cresswell received a thinly veiled message from Dudley Pound, the commander of the Royal Navy. "Hearty Congratulations. The petals of your flower are of rare beauty."

The typewriter-like device Balme's party had found was a fully-working Enigma machine – the ingenious coding instrument devised by the German military. Enigma was used for "scrambling" a message so that it became diabolically difficult to crack. And there were literally billions of possible combinations for each coded message.

Enigma had a keyboard layout similar to a typewriter, but it only contained the 26 letters of the alphabet. When a letter key was pressed, it sent a signal to a plugboard at the front of the machine. This was also arranged in a standard keyboard layout, with a variable arrangement of cable leads which could go from any direction – say from C to T, and then U to K. This was the first stage in the scrambling of a message.

From the plugboard the signal was then routed to a series of replaceable, interconnected rotating wheels, each with all 26 letters of the alphabet around the rim. These scrambled the original letter still further. There were between three and five of these wheels inside the Enigma, depending on the model. The wheels were chosen from a standard selection of eight.

From the wheels the signal was sent to a "lampboard" positioned behind the keyboard, lighting up another letter which the operator would write down. In this way, messages would be fed through for coding, and then transmitted via Morse code as ordinary radio signals.

Most famously carried by German submarines, Enigma coding machines (bottom left of picture) were also used by the German army.

Enigma, invented in 1919 by German engineer Arthur Scherbius, was a remarkable machine. Each keystroke, even of the same key, produced a different letter. If the operator pressed three Ps, for example, the rotating wheels could produce three different letters – K, J and F, for example. Even on machines with three wheels, it would not begin to produce the same sequence for the same letter until the key had been pressed 16,900 times. This was when the internal mechanism returned to its original position.

Enigma's complexity created its own problems. Messages from one machine to another could only be correctly decoded if both machines were set up identically. Each wheel, for example, had to be inserted in one specific position, and in a specific order. Likewise, the front plugboard had to be arranged in exactly the same way.

This created a particular difficulty for the German navy, whose ships and submarines would be away at sea for months on end. They were sent out with code books giving precise details for how their Enigma machine should be set up for each day of the weeks and months ahead, and which settings should be changed at midnight. It was, of course, essential that such codebooks or coding machines should never fall into enemy hands.

The machine captured by Balme, and all the accompanying material, was sent at once to Bletchley Park. This grand mansion and its grounds had been set up as British intelligence's code-breaking headquarters in 1939, just before the start of the war. Most of the work was done in a makeshift collection of prefabricated huts, with trestle tables and collapsible chairs. It was staffed by some of the greatest mathematical brains in the country. Chief among them was Alan Turing, a Cambridge and Princeton University professor. His ground-breaking work into decoding Enigma messages, using primitive computers, led directly to the kind of computers we all use today.

Turing's team had a gargantuan task. The Enigma code was complex enough to begin with. But to make it even more difficult, the code was changed every day, and coding procedures were regularly updated. In the course of the war, the Enigma machines themselves also went through several design improvements. On top of all this, at the height of the conflict 2,000 messages a day, from all branches of the German armed forces, were being sent to Bletchley for decoding.

Even with the brightest brains in the country, the staff of Bletchley Park could not crack the Enigma code without some direct assistance. They relied on the kind of lucky breaks David Balme's boarding party brought them. These came in dribs and drabs throughout the war. Balme's Enigma machine was not the first to fall into British hands, but it was certainly the most up-to-date. The books and documents he rescued were especially useful. They gave information on settings and procedures for encoding the most sensitive, top-secret information, which the Germans called *Offizier* codes.

Enigma was like a huge jigsaw puzzle. Any codebooks or machines that were captured helped to put the puzzle together for a few days or weeks, until the codes and machines changed. Then, instead of decoding sensitive and highly useful messages about U-boat positions or air force strikes, code breakers would find themselves churning out reams of meaningless gobbledygook. For the staff at Bletchley Park, such moments provoked heartbreaking disappointment.

They were well aware of how their work could save the lives of thousands of people.

In 1997 Balme recalled: "I still wake up at night, fifty-six years later, to find myself going down that ladder." But, thanks to the courage of men like him, the staff of Bletchley Park were provided with vital further opportunities to break their enemy's code.

THE BOOK-KEEPER'S
STORAGE PROBLEM

1942

SNOW FELL SOFT AND SILENT around the shores of Wannsee, cloaking the forest, parkland and elegant villas around the famous lake. Throughout the morning of January 20, 1942, one of the larger villas received a steady stream of chauffeur-driven cars. Arriving at the villa was a succession of 15 of the most senior members of the Nazi government and its elite SS armed forces. As they entered the marble entrance hall, their coats were swept from their shoulders by fawning functionaries, and their arrival was silently noted. Among them were representatives from the Chancellery, the Race and Resettlement Office, the Ministry of Foreign and Eastern Territories, the Justice Ministry, the *Gestapo*, and the SS. Most had come from nearby Berlin, but some of the army men had been called in from the horror and chaos of the Russian Front, or from other conquered territory in the East. For them, the placid winter scene at Wannsee seemed to belong to some strange parallel universe.

The villa where they assembled, with its marbled staircases and rooms lined with wooden panels, was a substantial three-floored mansion. It had once belonged to a Jewish businessman, but had long since been taken over by the German government. On that January day it was to be the scene of one of the most obscene conferences in human history.

Organizing the preparation of the conference, coordinating the arrival of the delegates, the staff to attend to them, and the buffet prepared for lunch, was Adolf Eichmann. An Austrian Nazi in his late 30s, he was head of the *Gestapo*'s Jewish affairs section. Eichmann was a curiously quiet and rather anonymous man, once memorably described as looking like a book-keeper. He lacked the charisma and spark of some of his more notable colleagues, but he had a reputation for carrying out orders with great thoroughness and efficiency. As the morning progressed, he noted with some satisfaction how well his conference was proceeding.

Last to arrive at Wannsee was Eichmann's boss, SS General Reinhard Heydrich. As head of the Reich Security Main Office, he was one of the most powerful men in Nazi Europe. Tall, blond and handsome, Heydrich was everything Eichmann was not. A former international-level fencer and naval officer, he looked like the epitome of the "Aryan"* superman – a creature from a Nazi propaganda film. In his most famous photograph, Heydrich stares out with merciless eyes and a cruel mouth. He looks like a stern headmaster about to administer a severe beating to a gaggle of rebellious pupils. No doubt that was the image he wanted to project to the world. In person, the brisk and efficient Heydrich could ooze charm and amiability. But those who crossed him would

*Aryan was the Nazi term for "pure-blood" Germans.

find themselves subject to chilling threats, made in the casual manner of a Roman emperor, secure in his power of life and death over those around him.

So the conference began. In a haze of cigarette smoke, and the slightly oiled and jovial atmosphere of men who have had a couple of glasses of wine or spirits before lunch, the purpose of the meeting was made plain. Heydrich announced that he had been charged by Hitler's deputy, Hermann Göring, with "the responsibility for working out the final solution of the Jewish problem" in Nazi territory. The various representatives around him were there to ensure the government cooperated effectively with this venture.

Like all supporters of the Nazis, these distinguished and often highly educated men were broadly sympathetic to Hitler's corrosive hatred of the Jews. During the nine years of Nazi rule, heightened and reinforced by a constant barrage of anti-Semitic propaganda, they had grown to think of all Jews with repugnance and fear – perhaps as people today would regard a swarm of diseased rats, or a particularly malignant virus.

Nonetheless, what Heydrich had to report was utterly

monstrous. So much so, that he still felt the need to couch his words to these hard line Nazis in innocuous phrases, to lessen the impact of what he was saying. He explained to the assembled delegates, with statistics gathered directly by Eichmann, that there was a "storage problem" with the eight million or so Jews in German-held territory. Originally, the Nazis had merely intended to expel them, but the war had closed the borders, making this impossible. Heydrich gradually led his delegates around to the view that the only possible option left to Germany, with regard to the Jews, was "evacuation". As the conference went on, it slowly dawned on those assembled around the polished oak table what "evacuation" actually meant. What they were talking about was the cold-blooded murder of eight million people – maybe even eleven million, if Germany succeeded in conquering all of Europe.

Of course, there were a few objections. Even among men like these, the idea of murder on this scale was too horrific to contemplate. But eventually, with the odd silky threat here, and a sharp exhortation there, Heydrich gained the approval of all those assembled. Once this "solution" was accepted, the delegates, with their customary efficiency, decided that it would be economic to house the Jews in concentration camps and put them to work on road and factory building projects, where "natural diminution" (that is, death from exhaustion and illness) would gradually reduce their numbers. The old, the sick, and children would not be suitable for such projects, so they would be disposed of as soon as possible.

Since the war began, SS troops in Poland and Russia, known as *Einsatzgruppen* ("action squads") had been systematically shooting Jews in their thousands. But their officers had reported how demoralizing and unpleasant their men had found the job – especially the killing of women and children. So, it was decided the most efficient way to eradicate the Jews that couldn't be used for work, would be gas. In special death camps, hundreds at a time could be herded into gas chambers disguised as shower rooms, to have the life choked out of them quickly and efficiently. Such chambers could dispose of, say, 600 an hour. Working around the clock, they could "evacuate" thousands of Jews a day. Within a year, if all went to plan, Europe would be *Judenfrei*, meaning "Jew free" in German.

Luckless Hungarian Jews await selection for the gas chambers of Auschwitz-Birkenau, in May 1944. Mothers and their children were usually selected for immediate dispatch. Men were more often worked to exhaustion before they were murdered.

Afterwards, when the delegates had gone, Heydrich, Eichmann, and *Gestapo* chief Heinrich Müller sat down by the fireplace. They smoked a celebratory cigar and drank a toast to a job well done. According to Eichmann, as the drink flowed they began to sing, and arm in arm they danced a jig around the plush chairs and oak tables of the Wannsee villa.

Four months later, Heydrich was mortally wounded in Prague when he was attacked by two Czech soldiers. He died on June 4. In retaliation, German troops murdered nearly 1,500 Czechs, loosely accused of aiding the assassins. Then, for good measure, they also destroyed the Czech village of Lidice, killing all its male inhabitants, and sending its women and children to concentration camps.

By then, the work agreed at Wannsee had begun. From the Gulf of Finland to the Caucasus mountains, from France's Atlantic coast to the island of Crete and the North African shores of Libya, in all areas controlled by the Nazis, Jews were gradually rounded up. Some were shot, or gassed in special vans designed for the process. But most were placed on freight trains, packed in their hundreds and thousands into cattle wagons, and transported to death camps – Treblinka, Sobibor, Majdanek, Belzec, Chelmno and Auschwitz – names which would haunt the lives of an entire post-war generation.

Map of Europe showing the main death camps

THE WAR OF THE RATS
1942-1943

ESPITE THEIR FAILURE to conquer Russia, the Nazi invaders still met with remarkable success. In the summer of 1942, the German army commanded huge swathes of the country. So much, in fact, that before the war 40% of Russia's population had lived in the areas the Germans now occupied. To the north, they had reached the city of Leningrad close to the Finnish border, and continued down past Moscow through the Voronezh front. To the south, they were close to the Volga river, and had got as far as the Caucasus mountains, barely a hundred miles from the Caspian Sea (see map). Millions of Soviet citizens had been killed and millions had fled east. Now, in the late summer of 1942, after more than a year of fighting, the German Sixth Army was fast approaching the industrial city of Stalingrad. Because it was named after

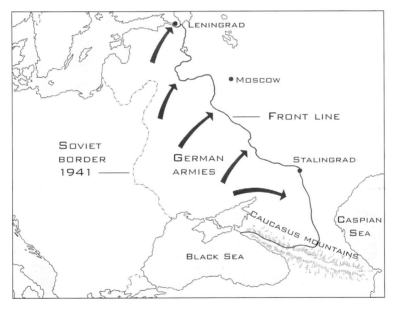

Map showing the greatest extent of German penetration into the Soviet Union in November 1942

Soviet leader Joseph Stalin, the city had great symbolic importance for both the Soviets and the Nazis. Both sides were determined to fight as if the outcome of the entire war depended on their victory. Perhaps it did.

The German Sixth Army's arrival at the outskirts of Stalingrad was foreshadowed by a vast cloud of dust thrown up by their marching feet, and the tanks, trucks and artillery that trundled through the parched steppe of late summer. Most of the soldiers, young and still fresh, were in good spirits. The odds were very definitely on their side. Despite occasional heavy fighting, most of those who had trekked the thousand or so miles from the German border to the banks of the Volga had every reason to feel they were as invincible as Nazi propaganda had told them they were. Hitler's armies had astonished the world with their string of victories.

But, when the Sixth Army got to Stalingrad, there were no longer vast open plains to sweep through, and they became bogged down in street fighting. It was the kind of warfare every soldier dreads. Intensely personal, horrific, terrifying hand-to-hand combat, where men fight men with grenades, bayonets, sharpened spades, and anything else they can grab to kill each other in the most brutal, bloody way. Among many of the personal accounts of the fighting to emerge was one by a young German army lieutenant. His numb description sums up the personal nightmare of Stalingrad so eloquently that it is mentioned in virtually all books and television documentaries about the battle:

"We have fought during fifteen days for a single house. The front is a corridor between burned-out rooms; it is the thin ceiling between two floors ... From floor to floor, faces black with sweat, we bombard each other with grenades in the middle of explosions, clouds of dust and smoke, heaps of mortar, floods of blood, fragments of furniture and human beings ... The street is no longer measured by dimension but by corpses ... Stalingrad is no longer a town. By day it is an enormous cloud of burning, blinding smoke; it is a vast furnace lit by the reflection of the flames. And when night arrives, one of those scorching, howling, bleeding nights, the dogs plunge into the Volga and swim desperately to gain the other bank. The nights of Stalingrad are a terror for them. Animals flee this hell; the hardest stones cannot bear it for long; only men endure."

In the early stages of the Battle of Stalingrad, these German soldiers fight with machine guns among houses that are still standing. When the battle ended, 99% of the Soviet city had been reduced to rubble.

The battle raged from August 1942 to February 1943, and in such fearful and exhausting circumstances, the morale of each side would be a major deciding factor in the outcome. The Germans arrived convinced that victory would soon be theirs. The Russians fought desperately to cling on to what remained of their front line positions. They were overawed by the German army who, after all, had yet to face a serious defeat. At one point early in the struggle, nine-tenths of Stalingrad was in German hands. So confident in victory was the commander of the German Sixth Army, General Friedrich von Paulus, that he had already designed a medal commemorating the capture of the city.

To begin with, the casualty rate among the Soviet army was unsustainable. Reinforcements, rushed to Stalingrad to prop up its crumbling barricades, would arrive at a railhead on the other side of the Volga. They would be bundled out of cattle wagons to be greeted by the terrifying sight of a city in flames. It looked, quite literally, like a vision of hell. From the railhead, men were quickly transferred across the river by ferry. Even if they survived the heavy machine gun and artillery bombardments, and the strafing of the *Stuka* dive bombers as they crossed, these soldiers would be lucky to live for 24 hours.

As each area of the city was overtaken by fighting, Stalingrad was reduced to little more than a huge pile of rubble. German soldiers described the fighting as *Rattenkrieg* – the war of the rats – as men scurried and burrowed through the debris.

The commander of the Russian forces at Stalingrad was General Vassili Chuikov. He quickly grasped that the key to survival in the city would be small, individual encounters with the enemy, rather than a war of tanks, artillery and bombers. The most lethal soldier of all would be the sniper. In the bizarre landscape of the city, with its acres of demolished or burned-out factories and apartment buildings, Stalingrad was perfect sniper territory. A soldier would feel he could be killed at any moment by a sharpshooter perched atop some derelict eyrie. A handful of good snipers could completely demoralize an entire front line regiment. Because of their importance to the defenders, Soviet snipers were rewarded well for their efforts. A marksman with 40 kills, for example, won the title "noble sniper" and was given a medal.

This highly specialized job requires both particular skills and an uncommon personality. It is one thing to kill a soldier when he is charging toward you with a bayonet. It is an entirely different matter to observe him coldly from a hiding place. He may be shaving, chatting to a friend, writing a letter home, or even squatting over a latrine. A sniper must kill him in cold blood, and at the moment when he is least likely to give away his own position. Sniping is a skill which requires great cunning and patience. Especially when one sniper is sent to stalk another. A sound knowledge of camouflage is essential. At Stalingrad, skilled snipers learned to fire against a white background, where the flash of their rifle shot could be less easily seen. Some snipers improvised special attachments to their rifles, which hid the flash of a shot. Some set up dummy figures to act as lures, returning to them regularly to move their position.

Early September was a particularly desperate time in the battle. It was then that Vasily Zaitsev, a sniper of the Russian 62nd Army, began to make a name for himself. In his first 10 days in the city, he managed to kill 40 German soldiers.

Zaitsev was a 22-year-old shepherd from the Elininski forest of the Ural mountains. He had learned to shoot as a young boy, and was already a skilled marksman before he even joined the army. He had the broad, open face of a Russian peasant. All of this made him ideal material for Soviet propaganda newspapers. Such papers were desperately trying to instill some confidence and fighting spirit into the soldiers of the city. Zaitsev's combination of ordinariness and special talent made him a perfect *people's hero*. Even his name was just right – Zaitsev is a surname derived from the word for "hare" in Russian. Animal cunning and speed were perfect attributes for a sniper. As his fame grew, his story was also taken up by national newspapers, newsreels and radio broadcasts.

Such was his success, the army had Zaitsev set up a sniper training school close to the front. Here, between forays to the German front lines, he passed on his skills to eager recruits. "Conceal yourself like a stone," he told them. "Observe, study the terrain, compile a chart and plot distinctive marks on it. Remember that if in the process of observation you have revealed yourself to the enemy… you will receive a bullet through your head." He taught his pupils how to use dummies, and other ruses, to lure enemy snipers into giving away their position. Sometimes he would taunt an opponent with a firing range target. Then, when he was confident he had discovered his enemy's hiding place, he would hurry back to where his dummy had been, and swiftly catch his opponent off guard. Snipers sometimes played these games with each other. Zaitsev warned his pupils never to become angry at such tactics. The way to stay alive as a sniper was to look before you leap. A sniper needed to be intimately familiar with the territory in which he operated. Anything different, a pile of bricks here, a slightly-shifted pile of wooded planks there, would tell an experienced soldier that an enemy sniper lay hidden and waiting for his next victim.

Among Zaitsev's pupils was a young woman named Tania Chernova. Like many Russian women, she fought as a front line soldier. Several of her family had been killed in the war, and Tania had a deep hatred for her enemy. She always called them "sticks" – targets – refusing even to think of them as human beings. She had a special skill as a sniper, and often fought alongside Zaitsev. Sharing the hardships of front line soldiers, they snatched meals eaten with a spoon kept in their boots, bathed in buckets of cold water, and slept huddled together in dark overcrowded shelters. As courtships went it was hardly flowers and candle-lit dinners, but in the intense atmosphere of the front, where death was often an instant away, the two became lovers.

From their careful monitoring of the Soviet newspapers and radio broadcasts, and their interrogations of captured Soviet soldiers, the Germans soon learned about Vasily Zaitsev. His worth to the Russians as a morale booster was obvious. The German Sixth Army high command also realized what a prize it would be to kill him. Besides, the success of Soviet snipers was making life so unpleasant for the German ground troops, that no one dared raise their head above the rubble in the hours of daylight.

An SS Colonel named Heinz Thorwald, head of the sniper training school at Zossen, near Berlin, was flown to Stalingrad to dispatch Zaitsev. He had several advantages over the Soviet sniper. He knew all about the techniques of his opponent, because Soviet newspapers and army training leaflets full of this information had been passed on to him. Zaitsev, on the other hand, knew nothing about him – although he had been tipped off that the Germans had sent one of their best snipers to kill him. For several days he kept his eyes and ears open for any clues as to the whereabouts of this Nazi "super-sniper" – as Zaitsev called him. Then, in a single day, his friend Morozov was killed and another comrade, Shaikin, was badly wounded. Both men were expert snipers. They had been outfoxed by someone of even greater talent.

Zaitsev hurried to the section of the front line where his comrades had been shot – the Red October factory district, a malignant landscape of twisted machinery and the skeletal framework of partially demolished buildings. Like a police inspector investigating a murder, he asked soldiers who had witnessed the shootings exactly what had happened, and where his comrades had been hit. Making use of his now considerable experience, he deduced that the shots had to come from a position directly in front of the area where these men had fallen. Across the lines, amid the tangled rubble, was the hulk of a burned-out tank. This was too obvious a spot for an experienced sniper. To the right of the tank was an abandoned concrete pillbox. But the firing slit there had been boarded up. Between these two landmarks, right in front of Zaitsev's own position, was a sheet of corrugated iron lying amid piles of bricks. This, he thought, was the perfect place for a sniper to hide, then crawl away under cover of darkness.

As he studied the landscape, Zaitsev caught sight of the top of a helmet moving along the edge of an enemy trench, and instinctively reached for his rifle. But then he realized, by the way the helmet was wobbling along, that this was a trap. Colonel Thorwald almost certainly had an assistant who had placed the helmet on a stick and was waiting for Zaitsev to reveal his position by firing at this dummy target.

Putting his theory to the test, Zaitsev placed a glove on a small plank and raised it above a brick parapet in front of the iron sheeting. At once a shot rang out, piercing the glove and plank in an instant. Zaitsev looked at his plank carefully. The bullet had gone straight through it. His quarry was obviously directly under the iron sheet. After dark, Zaitsev and his friend Kulikov scouted the area for suitable firing spots. The night wore on with occasional bursts of rifle fire, followed by sporadic mortar and artillery barrages. Every now and then a flare would shoot high into the air in a graceful arc, floating down in a bright blaze that cast harsh shadows over the still, sinister landscape.

When the sun rose the next morning it fell directly on them, so they waited. To have fired then, with the sunlight catching their rifles or telescopic sights, would have been too risky. But, by early afternoon, the sun had moved across the sky, and over to the German lines. At the edge of the iron sheet, something glistened in the bright light. Was it Thorwald's rifle, or just a piece of broken glass? Kulikov offered the German sniper a target. Very carefully he raised his helmet above the broken brick wall they sheltered behind. A shot rang out, piercing the metal helmet. Kulikov rose slightly and screamed, as if he had been hit. Unable to contain his curiosity Thorwald raised his head a little from behind the iron sheet, to try to get a better look. It was the chance Zaitsev had been waiting for. He fired a single shot, and Thorwald's head fell back. That night, Zaitsev crept up to his opponent's position to take his rifle as a souvenir. You can still see the telescopic sight on display at the Armed Forces Museum in Moscow.

The course of the battle of Stalingrad makes up one of the great horror stories of modern history. The Germans, together with their Italian, Hungarian and Romanian allies, lost 850,000 men. The Soviets lost 750,000. But Stalingrad was not just the scene of a vast, prolonged battle, it was also a city of half a million people. In the first two days of the fighting, 40,000 of them were killed in German bombing raids. By the end, a mere 1,500 were still alive among the rubble, although some who had lived in the city before the Germans came had already fled to other parts of Russia.

The battle ended when Soviet forces outside Stalingrad surrounded the Germans, cutting them off inside the city. "There is not a single healthy man left at the front...everyone is at least suffering from frostbite," ran a report by Sixth Army commanders to Berlin on January 18, 1943. "The commander of the 76th Infantry Division on a visit to the front yesterday came across many soldiers who had frozen to death." But Hitler refused to allow his starving, demoralized Sixth Army to give in. Von Paulus and his troops went through a further two weeks of needless suffering before he defied direct orders and submitted to the Russians. Of the 91,000 Germans who surrendered, only 5,000 would ever return home. The rest died in captivity.

Sad to say, there was to be no happy ending to the relationship between Vasily Zaitsev and Tania Chernova. Shortly after Zaitsev survived his encounter with Colonel Thorwald, Tania was critically wounded. She and a small squad of soldiers had been sent out to assassinate von Paulus. On the way to the German front lines, one of them stepped on a mine. In the explosion, Tania received a near fatal stomach wound. Zaitsev was told she was not expected to live. But Tania survived. Several months later, while recovering in a hospital in Tashkent, far behind the front lines, she too received terrible news. Zaitsev had been killed in an explosion in the final weeks of fighting in Stalingrad. Sunk in despair, for weeks afterwards she would just stare into space. Eventually she recovered her health and even married, although the wound she received meant that she could never have children. For Tania, like so many others, the war had consequences she would have to bear for the rest of her life.

Only in 1969, when she was in her late 40s, did she learn that Zaitsev was still alive. After the war he had married, and became the director of an engineering school. It was bittersweet news, because she still loved him. The explosion she had been told about had happened. Zaitsev had also been caught by a mine. It had blinded him temporarily, but he too had recovered.

Note

The identity of Colonel Thorwald is a thorny historical issue. In some accounts he is referred to as Major Koning or Konig. Zaitsev wrote about the duel described here in his post-war memoirs, but does not mention his rival by name. No one doubts Zaitsev's skill and achievements as a sniper, but some historians think the episode with Thorwald/Konig was made up, or at least heavily embroidered, by Soviet propagandists. The story about Tania Chernova is undoubtedly true, and was taken directly from her personal experience of the battle of Stalingrad given to American historian William Craig in his book Enemy at the Gates.

The Gentleman's Gentleman

1943-1945

LUDWIG MOYZISCH WAS NOT amused. He had been woken from a deep sleep and summoned to the house of the First Secretary to the German Embassy in Ankara, Turkey. In the middle of the night. What could possibly be this important?

It was October, 1943. Europe was deep into the Second World War. Neutral Turkey, uncomfortably positioned between

Nazi-occupied Europe and Soviet Russia, was teeming with spies. Moyzisch, a member of the German secret service – the SD (*Sicherheitsdienst*) – was one of these spies. He had a cover job as a trade representative at the German Embassy, and he was often expected to do odd, unexpected things at strange times of the day. Nonetheless, he was even more irritated when he got to the house. The First Secretary had gone to bed, and it was his wife who greeted Moyzisch at the door.

"There's a strange sort of character in there," she said, pointing to the drawing room. "He has something he wants to sell us."

Then she too left for her bed, telling him to be sure to close the door properly when he left.

Moyzisch was seething, and walked briskly into the drawing room. He was determined to sort this visitor out as soon as possible. His eyes searched around the clutter and paraphernalia of the room, and it took a few moments before he noticed a still, pale figure, sitting stock still on a sofa, his face hidden in shadow. Something about this man made Moyzisch stiffen suspiciously. His temper receded, and he concentrated on clearing his head.

The visitor stood up. He was small and squat, with thick black hair and a high forehead. Moyzisch later recalled his face as being "that of a man accustomed to hiding his feelings," but on this occasion his dark, piecing eyes darted around the room, betraying his unease.

The man went over to the door, and suddenly jerked it open, to see if anyone was hiding behind it. Moyzisch's irritation returned. He was a spy, not one of the Marx Brothers, and this was not a silly film. But he kept his silence and let his visitor do the talking.

"I have an offer to make to you," the man began, talking in fluent but heavily accented French. "But first I must ask for your assurance that nothing I say now will go beyond you and your chief. If you betray me, your life will be as worthless as mine. I'll see to it if it's the last thing I do."

With that, he drew his hand across his throat.

Moyzisch looked at the man coldly. Certainly, he could not take a threat like that seriously. But he was a professional spy, and his training told him to wait and see what else this stranger had to say. It was certainly interesting. . .

"I can deliver to you photographs of top secret

information – extremely secret information – from the British Embassy. But if you want it, you'll have to pay me a great deal of money. I'll risk my life for you, so I want you to make it worth my while."

Moyzisch spoke for the first time: "And what sort of sum would you be thinking of?"

"I want £20,000 – sterling – in cash."

Moyzisch's mask slipped. He could not resist a sneer.

"That's completely impossible," he replied. "What on earth have you got that would be worth such a huge sum of money?"

In 1943, such an amount was a veritable fortune.

"Well, think about it," said the stranger. "I'll give you three days to decide. Then I'll call you at the German Embassy and identify myself as "Pierre". I shall ask if you have any letters for me. If the answer is yes, I shall come and see you. If no, then you shall never hear from me again. If you're not interested, there are others who certainly will be."

Something about this man made Moyzisch hesitate to dismiss him. He almost certainly meant to take his information to the Soviet Embassy in Ankara if the Germans turned him down, and he certainly did mean business. Moyzisch agreed to this arrangement and the man got up to leave. Just as he got to the door he turned and smiled slyly.

"I'll bet you're dying to know who I am. Well, I'll tell you. I'm the British Ambassador's valet."

Before Moyzisch could say any more the door slammed shut, and the strange little man was gone.

The next morning Moyzisch arranged to see the German ambassador, Franz von Papen. The sum of money this man demanded was so huge they would have to ask permission to give it to him from the German Foreign Secretary, Joachim von Ribbentrop, himself. They were certain he would say no. But a reply came back accepting the arrangement. A special courier was being sent from Berlin with the money.

Moyzisch gave his stranger a code name – *Cicero*, after a famous Roman orator – and made preparations for his visit. Sure enough, the phone call from "Pierre" came and they arranged to meet at the Embassy at 10:00pm that night.

Moyzisch was well prepared. He arranged for a darkroom, complete with a photographic technician, to be made ready, so he could check the film on the spot. The strange man turned up right on time, and the two of them began a tentative, suspicious exchange. Cicero wanted the money first, and then he would hand over the film. Moyzisch wanted the film to check if it was genuine, then he would hand over the money. They came to a compromise. Moyzisch counted out the £20,000 in front of him, then returned it to the safe and took the film to the darkroom.

The results were spectacular: unquestionably authentic top secret documents, all with recent dates. Cicero got his money, and a further arrangement was reached whereby the Germans would pay him £15,000 for every subsequent delivery. The money was an astronomical amount, but then, the information was simply extraordinary.

The next night Cicero returned again with yet more film. When he left he asked Moyzisch to drive him back to the British Embassy. The German was astonished.

"But why not?" said Cicero, simply. "That's where I live."

More films followed, each revealing documents containing highly sensitive information. The Germans could not believe their luck. Cicero was simply too good to be true, and they suspected he was playing a game of double-bluff with them, supplying fake information to confuse and mislead the German Secret Service.

Moyzisch was instructed to find out all he could about their contact in the British Embassy, and soon built up a picture of Cicero. His actual name was Eleyza Bazna. He was an Albanian who had made his way to Turkey and settled in Ankara. Here he found work as a chauffeur, then a butler, and then as a valet to high ranking diplomats. He had worked for the Yugoslav ambassador and a German diplomat who had fired him for reading his mail. Finally, he had found work at the British Embassy as the valet for a high ranking official.

Bazna was very good at his job. He was servile, efficient, and had a knack of being able to second-guess what his master wanted. He was intelligent too, and spoke several languages fluently. When the position of valet at the residence of the ambassador Sir Hughe Knatchbull-Hugesson came up, Bazna got the job.

What Sir Hughe didn't know was that his new manservant had several interests which were to prove quite counter-productive. One was photography, another was Mara, a maid at the Embassy, and the third was snooping around in

Embassy files. When Bazna discovered how easy this was, it became a full time passion.

Bazna found out that his new master was a man of punctilious habits. Everything in Sir Hughe's life was run like clockwork. He liked to bathe morning and evening, play the piano after lunch, and have his meals at exact times of the day. When he went out in his purple Rolls-Royce, he knew exactly when he was leaving and when he would return.

Another of Sir Hughe's habits could not have been more accommodating – he liked to read top secret documents in his residence, and kept them in a safe there.

One evening, while Sir Hughe was having his bath, Bazna slipped into his bedroom, on the excuse of laying out his evening clothes, and made a wax impression of the safe key. He then had a replica key made up by a friend. After that, everything Sir Hughe kept in his safe was given a thorough read by his manservant.

Such a routine was perfect, and the more Bazna snooped, the more daring he became. On one occasion, after Sir Hughe had taken a sleeping pill, Bazna even read and photographed his secret papers on a bedside table.

And what secrets they were! Plans to launch air attacks from Turkey against Nazi ally Romania... Details of meetings between the American president Franklin Roosevelt, British Prime Minister Winston Churchill, and Soviet leader Joseph Stalin... Best of all for the Germans, Bazna passed on news of the forthcoming Allied invasion of Europe from England to France. Bazna even gave the Nazis its codename – *Operation Overlord.*

But, bizarrely, the Nazis still believed such information was too good to be true. Although they thought Bazna was genuine, they assumed the information he was supplying was fake – deliberately planted by British intelligence for him to find and pass on to the Germans.

Bazna cared little for what the Germans did with his information, and even less for what they thought of it – just as long as the bank notes kept coming in. The money was piling up. He made no great effort to hide it, and kept it under his bedroom carpet.

Not all of his ill-gotten gains were saved for a rainy day. Bazna began to spend extravagantly. A country cottage was rented and equipped with every modern convenience. In another alarming breach of secrecy, Bazna even called it "Villa Cicero" after his German code name, and had a little plaque with this put up above the door. He and girlfriend Mara became regular customers at the ABC Store on Ataturk Boulevard – the most fashionable shop in all of Turkey. Their clothes and jewels would have shamed high society socialites.

Moyzisch became irritated with the way Bazna flaunted his wealth, especially when he began to wear a gold watch. Even Mara, who believed he was working for the Turks, started to chide him.

"People are going to start to wonder about how we can afford such wonderful clothes. You're just a valet after all."

"Don't you worry," he smiled. "They're all too stupid."

But they weren't. Curiously, it was the Turks who first started to take an interest in Bazna. They were neutral in the war. As the conflict dragged on, they began to wonder which side it would best suit their own interests to support. One night, after Bazna had dropped off more film at the German Embassy, and Moyzisch was driving him home, they noticed a large black car was following them. Moyzisch slowed, the car slowed. Moyzisch speeded up, the car speeded up. Desperate to shake them off, Moyzisch hit the accelerator and sped through Ankara's fashionable boulevards at a death-defying 190kmph (120mph).

Later that week, Moyzisch bumped into a Turkish official.

"My dear man," said the Turk, "you really are a most reckless driver. You should take more care – especially at night."

It was a warning, and the first hint that Bazna's spying days were numbered.

More alarming events followed. At the British Embassy a team of security experts arrived to install a security system on the ambassador's secret documents. But Bazna heard Sir Hughe discussing the system with one of these men, and was able to work out a way of bypassing it.

Secrets still continued to flow from the British Embassy to Germany, but Bazna was about to be given away by a spy of far greater daring than he. In the German Foreign Ministry worked Fritz Kolbe, a German who hated the Nazis. Kolbe had direct access to all the material that Cicero was supplying to the Germans in Ankara, and he alerted the Americans.

The Americans then told the British that they must have a spy on the loose inside their Embassy.

But still British intelligence could not establish Cicero's identity. His eventual betrayer came from within the German Embassy. Moyzisch had a surly, deeply inefficient secretary named Nellie Kapp. She was blonde, 20 years old, and pouted and sulked her way through the working day. She was so lazy that Moyzisch really wanted to get rid of her – the only reason he didn't was that her father was a high-ranking German diplomat.

But curiously, Nellie, for all her faults, did at least show quite an interest in Moyzisch's work. This was because Nellie was also a spy. She worked for the American Office for Strategic Services (OSS) and had had a key cut to fit Moyzisch's safe. She too photographed everything that passed through it. Before long, she had a very good idea that Cicero was Eleyza Bazna.

By the end of March 1944, Nellie had done her job, and decided it was time to escape. After all, if staff at the German Embassy discovered she had been spying on them, she would be tortured and then shot. She cut her hair, dyed it black, and took a plane out of Turkey.

Meanwhile, the British secret service was still not quite sure Bazna was their man, so they set a trap. One night a British security officer, Sir John Dashwood, settled down in Sir Hughe's office with a glass of whisky. He switched the lights off and waited. Soon enough, the door opened, the light came on, and there stood Bazna, key in hand. The two men looked at each other. Not a word was said. Then Bazna turned and left. It was all over.

Bazna could not be arrested, as he had broken no Turkish law. After a furious row with a spluttering, highly indignant Sir Hughe, he rounded up his possessions, including all the money under his carpet. Then he left the Embassy for good, to lay low in one of Ankara's more exclusive districts.

Moyzisch, meanwhile, was having a very uncomfortable time. His secretary had vanished under extremely suspicious circumstances, and now his best agent had been uncovered. His masters in Berlin were extremely displeased, and had sent him a stream of telegrams demanding his immediate return to Germany. Moyzisch feared for his life. To buy some time, he telegraphed back that he was ill, and could not travel. Shortly afterward, he received a phone call at his home.

"I'm calling on behalf of the British," said a mysterious voice. "If you go back to Germany you will be shot. Come over to us and save your life."

It was a terrible dilemma to be in, and Moyzisch was reluctant to betray his country. He was a loyal Nazi who had joined the party before Hitler came to power. Even now, he still believed in the Nazi's evil cause. But, fortunately for him, he never had to make the decision. Shortly after, the Allies did indeed invade France, as Cicero had predicted, and the war turned very definitely against Germany. The Turks took this as a cue to join the Allies. All German diplomats, including Moyzisch, were arrested and detained for the rest of the war.

Bazna was extremely pleased with himself. He was still alive, and he was fabulously rich. He took himself, and £300,000, off to Portugal, and then to South America. But here the world turned sour. Bankers turned up at a luxury villa Bazna had rented, and told him that all the banknotes he had placed with them were counterfeit.

Bazna took the news well. He laughed out loud at the Germans' deception. They had decided his information was useless, and they were not going to pay real money for it. But what followed was far from funny, at least for him. Bazna was arrested, and sent to prison for passing forged banknotes. When he was released he headed for Germany, and asked the West German government to compensate him for his lost *earnings*. Unsurprisingly, his request was not successful. He died, lonely and poverty-stricken, in Istanbul in 1971.

Ludwig Moyzisch did rather better after the war. He gave evidence at the Nuremberg trials of Nazi war criminals and then returned to civilian life in Austria. Here he took up his bogus embassy alias for real – becoming an export manager for a textile firm. He wrote a book, *Operation Cicero*, about his spying activities, which was later made into a film called *Five Fingers*, starring James Mason.

ODETTE'S ORDEAL

1942-1945

O N A MAY DAY IN 1943, several German officers sat beneath a cut-glass chandelier in an elegantly decorated room filled with sunlight. The room served as a court at 84 Avenue Foch, Parisian headquarters of the German *Gestapo*, the Nazi secret police, whose brutal methods were feared throughout Europe.

The court's attention was focused on a bedraggled French

woman who sat before them. She had just spent a month in prison, where she had been forbidden to bathe, exercise or change her clothes. Her feet were bandaged where she had been tortured, but she looked far from broken – in fact she seemed to project a curious, detached kind of dignity, as if she were indifferent to her surroundings. Her name was Odette Sansom, housewife turned British spy, and she was on trial for her life.

Odette, who spoke no German, soon became bored, and her eyes wandered around the room. But when the bemedalled colonel who was obviously in charge of the proceedings stood up and read a statement to her, she knew the trial had ended.

She shrugged wearily and told the court she did not speak German. The colonel frowned and explained in halting French that she had been sentenced to death on two counts. One as a British spy, the other as a member of the French Resistance.

Odette looked on the stiff, pompous men before her with scorn, and a giggle rose inside her. "Gentlemen," she said, "you must take your pick of the counts. I can die only once."

Odette had led a life that hardened her to the tribulations she now faced. She was born Odette Brailly, in Amiens,

France, in 1912. When she was four, her father had been killed in the First World War. At seven, she caught polio and was blinded for a year, and then spent another year unable to move her limbs. These disabilities turned her into a fiercely independent character. The teenage Odette was remembered as a loyal friend and merciless enemy.

During the First World War, her mother had provided lodgings for English officers. Odette had liked them all immensely, and grew up determined to marry an Englishman. At 19 she did. His name was Roy Sansom. They moved to England in 1932. Odette's years before the Second World War were spent raising three daughters and living the life of an English housewife in Somerset.

War broke out in 1939 and, in less than two years, Nazi Germany had conquered almost all of Europe. When France fell in 1940, it caused Odette much grief. Cut off from her family, she worried constantly about their safety.

In the spring of 1942, Odette heard a government radio broadcast appealing for snapshots of French beaches. An invasion of France from Britain was being planned, and such photos would help decide which beaches were best for landing troops. Odette had spent her childhood by the sea, so wrote to offer her help.

Shortly afterwards an official letter arrived asking her to come up to London. Here she met a man in a shabby back room office, in a building off Oxford Street. They talked for a while and she placed an envelope of her photos on his desk. To Odette's surprise, he pushed them to one side and looked at her closely.

"Actually," he said with a brisk smile, "we're not really interested in your photos. What we'd really like you to do is go to France as a spy."

Odette was flabbergasted.

"Look, I'm a housewife," she said with some exasperation. "I'm not particularly bright and I don't know a thing about spying. I'm sorry. I'll have to say no to you."

"Very well," said the man, who seemed quite unperturbed. "That's quite understandable. But, here, take my number. If you change your mind, just telephone."

Over the next week Odette could not decide what to do. She was torn between her own patriotic feelings for France, and the responsibility she felt for her three children in

England. Eventually she decided she would train as a spy, and found a convent boarding school for her daughters. Odette's work was so secret she could not even tell her family and friends what she was doing. She told them instead that she had joined the Army to work as a nurse.

She joined a branch of the British secret service called the Special Operations Executive (SOE) which sent agents overseas. As soon as her training began, the dangers that would face her were made alarmingly clear. "In many ways it's a beastly job," said her commanding officer, Major Buckmaster. "You will be living a gigantic lie for months on end. And if you slip up and get caught, we can do little to save you." In wartime, the fate of a captured spy was almost always execution.

Physical fitness and combat training toughened Odette. She also learned specialized skills, such as which fields were best for aircraft to make secret landings, and how to tell the difference between various kinds of German military uniforms.

Buckmaster had mixed feelings about Odette. He felt she had a temperamental and impulsive nature which could endanger her and any other agents she would work with. "Her main asset is her patriotism and keenness to do something for France," he wrote in a report. "Her main weakness is a complete unwillingness to admit that she could ever be wrong."

In Odette's final days in England, before she went to France, the British secret service made sure her appearance looked as French as possible. She was given a new wardrobe of authentic French clothes, as anything with an English label on it would betray her. But tiny details were taken care of too. The English fillings in her teeth, for example, were taken out and replaced with French ones, and even her wedding ring was replaced with one that had been made in France.

On Odette's last meeting with Major Buckmaster, he supplied her with several different drugs to help with her work. There were sickness pills, energy pills, sleeping pills and, most sinister of all, a brown, pea-sized suicide pill. Buckmaster told her it would kill her in six seconds.

"It's rather a horrible going away present," he said, "so I've also brought you this," and gave her a beautiful silver compact.

Odette was flown over to France in November 1942. She began working in Cannes with a group of secret service agents led by a British officer named Peter Churchill. She acted as a courier, delivering money to pay for the work of the French Resistance. The British secret service worked closely with the Resistance, organizing bands of guerrilla fighters, assisting in sabotage operations and sending back information to England.

Odette picked up stolen maps and documents from the Resistance to pass back to Britain. She found "safe houses" for other spies and suitable locations for aircraft to land with agents or drop weapons by parachute. Peter Churchill was impressed with her. His new agent was quick-thinking, and capable. He thought she was very funny and seemed to possess an unstoppable determination.

Her job was very difficult and danger lurked at every turn. The Germans were constantly arresting Resistance members, and anyone Odette met in her work could be a double-agent. Eventually the group was betrayed by a traitor named Roger Bardet, who worked for German Military Intelligence – the *Abwehr*. Churchill and Odette were arrested on April 16,

1943. Even as they were being bundled off at gunpoint, Odette had the presence of mind to hide Churchill's wallet, which contained radio codes and names of other agents, by stuffing it down the side of a car seat on their way to prison.

There was no point denying they were British agents, but Odette spun a complex tale for her captors, hoping at least to save Peter Churchill's life. She said that that they were married to each other, and Churchill was related to the British Prime Minister, Winston Churchill. This was a complete lie. She claimed her "husband" was an amateur dabbler who had come to France on her insistence. It was she who had led the local resistance ring, and she who should be shot. She told the story so convincingly the Germans swallowed it completely.

A month after their arrest, both of them were taken to Fresnes – a huge jail on the outskirts of Paris. Odette was placed in cell No. 108, and a campaign to break her spirit began. Outside her door a notice read: "No books. No showers. No packages. No exercise. No privileges."

This was where Odette's interrogation by the *Abwehr* began in earnest. But she also began her own campaign to survive. With a hairpin she carved a calendar on the wall and marked every day. A grate set high in the wall covered an air vent which led to the cell below, and she was able to talk to a fellow prisoner named Michelle. This was a great comfort, as part of her punishment was that she was allowed no contact with other prisoners. Apart from frequent visits to her interrogators, she had no human contact other than an occasional visit by a German priest named Paul Heinerz.

The window in Odette's cell was made of opaque glass. Michelle whispered up to her: "Break that glass pane at once! If you can see even a little blue sky, or the crescent of the moon, it will be a wonderful sight in your dreary cell. The guards, they'll punish you to be sure. They'll probably stop your food for a few days. It's tasteless slop anyway! Believe me, when you can see outside, you'll feel it's been worth it." Odette didn't think twice.

After two weeks of interrogation, the *Abwehr* realized their prisoner was not going to tell them anything useful and Odette was taken instead to *Gestapo* headquarters at 84 Avenue Foch. On her very first visit she was given a large meal. But despite her ravenous hunger, she only ate a little. She knew the meal was intended to make her sleepy and dull-witted.

Her interviewer this time was a sophisticated young man, with Nordic good looks, who smelled of cold baths and eau de Cologne. He was polite, but Odette knew she was dealing with someone who was prepared to be far more brutal than the *Abwehr*. She was right – this urbane young man was actually a trained torturer. But his questions about Odette's Resistance activity were met with her stock response: "I have nothing to say." The interview came to an end and Odette was returned to Fresnes for the night.

She knew her visit to the *Gestapo* the next day would be more difficult. The suave young man told her he had run out of patience. Her stomach turned over as a shadowy assistant slipped into the room and stood menacingly behind her. First this man applied a red-hot poker to the small of her back. Still Odette would not talk. Then he removed her toenails one by one.

Throughout this torture Odette gave no cry, although she expected to faint several times. As she was asked the same set of questions, she replied with the same answer: "I have nothing to say."

The young man offered her a cigarette and a cup of tea – a standard tactic by torturers, who hope to catch their victims off guard by showing them unexpected kindness. Although she was in great pain, Odette felt elated. She had kept silent and won her own victory over these inhuman thugs.

Her questioner told her they were now going to remove her fingernails, and Odette's courage wavered. But help came from an unexpected quarter. Just as they were about to start on her hands, another *Gestapo* man came into the cell. "Ach, stop wasting your time," he said. "You'll get nothing more from this one."

Odette was taken back to her cell at Fresnes, where she bound her injured feet in strips of wet cloth. Then she lay on her cell bed, sick with fear at what the *Gestapo* would do next. Michelle called throughout the night but she was too weak to answer. Father Heinerz visited. He was so disgusted he could not speak. He kissed her head and left. A few days later, she was summoned to the *Gestapo* court in the chandeliered ceiling room at Avenue Foch, and sentenced to death.

Returning to her cell after the trial, Odette felt unexpectedly calm. Throughout her torture, she had not betrayed her fellow agents. Most of those she knew were still free to continue their work fighting against the Nazis. Alone on her bunk, she bid a silent good night to each of her three daughters and fell sound asleep. But in the early hours she woke with a start. There was no date for her execution. From now on, every footstep outside her door could turn out to be a guard detachment, arriving to escort her to a firing squad.

Despite this constant threat, Odette was determined not to give up hope. Her story about being related to Prime Minister Churchill had been widely repeated among the prison authorities. Many of the staff who guarded Odette were unusually courteous with her. Like many people in 1943, they had realized the war was going badly for Germany and thought that it would pay to keep on the right side of one of the relatives of Winston Churchill.

As summer turned to autumn, Odette fell gravely ill and was moved to a warmer cell. She was also given a job in the prison sewing room and ordered to make German army uniforms. This she refused to do, saying she would make dolls instead. Amazingly, the prison staff let her do this.

Over the winter her health improved but, in May 1944, news came that she was to be transferred to a prison in Germany. As she left, Odette caught sight of one of her interrogators and waved at him gaily, shouting, "Goodbye, goodbye." She was determined to let him know he had not broken her spirit.

In the van that took her away were seven other women. They all immediately recognized each other as fellow SOE agents. All instinctively felt they were being taken to Germany to be executed, but they were still delighted to see each other. Their instincts were right. Within a year, all but Odette would be dead.

On the way through Paris, they stopped at Avenue Foch where a *Gestapo* officer asked if there was anything they wanted. Odette ordered a pot of tea... not as it is made in France or Germany, but in the English manner. "One spoonful for each person and one for the pot. With milk and sugar please." The tea duly arrived, with china cups and saucers.

Odette was placed on an east-bound train with an armed guard, and spent the next few weeks in several prisons. Once she was presented to a Nazi newspaper reporter who crowed that there were now three Churchills in German prisons, and he was to write a feature on her. Odette dismissed him with a barbed remark, but this was good news. If the Nazis were publicizing her imprisonment, they were hardly likely to execute her immediately.

In July 1944, she was taken to Ravensbrück concentration camp for women on the shore of swampy Lake Fürstenburg. Even the name of the camp – the "Bridge of Ravens" – sounded sinister.

Inside its barbed-wire perimeter were row upon row of shabby prisoners' huts, patrolled by guards with whips and savage dogs. All of Ravensbrück's inmates had shaven heads, to cut down on the lice that constantly plagued them. Prisoners who had been there for months or years had been so badly fed they looked like walking skeletons.

Smoke from the camp crematorium constantly filled the sky, scattering a ghastly pall of dust and ashes over the stark, grey interior. The Nazis sent their enemies here to be worked to death and, every morning, those who had died in the night were carried away in crude wooden handcarts. As a young girl walking the cliffs of Normandy, Odette had sometimes wondered where she would die. As she entered Ravensbrück, she felt she knew the answer.

The commandant of the camp, a German officer named Fritz Sühren, was eager to meet Odette. When she was taken before him, she noticed how clean and well fed he looked. Like most of her captors, Sühren was interested in her connection with Winston Churchill. He ordered her to be placed in "the bunker" – the camp's own solitary confinement cells.

Odette's bunker cell was pitch black and for three months she was kept there in total darkness. But she had been blind for a year of her childhood. She was used to the dark. She passed the time thinking about her three daughters, and how they had grown from babies into young girls. She decided to clothe them in her imagination, stitch by stitch, garment by garment. So completely did she fill her days deciding on the fabric, shades and style of these clothes, that whenever she was visited by camp guards, it seemed like an interruption, rather than the chance to make contact with another human being.

Odette's ordeal

In August, southern France was invaded by French, British and American forces. This was where Odette had done most of her Resistance work. As a spiteful punishment, the guards turned the central heating in her cell to maximum. Odette wrapped herself in a blanket soaked in cold water, but this did not stop her from becoming terribly ill. Near death, she was taken to the camp hospital. It was a strange way to treat someone who had been sentenced to execution. Perhaps the Nazis were still hoping they could break her and she would tell them about her Resistance work.

Away from the bunker, Odette recovered her strength and was returned to her cell. On the way back she found a single leaf that had blown into the treeless camp, and scooped it into her clothing. In her dark world she would trace its spine and shape with her hands, and think about how the wind had blown a seed into the earth which had grown to a tree with leaves and branches that rustled in the wind and basked in the sunlight.

Over the next few months she overheard the execution of several of her fellow agents, all of whom were shot during the winter.

On April 27, 1945, Sühren visited her. He stood at the cell door then drew his finger across his throat. "You'll leave tomorrow morning at six o'clock," he said. Odette wondered if the end had come at last. On April 28 she would be 33. It would be a pity to be shot on her birthday.

When morning came she could hear the chaos that had overtaken the camp. Sühren arrived and bundled her into a large black van with a handful of other inmates. Through the window she could see the guards fleeing from the camp.

The van, together with an escort of SS troops, drove west. It soon became clear to Odette that the war was almost over. For the next three days Sühren, his SS escort, and his small band of prisoners, drove from one camp to another as Germany collapsed into anarchy. Many of the prisoners in these camps, so near to freedom but so close to death, were almost hysterical. Some whooped and screamed, making huge bonfires of anything they could find to burn. Others collapsed from hunger, or rushed at their guards only to be gunned down. It all seemed like a delirious nightmare.

On the fourth day away from Ravensbrück, a guard grabbed Odette and dragged her before Sühren. She was told not to bring her few belongings, and was certain she was to be executed. Thrown into Sühren's large staff car, and with an escort of SS guards in two other cars, she sped away from the camp.

After two hours, the three cars stopped by a deserted field and Sühren barked, "Get out." But this was not to be Odette's place of execution. Instead Sühren offered her a sandwich and a glass of wine, and told her he was handing her over to the Americans. At first she thought this was a cruel joke, but he seemed serious enough. Clearly he thought safely delivering Winston Churchill's relative would get him off to a good start with his captors.

The SS guards spent the next few hours burning incriminating Ravensbrück documents. Then, at 10:00 that night, they drove into a village which had been occupied by American soldiers. Sühren marched up to an officer and said, "This is Frau Churchill. She has been a prisoner. She is a relative of Winston Churchill." He handed Odette his revolver and surrendered.

The Americans offered her a place to sleep, but Odette wanted to spend her first night of freedom out in the open.

She walked over to Sühren's abandoned open-topped car and sat in the front seat, feeling neither triumph nor elation, just utter exhaustion. Nearby was a party of SS soldiers who had been part of Sühren's escort. One came over and gave her his sheepskin coat to ward off the chill of the night.

To Odette, this act of kindness by a former enemy seemed part of a strange dream, and she expected to wake at any moment and find herself back in the bunker at Ravensbrück. But the dream continued. She nestled into the coat and stared up at the stars. The village clock chimed its quarter hours throughout the night, and it was so quiet she could hear her heart beating.

Following her release, Odette returned to England, after ensuring that Fritz Sühren's American captors were aware that he had been commandant of Ravensbrück. (He was later tried as a war criminal and executed.)

She had several operations on her injured feet before she was able to walk properly again. In 1946, she became the first woman to be given the *George Cross*, Britain's highest civilian award for bravery, "for courage, endurance and self sacrifice

French housewife turned spy Odette Sansom. Her extraordinary spirit and resilience was forged by a childhood blighted by polio.

of the highest possible order." She always insisted that the medal had not been given to her personally, but in recognition of the bravery of all French resistance workers.

The medal was stolen a few years later. But following a series of outraged newspaper articles in Britain's national press, it was returned with a letter of apology from the anonymous burglar.

In 1948, after her first husband had died, she married Peter Churchill, the man she had suffered so much to protect. But after eight years they parted, and Odette later married Geoffrey Hallowes, another secret service veteran. In later life she co-founded the British "Woman of the Year" award, worked for charities and spent many hours writing to thousands of people with problems, who had contacted her for advice or inspiration.

Odette Sansom's life as a secret agent was portrayed in the 1950 British film *Odette*, starring Anna Neagle. It was partially shot at Fresnes Prison, Paris, where Odette herself had been held prisoner. She worked as an advisor on the film, but seeing Anna Neagle relive her worst moments was a very painful experience.

She returned to Ravensbrück in 1994, for a ceremony to unveil a plaque commemorating the courage of the British SOE women who had died there. Looking back on the war, Odette wrote: "I am a very ordinary woman, to whom the chance has been given to see human beings at their best and at their worst."

She died in 1995, aged 82.

STAUFFENBERG'S
SECRET GERMANY

1943-1944

ON A SPRING MORNING in 1943, American fighter planes screamed low over a Tunisian coastal road, pouring machine-gun fire onto a column of German army vehicles. Fierce flames bellowed from blazing trucks and smeared the blue desert sky with oily, black smoke. Amid the wreckage on the ground lay Colonel Claus von Stauffenberg, one of Germany's most brilliant soldiers. He was badly wounded, and fighting for his life.

Stauffenberg was quickly transported to a Munich hospital and given the best possible treatment. His left eye, right hand and two fingers from his left hand had been lost in the attack. His legs were so badly damaged that doctors feared he would never walk again.

Willing himself back from the brink of death, Stauffenberg was determined not to be defeated by his injuries. He refused all pain-killing drugs, and learned to dress, bathe and write with his three remaining fingers. His recovery was astounding. Before the summer was over he was demanding to be returned to his regiment.

Hospital staff were amazed by their patient's stubborn persistence, and admired what they thought was his patriotic determination to return to active service. But it was not to fight for Nazi leader Adolf Hitler that the colonel struggled so hard to recover. What Stauffenberg wanted to do was kill him.

Stauffenberg had supported the Nazis once, but his experience in the war had turned him against them. In Poland, in 1939, he had witnessed SS soldiers killing Jewish women and children by the roadside. While fighting in France in

1940, he had seen a Nazi field commander order the execution of unarmed British prisoners. Worst of all had been Hitler's war against the Soviet Union. Not only had this invasion been fought with great brutality to Russian soldiers and civilians alike, but Stauffenberg had been sickened by Hitler's incompetent interference in the campaign, and his stubborn refusal to allow exhausted troops in impossible situations to surrender.

After one disastrous battle, Stauffenberg asked a close friend: "Is there no officer in Hitler's headquarters capable of taking a pistol to the beast?" Lying in his hospital bed, Stauffenberg realized he was just the man for the job.

Like most people, Stauffenberg had his flaws. Although he was untidy in his personal appearance, he was incredibly strict about orderliness and punctuality. He had a ferocious temper, and could become enraged if an aide laid out his uniform less than perfectly. But Stauffenberg was blessed with a magnetic personality and he was a brilliant commander. He also had a sensitive nature, which encouraged fellow officers to confide in him. All these aspects of his character made him an ideal leader of any opposition to Hitler.

As soon as Stauffenberg was well enough to come out of hospital, he was appointed Chief of Staff in the Home Army. The Home Army was a unit of the German Army made up of all soldiers stationed in Germany. It was also responsible for recruitment and training. Stauffenberg quickly established that the deputy commander of the Home Army, General Olbricht, was not a supporter of the Nazis either. He too was willing to help Stauffenberg overthrow Hitler. Between them, they began to persuade other officers to join them.

Stauffenberg and his fellow plotters soon devised an ingenious plan to get rid of Hitler. In the previous year, the Nazis had set up a strategy called *Operation Valkyrie*, as a precaution against an uprising in Germany against them. If such a revolt broke out, the Home Army had detailed instructions to seize control of all areas of government, and important radio and railway stations, so the rebellion could be quickly put down.

But, rather than protect the Nazis, Stauffenberg and Olbricht intended to use *Operation Valkyrie* to overthrow them. They planned to kill Hitler and, in the confusion that followed his death, they would set *Operation Valkyrie* in motion, ordering their soldiers to arrest all Nazi leaders and their chief supporters – especially the SS and the *Gestapo*.

The plot had two great flaws. Firstly, killing Hitler would be difficult, as he was surrounded by bodyguards. Secondly, when the head of the Home Army, General Friedrich Fromm, was approached by the conspirators, he refused to take part. Like everyone in the armed forces, he had sworn an oath of loyalty to Hitler, and he used this as an excuse for not betraying him. Fromm also feared Hitler's revenge if the plot should fail. Without Fromm's help, using Valkyrie to overthrow the Nazis would be considerably more difficult.

But the plotters were not deterred and Stauffenberg still threw himself into the task of recruiting allies. He referred to his conspiracy as "Secret Germany" after a poem by his hero, German writer Stefan George. Many officers joined Stauffenberg, but many more wavered. Most were disgusted by the way Hitler was leading the German army but, like Fromm, they felt restrained by their oath of loyalty or feared for their lives if the plot should fail.

The plotters took care to avoid being discovered by the

Gestapo. Documents were typed wearing gloves, to avoid leaving fingerprints, on a typewriter that would then be hidden in a cupboard or attic. Stauffenberg memorized and then destroyed written messages, and left not a scrap of solid evidence against himself. And such was his good judgment in recruiting plotters that not a single German officer he approached to join the conspiracy betrayed him.

But by the summer of 1944, time was running out. The *Gestapo* had begun to suspect a major revolt against Hitler was being planned. They were searching hard for conspirators and the evidence to condemn them. The longer the plotters delayed, the greater their chance of being discovered.

By this time, the plotters had decided the best way to kill Hitler would be with a bomb hidden in a briefcase. As part of his Home Army duties, Stauffenberg attended conferences with the German leader, who thought the colonel was a very glamorous figure and had a high regard for his abilities. Because Stauffenberg had such close contact with Hitler, he volunteered to plant the bomb himself.

In order to give him time to escape, the bomb would be primed with a ten-minute fuse. This device was quite complicated. To activate the bomb, a small glass tube containing acid needed to be broken with a pair of pliers. The acid would eat through a thin steel wire. When this broke, it released a detonator which set off the bomb.

On July 11, Stauffenberg went to Hitler's headquarters at Rastenburg in East Prussia for a meeting with Hitler, and two other leading Nazis, Heinrich Himmler and Herman Goring. He hoped to wipe out all three, but when Himmler and Goring did not arrive he decided to wait for a better opportunity.

On July 15, Stauffenberg was again summoned to Rastenburg. On this occasion, *Operation Valkyrie* was set in motion before the meeting. But unfortunately, at the last moment, Hitler decided not to attend the conference where Stauffenberg was due to plant his bomb. A frantic phone call to Berlin called off *Valkyrie* and the conspirators covered their tracks by pretending it had been an army exercise.

Their chance finally came on July 20, 1944, when Stauffenberg was again summoned to Hitler's headquarters at Rastenburg. Together with his personal assistant, Lieutenant Werner von Haeften, he collected two bombs and drove to

Rangsdorf airfield south of Berlin, and from there took the three hour flight to Rastenburg.

Arriving in East Prussia at 10:15am, they drove through gloomy forest to Hitler's headquarters. Surrounded by barbed wire, minefields and checkpoints, the base – fancifully known as "The Wolf's Lair"– was a collection of concrete bunkers and wooden huts. It was here, cut off from the real world, that Hitler had retreated to wage his final battles of the war.

The conference with Hitler was scheduled for 12:30pm. At 12:15pm, as conference staff began to assemble, Stauffenberg requested permission to wash and change his shirt. It was such a hot day this seemed perfectly reasonable.

An aide ushered him into a nearby washroom, where he was quickly joined by Haeften, and they set about activating the two bombs. Stauffenberg broke the acid tube fuse on one but, as he reached for the second bomb, they were interrupted by a sergeant sent to hurry Stauffenberg, who was now late for the conference.

One bomb would have to do. But there was further bad news. Stauffenberg had hoped the meeting would be held in an underground bunker – a windowless, concrete room where

Taken several days before the July 20th assassination attempt, this shows Colonel Claus von Stauffenberg (far left) with Adolf Hitler (middle) at the 'Wolf's Lair' headquarters. Stauffenberg carries a suitcase bomb, but on this occasion he decided not to detonate it.

the blast of his bomb would be much more destructive. But instead, he was led to a wooden hut with three large windows. The force of any explosion here would be a lot less effective.

Inside the hut, the conference had already begun. High-ranking officers and their assistants crowded around a large, oak, map table, discussing the progress of the war in Russia. Stauffenberg, whose hearing had been damaged when he was wounded, asked if he could stand near to Hitler so he could hear him properly.

Placing himself to Hitler's right, Stauffenberg shoved his bulging briefcase under the table, to the left of a large, wooden support. Just then, Field Marshal Keitel, who was one of Hitler's most loyal generals, suggested that Stauffenberg should deliver his report next. But with less than seven minutes before the bomb would explode, he had no intention of remaining inside the hut. Fortunately, the discussion on the Russian front continued and Stauffenberg made an excuse to leave the room, saying he had to make an urgent phone call to Berlin.

Keitel, already irritated by Stauffenberg's late arrival, became incensed that he should have the impertinence to leave the conference, and called after him, insisting that he should stay. But Stauffenberg ignored him and hurried off. Like all the conspirators, he hated Keitel, whom he called Lakeitel – a pun on the word *Lakei* meaning "toady" or "lackey" in German.

There were less than five minutes to go. Stauffenberg hurried over to another hut and waited with his friend General Erich Fellgiebel, the chief of signals at the base, who was one of several Rastenburg officers who had joined Stauffenberg's conspiracy. The seconds dragged by.

Inside the conference room, an officer named Colonel Brandt leaned over the table to get a better look at a map. His foot caught on Stauffenberg's heavy briefcase, so he picked it up and moved it to the opposite side of the heavy, wooden support. An instant later, at 12:42 precisely, the bomb went off.

At the sound of the explosion, Haeften drove up in a staff car and Stauffenberg leapt in. The two of them had to escape to the airfield quickly, before "The Wolf's Lair" was sealed off by Hitler's guards. The hut looked completely devastated and, as they drove away, both felt confident no one inside could have survived.

They were wrong. Brandt and three others had been killed but, in moving the briefcase to the other side of the wooden support, Brandt had shielded Hitler from the full force of the blast. The German leader staggered out of the hut, his hair smoldering and trousers in tatters. He was very much alive.

Fellgiebel watched in horror. Hitler's death was an essential part of the plot. But, nonetheless, shortly before 1:00pm he sent a message to the War Office in Berlin, confirming the bomb had exploded and ordering Olbricht to set *Valkyrie* into operation. He made no mention of whether Hitler was alive or dead.

But back in Berlin, Olbricht hesitated because he was uncertain whether Hitler was dead. Until he knew more, he was not prepared to act. Meanwhile Stauffenberg, flying back to Berlin, was cut off from everything. During the two hours he was in the air, he expected his fellow conspirators to be carrying through *Operation Valkyrie* in a frenzy of activity. In fact, nothing was happening. Unfortunately for the plotters, Stauffenberg could not be in two places at once. He was the best man to carry out the bomb attack in Rastenburg, but he would also have been the best man to direct *Operation Valkyrie* in Berlin.

At Rastenburg, it did not take long to realize who had planted the bomb. Orders were immediately issued to arrest Stauffenberg at Berlin's Rangsdorf airfield. But the signals officer responsible for sending this message was also one of the conspirators, and the order was never transmitted.

Only after an hour and a half, at 3:30pm, did the Berlin conspirators reluctantly begin to act. Home Army officers were summoned by Olbricht and told that Hitler was dead and *Operation Valkyrie* was to be set in motion. But General Fromm was still refusing to cooperate, especially after he phoned Rastenburg and was told by General Keitel that Hitler was alive.

At 4:30pm, the plotters grew bolder and issued orders to the entire German army. Hitler, they declared, was dead. Nazi party leaders were trying to seize power for themselves. The army was to take control of the government immediately, to stop them from doing this.

Stauffenberg arrived back in Berlin soon afterwards. He too was not able to persuade Fromm to join the conspiracy. Instead the commander-in-chief erupted into a foaming tirade against him. Banging his fists on his desk, Fromm demanded that the conspirators be placed under arrest and ordered Stauffenberg to shoot himself. When Fromm began to lunge at his fellow officers, fists flailing, he had to be subdued with a pistol pressed to his stomach. Then he meekly allowed himself to be locked in an office. Other officers at Home Army headquarters who were still loyal to the Nazis were also locked up.

Stauffenberg now began to direct the conspirators with his usual energy and verve. For the rest of the afternoon, they worked with desperate haste to carry out their plan. Stauffenberg spent hours on the phone trying to persuade reluctant or wavering army commanders to support him. He was still convinced Hitler was dead, but many of the people he spoke to would not believe him. At the time, it was widely believed that the Nazi leader employed a double who looked and acted just like him. What if Stauffenberg had killed the double rather than the real Hitler, they thought.

From Paris to Prague, the army attempted to take control and arrest all Nazi officials. In some cities such as Vienna and Paris there were remarkable successes, but in Berlin it was another story. Here, the plotters were foiled by their own decency. They had revolted against the brutality of the Nazi regime and, ironically, only a similar ruthlessness could have saved them. If the conspirators had been prepared to shoot anyone who stood in their way, they might have succeeded.

They failed to capture Berlin's radio station and army communication bases in the capital. All through the late afternoon, their own commands were constantly contradicted by orders transmitted by commanders loyal to the Nazis.

By early evening it became obvious to Stauffenberg that the plot had failed yet, true to his character, he refused to give up. He insisted that success was just a whisker away and he continued to encourage his fellow plotters not to give up hope. But the end was near.

The War Office was now surrounded by hostile troops loyal to Hitler and, inside the building, a small group of Nazi officers had armed themselves and set out to arrest the conspirators. Shots were fired, Stauffenberg was hit in the shoulder and Fromm was released.

Fromm could only do one thing. Although he had refused to cooperate with the plotters, he had known all about the plot. No doubt the conspirators would confirm this – under torture or of their own free will. Fromm had to cover his tracks. He sentenced Stauffenberg, Haeften, Olbricht and his assistant Colonel Mertz von Quirnheim to immediate execution.

Stauffenberg was bleeding badly from his wound, but seemed indifferent to his death sentence. He insisted the plot was all his doing. His fellow officers had simply been carrying out his orders.

Fromm was having none of this. Just after midnight, the four men were hustled down the stairs to the courtyard outside. By all accounts, they went calmly to their deaths. Lit by the dimmed headlights of a staff car, the four were shot in order of rank. Stauffenberg was second, after Olbricht. An instant before the firing squad cut Stauffenberg down, Haeften, in a brave but pointless gesture, threw himself in front of the bullets. Stauffenberg died moments later, shouting: "Long live our Secret Germany."

There would have been more executions that night, had not *Gestapo* chief Kaltenbrunner arrived and put a stop to them. He was far more interested in seeing what could be learned from the conspirators who were still alive.

Still, the *Gestapo* torturers had been cheated of their greatest prize. Stauffenberg and his fellow martyrs were buried that night in a nearby churchyard. They had failed, but their bravery in the face of such a slim chance of success had been truly heroic.

If Stauffenberg and his conspirators had succeeded with *Operation Valkyrie*, the war in Europe might have ended much earlier. As it was, it continued for almost another year. In those final months of the Second World War, more people were killed than in the previous five years of fighting.

Hitler described the conspiracy as "a crime unparalleled in German history" and reacted accordingly. Although Stauffenberg, von Haeften, Olbricht and Mertz were dead and buried, Hitler demanded that their bodies be dug up, burned, and the ashes scattered to the wind.

Following brutal interrogation, the main surviving conspirators were hauled before the Nazi courts. They refused to be intimidated, knowing the regime they loathed was teetering on the brink of defeat. General Erich Fellgiebel, who had stood with Stauffenberg as the bomb exploded at Rastenburg, was told by the court president that he was to be hanged. "Hurry with the hanging, Mr. President," he replied, "otherwise you will hang earlier than we."

Gestapo and SS officers investigated the plot until the last days of the war. Seven thousand arrests were made, and between two and three thousand people were executed. Among them was General Fromm. Although he had never joined the conspirators, he was shot for cowardice in failing to prevent them from carrying out their revolt.

Stauffenberg's personal magnetism continued to exert an extraordinary influence, even from beyond the grave. SS investigator Georg Kiesel was so in awe of him, he reported to Hitler that his assassin was, "a spirit of fire, fascinating and inspiring all who came in touch with him."

THE LOST HERO

1944-1945

HATRED AND PERSECUTION of the Jews in Germany, and the territories the Nazis conquered, was common knowledge during the war. But what was not known almost until the war ended was that random murder had turned into full scale genocide. Then, in 1944, two Jews named Rudolf Vrba and Alfred Wetzler escaped from Auschwitz – a massive concentration and extermination camp in Poland. They compiled a report giving clear details of the gas chambers – the final destination of Jews swept up in the mass deportations that followed the Wannsee Conference. Their report added to mounting evidence confirming the unthinkable – the Nazis were setting out to murder every single Jew in Europe.

When British prime minister Winston Churchill read the report in July 1944 he wrote, "This is the greatest, most horrible crime ever committed in the whole history of the world." American president Franklin Roosevelt had already established the US War Refugee Board with the intention of funding any neutral states prepared to offer help to the Jews. Now he issued a proclamation to all of the Axis powers, warning them that they would be held personally responsible if they supported the Nazis in their persecution of the Jews. But really there was little practical that the Allies could do to stop the rail deportations and mass killings. They were, after all, being carried out far behind the front lines. A resentful debate still continues to this day regarding measures the Allies could have taken to hinder the Nazi's *Final Solution*.

While Vrba and Wetzler's Auschwitz report was circulating in government departments in Washington and London, the Nazis began to round up the 850,000 Jews in Hungary. Until early 1944, they had been protected by the Hungarian government. The leader of Hungary, Admiral Miklós Horthy, was a supporter and ally of Hitler's, but he had no sympathy for the Nazis' anti-Semitism, and even spoke out against what he called the, "inhuman, cruel persecution of the Jews." But, in March 1944, Hitler became suspicious that the Hungarians might make a separate peace with the Allies, and sent German troops to occupy the country. The Nazis allowed Horthy to stay as leader, to give the impression that the Hungarians were still in charge of their own destiny. Even so, Hungarian Jews immediately became the target for violent, often fatal, attacks. Adolf Eichmann and SS troops arrived, to organize the deportation of the Jewish population.

Between May and July, Eichmann worked with great efficiency. Some 437,000 Jews were rounded up, packed into freight trains, and sent to Auschwitz (see the map on page 291). Of this number at least 365,000 were killed. By midsummer the lives of the remaining Jews left in Hungary were hanging by a thread. Not only were the German troops after them, but Hungary had its own brand of anti-Semitic fascists too, known as the *Arrow Cross*. This militaristic organization was a strange brew of fanatical Catholics and pro-Nazi supporters, and they attacked Hungarian Jews with as much zeal as the Nazis.

Word of these deportations soon reached the Allies. The United States appealed to neutral nations with legations (diplomatic offices) or embassies in Budapest, the Hungarian capital. They could help by granting some kind of protective status to Hungary's Jews. The Swedish legation issued "protective passes" – which declared that the holder should be treated as if he or she were a Swedish citizen. Swedish diplomats stationed in the United States offered more direct help. They recommended a 32-year-old businessman named Raoul Wallenberg to act as a special emissary to help the Jews of Hungary.

Wallenberg came from a long line of bankers, diplomats, politicians and military men, in one of the most famous families in Sweden. He was born in August 1912, three months after his navy father died of cancer. He was a curious character – a sensitive, gentle soul who was also quite fearless. As a child he hated fox hunting and once let all the dogs on the family estate escape on the night before a hunt. His family had intended him to become a banker, but Wallenberg was more interested in architecture and trade. He trained as an architect at Michigan University in the United States. His girlfriend there worked with physically handicapped children, and he would often help look after her pupils.

In the 1930s, Wallenberg worked for a while in Haifa, in Palestine, where he met Jewish refugees fleeing from the Nazis. Returning to Sweden, he set up a successful food import and export business, the Mid European Trading Company, with a Jewish Hungarian partner named Koloman Lauer. When the Second World War broke out, Sweden remained neutral. This meant Wallenberg was able to travel around Germany, her allies and conquered territory as he wished, cutting business deals with Nazi officials and their collaborators. His work often took him to Budapest.

Wallenberg was more than happy to help, and set off for Hungary at once by train. He reached the capital on July 9, 1944, arriving with $100,000 donated by American Jewish charities to fund his activities. Although he knew what the Germans intended to do to the Jews, he also understood the bizarre mentality of most Nazi officials. The men who ruled Germany and its conquered territories had such warped priorities that destroying the Jews was often more important to them than delaying or defeating the approaching Soviet army. But, at the same time, these same men were usually so corrupt that they were also quite open to whatever bribes Wallenberg could put their way. It was a strange combination, but it created a small corridor of opportunity in which Wallenberg could operate.

Because he had made plenty of business trips to occupied Europe, he also understood how to handle the low-ranking officials. He knew that ordinary soldiers and policemen had a deep fear and exaggerated respect for authority. Wallenberg had an inherent advantage. He was tall and well-spoken, and in several languages too, including German, Russian and English. As a wealthy aristocrat from a prominent Swedish family, he had a natural air of authority, which he could use to his benefit. Here in Budapest, he was the perfect example of a man and his circumstances matching perfectly. His sensitivity, his plain decency, his keen knowledge of human character and quick-thinking intelligence all allowed him to survive in what would soon become a treacherous madhouse.

With the help of other Swedish diplomats, Wallenberg immediately set about manufacturing a fictitious Swedish citizenship, a protective pass, known as a *Schutzpass*. The Swedes in Budapest had already made similar passes, but Wallenberg's design was a major improvement. Knowing how much both the Nazis and the Hungarians admired impressive-looking documents, Wallenberg cooked up a formidable-looking pass in blue and yellow. It had coats of arms, official stamps, signatures, and the three crown symbol of Sweden. He was given permission to manufacture 5,000 of these passes but actually made 15,000 of them. Other meaningless identification documents were also created, to wave at guards and policemen to convince them that the bearer should be left alone. Such passes declared that the holder was emigrating to Sweden, and was a Swedish citizen, and that the protection

Raoul Wallenberg (seated) at work in Budapest in November 1944, photographed with some of the Hungarian Jews he is trying to save.

offered by the pass should also be extended to the holder's family.

Shortly after Wallenberg arrived in Hungary, he came across Adolf Eichmann. They arranged to meet in a nightclub in Budapest in early August. Here Wallenberg offered to buy a substantial amount of Nazi-owned property in the capital. Eichmann knew that he wanted these buildings to provide sanctuary for Jews, and so he brushed aside his offer. He was unimpressed with Wallenberg, dismissing him as, "a soft… and decadent diplomat."

At the time, Eichmann was meeting resistance to his deportations from several quarters. Although Horthy no longer had the power he had wielded before German troops took over his country, he was still making some efforts to protect Hungarian Jews. Various factions within the Nazi party were also squabbling about how and when to carry out the deportations, which delayed their implementation as well. As a result, the deportations were put on hold, and Eichmann returned to Germany.

By early autumn, Wallenberg's efforts to protect

Hungarian Jews had been so successful he was contemplating returning home. But events took a turn for the worse. Admiral Horthy had become convinced that Hungary should withdraw from the war. So, on October 15, a pre-recorded speech by him was broadcast on Hungarian national radio, announcing the end of the war as far as Hungary was concerned. The speech was greeted with delight, and people danced in the streets. But Horthy had underestimated the ruthless determination of his Nazi allies. Minutes after the broadcast had finished, another announcement was made, claiming Hungary was still at war. Suddenly, the airwaves were filled with the sound of Nazi marching songs. This almost instant change of heart was brought in part because SS troops had kidnapped Horthy's son. They threatened to execute him unless the Admiral changed his mind. Horthy stepped down as leader, and went into exile in Bavaria. His son was sent to a concentration camp. The fascist Arrow Cross party took control of the country, under the leadership of Ferenc Szálasi.

Szálasi's government immediately announced they would no longer recognize the Swedish *Schutzpasses*. But Wallenberg had a trick up his sleeve. He was friendly with a young

Austrian aristocrat named Liesel Kemény, who had recently married the new Hungarian foreign minister. Wallenberg told Kemény that the Jews were being deported to be exterminated. If her new husband allowed this to happen he would be hanged after the war as part of a government that had permitted such an atrocity to take place. Madame Kemény talked her husband into persuading the new government to recognize the *Schutzpass* after all.

But, with Horthy gone, armed thugs of the Arrow Cross were unleashed to murder Jews on the streets. Eichmann and his SS troops returned. Jewish community leaders were summoned to a meeting with him. "You see I am back again," Eichmann hissed at them, like some pantomime villain. "You forget Hungary is still in the shadow of the Reich. My arms are long and I can reach the Jews of Budapest as well." The deportations began again. At this stage of the war, the massive resources that had been available to the Nazis in the initial stages of the Final Solution were no longer theirs to command. The Russians were fast approaching from the east, cutting rail links. Fuel, locomotives and freight wagons were scarce. But Eichmann's determination was undimmed. When trains could not be found to transport the Jews, they were marched out of Budapest instead.

With the Arrow Cross to help him, Eichmann worked fast. In a few dark autumn days, 80,000 Jews were rounded up in Budapest and marched out of the capital to Austria. Jews deported from Budapest usually went straight to Auschwitz, but this group was earmarked to be worked to death in armament factories. If anyone faltered on the march, they were shot where they dropped, and many others simply froze to death during overnight stops, or died from plain exhaustion. But, whenever columns of Jews were marched off, Wallenberg soon followed after them with food and medical supplies. He would hand out protective passes, and always managed to bring back a few hundred people from the thousands who left.

His bravery on these occasions was extraordinary. He would rush into a crowd of frightened Jews assembled for deportation, right under the bayonets and rifles of jittery, ill-tempered guards. Then he would shout, "Who here has Swedish papers?" while handing them out to those around him. Sometimes, Wallenberg arrived when a train packed with

Jews was due to depart for Auschwitz. He would stand in front of the locomotive to prevent it from leaving, then clamber down the roof of the freight carriages, handing out his Schutzpasses to any hands that appeared through the narrow slats at the sides. Sometimes he would just stuff bundles of passes into the trains. Occasionally, he would be roughly manhandled by the guards, or have warning shots fired above his head. Wallenberg had no official right to behave as he did. But he always acted as if he had complete authority, and was a man whose orders should not be disobeyed.

It was in early November that Wallenberg met Eichmann again face to face, this time at *Gestapo* headquarters in Budapest. Eichmann greeted his mild-mannered opponent with open hostility and plain threats, but was taken aback when Wallenberg presented him with a gift of Scotch whiskey and cigarettes. Unlike many Nazi chiefs, Eichmann was not someone who could be bribed. But the shrewd Wallenberg had correctly guessed that the vanity of a man from his humble background would be tickled by a gift from a Swedish aristocrat. The two men shared a drink and Eichmann became quite friendly, even offering to let a small trainload of Jews leave for Sweden, in exchange for a ransom. But Wallenberg knew he couldn't be trusted, and Eichmann's feelings toward him rapidly turned murderous. A few days after the meeting, a German military vehicle attempted to ram Wallenberg's car. It failed. But, thereafter, Wallenberg made a point of regularly changing the house where he slept.

Using money provided by the US War Refugee Board, an "international ghetto" was set up. Rows of houses were bought, 72 in all, and over 15,000 Jews sheltered in them. Sometimes Jewish men who looked particularly "Aryan" (see page 285) dressed in stolen SS uniforms to stand guard outside the houses. Following Wallenberg's example, diplomats from Spain, Portugal and Switzerland also provided safe havens and passes too, renting buildings that would become hiding places for Jews.

Throughout November, as the cold central European winter settled on the capital, the deportations and killings continued. With Russian troops fast approaching, an air of anarchy overtook Budapest, and any semblance of law and order evaporated. Nazi troops and Arrow Cross thugs knew their days were numbered. In their twisted ideology, the Jews were considered the source of all their troubles, and in their final days of power they worked all hours to kill as many as could be found. Houses that were supposedly safe Swedish legation territory were broken into at random, and those sheltering inside were slaughtered.

During this time Eichmann declared: "I know the war is lost, but I am still going to win my war." Despite the obvious attempts Eichmann had made on his life, Wallenberg still thought it was worth inviting him to dinner in a final bid to dissuade him from continuing. So, in mid-December, Wallenberg and Eichmann had their last encounter. A meeting was duly arranged and they, and other dinner guests, met in an imposing hilltop mansion overlooking Budapest.

It was a strangely theatrical evening. Fine food and wines were served on elegant china dishes, and a surprisingly cordial atmosphere was established. After the meal the guest retired to the sitting room for coffee and brandy. The room had a fantastic view over the city. In a well-documented scene that could have come from a Hollywood movie, Wallenberg pulled back the curtains, revealing a horizon lit up with flashes of artillery and rockets from the approaching Soviet army.

"Look how close the Soviets are," Wallenberg said to Eichmann. "Your war is almost over. The Nazis are doomed, finished, and so are those who cling to this hatred until the very last. It's the end of the Nazis, the end of Hitler, the end of Eichmann."

Here, in a moment of cold-blooded frankness that would have shamed the Devil, Eichmann replied, "I agree with you. I've never agreed with all of Hitler's ideology, but it has, after all, given me a good career… Soon, this comfortable life will end. No more planes bringing women and wine from France. The Russians will take my horses, my dogs, and my palace… They'd probably shoot me on the spot. For me there's no escape, no liberation. There are, however, some consolations. If I continue to eliminate our enemies to the end, it may delay our defeat… and then, when I finally walk to the gallows, at least I'll know I've completed my mission."

The Germans left soon after. Eichmann thanked Wallenberg for, "an exceptionally charming and interesting evening." Then he sneered, "Now don't think we're friends.

We're not. I plan to do everything I can to keep you from saving your Jews. Your diplomatic passport won't protect you from everything. Even a neutral diplomat can meet with an accident."

By Christmas Eve, Russian troops were at the gates of Budapest. Eichmann fled, but his final order was for the remaining 70,000 Jews of Budapest to be rounded up and executed. So August Schmidthuber, the German general charged with the task of defending the capital, mustered 500 of his men and armed them with heavy machine guns. But Wallenberg was alerted to the forthcoming massacre. He sent word to Schmidthuber that he would hold him personally responsible and see to it that he was hanged as a war criminal when the war ended. The massacre was called off just minutes before it was due to begin. Wallenberg had won probably his greatest victory.

Two days later, on January 13, Soviet troops began to arrive in the outskirts of Budapest. Wallenberg was ecstatic, and convinced his troubles were over. For months he had risked his life and, against extraordinary odds, he had survived. But only when he came up against a supposed friendly army did his luck desert him. His naiveté, which had allowed him to act with such bravery, betrayed him.

Wallenberg had great plans for post-war Budapest, and he outlined to Soviet officers an idea he had to help the Jews after the war. He was invited to discuss matters further behind the Russian lines, and drove away from the capital with a Red Army escort. His friends in Budapest and Sweden never saw him again.

What happened next has been the source of much speculation. Even today, nearly 60 years later, the precise truth is still uncertain. The most likely explanation was that the Russians thought Wallenberg was an American spy. He was arrested and held in a cell – probably in the infamous Lubyanka prison in Moscow, home of the much-feared Soviet secret police.

His best chance of a return home seems to have come in 1946, when the outgoing Swedish ambassador in Moscow was summoned for a final meeting with Soviet dictator Joseph Stalin. Stalin asked him if he had any special requests. In reply the ambassador asked that if Raoul Wallenberg was in Soviet hands, perhaps they could see to it that he was released. But then, tragically, the ambassador admitted to Stalin that he thought Wallenberg was dead. He may as well have signed Wallenberg's death sentence. Stalin was no less ruthless than Hitler. If the Swedes thought Wallenberg was dead, it would be far simpler just to kill him than to admit he had been wrongly imprisoned. Today, the most reliable records available indicate that Wallenberg was executed in his Moscow cell on July 17, 1947.

While Wallenberg had devoted his life to thwarting the evil work of a dying regime, another set of circumstances conspired against him. History would show him to be one of the first victims of the Cold War – the sullen peace between the Soviets and the Western Allies that followed the defeat of Nazi Germany. The war produced more than its fair share of senseless moments, but for a man who had saved anything up to 100,000 lives through sheer bare-knuckle courage, it was a desperately unjust fate.

"...LIKE RUNNING THROUGH RAIN AND NOT GETTING WET."

1945

THE PHOTOGRAPH THAT greeted American newspaper readers on the Sunday morning of February 25, 1945, would become one of the most famous images of the Second World War. It shows a cluster of six US Marines, their uniforms stained and dusty from three days of continual combat, raising a fluttering Stars and Stripes on a long iron pole. The shot catches them in such a classic pose – pole at 45°, their bodies straining with the heavy weight and biting wind, one man crouching at the base, others reaching up as the pole is raised beyond their grasp – the image seemed to echo heroic marble figures in a Roman statue. But photographer Joe Rosenthal, who took the picture, did not even look in his viewfinder when he captured this particular moment of history. It was a lucky fluke.

A reader who scrutinized the shot would get the impression that the men were atop some barren hill, for a pale horizon could be dimly seen below them. The hill was Mount Suribachi on the Japanese island of Iwo Jima, 1,045km (650 miles) south of Tokyo. It was the first piece of Japanese territory to be invaded in 4,000 years.

The story that accompanied the photo told how the men in the shot had struggled up Iwo Jima's Mount Suribachi in the teeth of fierce fire from fanatical Japanese defenders, who rolled grenades down the mountain to explode among them with devastating effect. Then, overcoming ferocious opposition, the Marines raised their flag in a hail of deadly sniper fire. But it was all a work of fiction. To start with, the Stars and Stripes had been raised earlier that day, and the flag

"...LIKE RUNNING THROUGH RAIN AND NOT GETTING WET."

Joe Rosenthal's photo of US Marines at Iwo Jima became one of the most famous images of the war. Three of the six men pictured here would die before the island was conquered.

in the famous shot was a replacement. It was bigger than the original, which had been quickly removed as a regimental souvenir. The men who planted the flag had walked up the hill unopposed. Why journalists felt the need to manufacture such a story is a mystery, for the actual events at Iwo Jima were far more heroic and harrowing than any overblown propaganda report.

Pacific islands conjure comforting images of white sand, blue sea and sunshine. Not Iwo Jima. It is a bleak volcanic slab of black ash and scrubby vegetation, shaped like an overloaded ice cream cone, and frequently lashed with driving rain. The name means "sulphur island"*. That evil-smelling chemical similar to rotten eggs, emanates from the dormant volcano that makes up the glowering hillside at its southern tip. The island is so small 20 square km (8 square miles) – that it only takes five or six minutes to drive across it.

During the war, many Pacific islands inhabited by Japanese soldiers were simply cut off from supplies by the allies, and left to starve or surrender. But Iwo Jima was a

* "Sulphur" is spelled "sulfur" in the United States.

notable exception. Its importance lay in two Japanese air force bases inland from its stone and ash beaches. From here fighter planes scythed into the huge, silver US *B-29* bombers that passed daily back and forth to pound the factories and cities of mainland Japan. Iwo Jima, in American hands, would provide these bombers with a base closer to Japan, especially one for emergency landings on their return journey.

The battle at Iwo Jima was one of the fiercest, and certainly the most famous, of the war in the Pacific. On one side were the soldiers of Imperial Japan. Since the 1930s, they had been fighting to build a Japanese empire in the Pacific – conquering territories that were once part of the empires of fading European powers. These soldiers fought with suicidal bravery and infamous cruelty. They had only contempt for enemy soldiers who surrendered when defeat seemed inevitable. Even when facing certain capture, most would kill themselves rather than fall into enemy hands.

On the other side was the United States. Like their Japanese counterparts, American soldiers fought with unquestionable bravery, but it was not part of their culture to sacrifice themselves needlessly if defeat was inevitable.

America had been at war with Japan since 1941, when the Japanese naval air service had launched a ferocious surprise attack on the American fleet at its Hawaiian base in Pearl Harbor. The architect of this attack, Admiral Yamamoto Isoroku, was never convinced of its wisdom. "I fear we have only succeeded in awakening a sleeping tiger," he said in response to congratulations following its success. Yamamoto was right. The United States was the richest, most powerful nation on Earth. Once war broke out, President Roosevelt devoted the entire resources of his country to winning it. The invasion fleet sent to attack Iwo Jima was an extraordinary 110km (70 miles) long. Aboard its 800 warships were over 300,000 men, a third of whom were intended to fight on the island itself.

The Japanese knew the strength of their enemy all too well. Many senior soldiers and diplomats had visited or lived in America before the war. The commander of Iwo Jima, Lieutenant General Tadamichi Kuribayashi, was one of them. His strategy in defending his tiny island was grimly effective. His orders to his 21,000 soldiers were brutally frank. They were outnumbered and outgunned, with no hope of rescue.

The island was sure to fall – eventually. But they had a sacred duty to defend this Japanese territory to the death. Every man was instructed to kill at least ten Americans before he died. Kuribayashi, and his masters in Japan knew that American troops were heading inexorably toward the mainland, intent on conquering their country. They hoped that American losses on Iwo Jima would

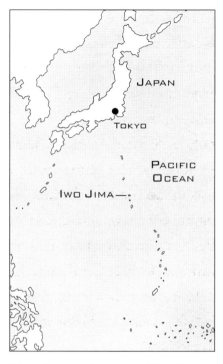

Map showing location of Iwo Jima

be so appalling that the American public would force President Roosevelt to come to a compromise peace with Japan, so preventing an invasion, and the resulting national humiliation.

So, in the months before the invasion, Iwo Jima was turned into a formidable fortress. Pillboxes and concrete gun emplacements littered the island. Every cave held a unit of soldiers, and linking them all up was an intricate network of tunnels. There were even underground hospitals large enough to treat 400 wounded men. Japanese soldiers were not on Iwo Jima; they were in it. "No other given area in the history of modern war has been so skillfully fortified by nature and by man," stated one post-war report.

The soldiers sent to seize this tiny island were from the 3rd, 4th, 5th and 21st divisions of the US Marines, under the overall command of Lt. General Holland M. "Howling Mad" Smith. The Marines Corps prided themselves on their skill at seaborne assaults, and their fierce fighting spirit and intense loyalty. But the majority of those sent to Iwo Jima had never been in combat before. Most, in fact, were boys of 18 or 19. They were fated to be thrown into the most savage of battles at an age when many other young men would be grappling with their final year in high school, first year at college, first job, first love… most had not even left home. Some were even younger – boys of 16 and 17 who had lied about their age when they were recruited. It was little wonder that when such boys died at the point of a Japanese bayonet, or blown in half by shell or mortar, their veneer of manly toughness seared away, their last words were often a frantic, desperate cry to their mothers.

The attack began on the morning of February 19. A pink winter sunrise and pale blue sky greeted the thousands of Marines aboard the invasion fleet. They had spent a sleepless night in preparation for the assault, and their day began at 3:00am, when they were all heartily fed with steak and eggs for breakfast. Then, around 7:00am, they filed off their vast, troop carrying boats, down metal steps to fill the holds of the smaller landing craft that would take them to the island. Here, one boy who had never been in combat, recalled some sardonic advice he received from an older soldier. "You don't know what's going to happen. You're going to learn more in the first five minutes there than you did in the whole year of training you've been through."

The naval shelling of the island stopped at 8:57am. Five minutes later, clumsy amphibious tanks emerged from landing craft onto the soft beaches which ran for 3km (two miles) down the south side of the island. They trundled directly underneath the baleful gaze of Mount Suribachi. Such was the operational efficiency of the US navy, the invasion was only an extraordinary 120 seconds behind the carefully planned schedule that had begun when the fleet left Hawaii.

The fear that clutched the hearts of troops approaching an enemy shoreline was intense. Each man knew that when the heavy steel door at the front of his landing craft was lowered into the frothing sea at the edge of the beach, he could be exposed to lacerating machine gun fire. That is, if he hadn't already been blown to pieces by a shell before his boat even reached the shore.

Yet when the doors of the first wave of landing craft went down at Iwo Jima, the Marines were greeted only by the corrosive smell of sulphur. Although shells from their ships and planes were whistling over their heads and on to the island, the Japanese themselves were eerily silent. At first many soldiers assumed the relentless 74-day bombardment of the island by US bombers, navy battleships and carrier aircraft, had wiped out the island's defenders. But Kuribayashi had ordered his men to hold their fire while the beach filled up with American troops, tanks and supplies.

"...LIKE RUNNING THROUGH RAIN AND NOT GETTING WET."

When the Japanese bombardment began an hour after the US invasion, it was catastrophic.

Amid the chaos of disembarking tanks, and bulldozers whose caterpillar tracks churned up the soft sand, hordes of wet, bewildered men milled around the beach. Then these men became aware of another more terrible distraction. All at once a lethal rain of shells, bullets and mortar fire fell upon them. One officer recalled that Mount Suribachi suddenly lit up like a Christmas tree – only, instead of lights and tinsel, the flashes he could see were gun and shellfire. The whole mountainside had been turned into a fortress, seven stories of fire platforms and gun emplacements, all hollowed out of its interior.

There was nowhere to hide. Marines hugged the soft sand as bullets flew over them so low they ripped the clothes and supplies in their backpacks to shreds. The carnage was hideous. Men were torn apart by shells, their bodies spread over the beach, causing even hardened veterans to vomit in horror. Others, caught directly by high explosive shells, were simply vaporized, and left no trace of human remains.

One Marine novice, having no real idea how this compared with other battles, yelled over to his commander.

"Hey, Sergeant… is this a bad battle?" The sergeant shouted back, "It's a ******* slaughter." A minute later the sergeant was blown to pieces by a mortar. Press photographer Joe Rosenthal was on the beach that day. "…not getting hit was like running through rain and not getting wet," he remembered. Another Marine, Lloyd Keeland, recalled: "I think your life expectancy was about 20 seconds…"

In that first hour of shelling the success of the invasion hung in the balance. But although it took a terrible toll, there were too many Marines already there, and too many still coming ashore, to wipe them off the island.

There were several things about the fighting on Iwo Jima that made it especially horrific. Such was the intensity of the Japanese bombardment that it didn't matter whether a soldier crouched in a foxhole or charged through open land. He would be killed either way. Another was that the enemy was completely invisible. Often, American soldiers only saw their Japanese adversaries when they were dead. For the rest of the time, Marines were fired upon by an unseen foe who could all too clearly see them.

"...LIKE RUNNING THROUGH RAIN
AND NOT GETTING WET."

Once off the beach, Marines headed into thin scrub and grasses, and terrain peppered with blockhouses, pillboxes, caves and rocks – almost all of which held or sheltered Japanese soldiers. Every one had to be attacked, and every one caused some casualties, before a hail of machine gun bullets, or a grenade or flame-thrower put an end to its defenders. But, more often than not, it didn't. The tunnel system that linked the Japanese strongpoints meant that a "neutralized" blockhouse could quickly become a lethal one again, with Japanese soldiers who had crawled through the tunnels, shooting at the backs of unsuspecting Marines.

Yet, despite the slaughter, the Marines were winning. The dreadful opening bombardment had not driven them off the beach, and by noon 9,000 men had come ashore. Even by mid-morning, one company from the 28th Marine Regiment had managed to cross the 650m (700 yards) that separated the furthest southern landing beach from the island's western shore. Their casualties were daunting – of the 250 men in the company, only 37 were still standing.

As night fell, the fighting subsided. 30,000 men had managed to come ashore. But as exhausted Marines lay huddled in shallow holes and trenches, they were assailed by Japanese soldiers, who sneaked out one by one to claim an unwary life before melting away into the darkness.

The next dawn brought fierce winds and high seas – making further landings difficult. As other Marine forces began cautiously to infiltrate the northern interior of the island, the great plan for the day was to attack Suribachi itself. The task was given to Colonel Harry "the Horse" Liversedge, and the 3,000 Marines of his 28th Regiment. All that day, they edged up to the base of the mountain.

The weather on the third morning on the island brought no respite. It was a grim day to die. As the 28th Marine Regiment prepared for its assault on Suribachi, a Marine artillery barrage from behind their lines opened up for an hour. Then US carrier planes swooped in to plaster the mountain with rockets. But the designated hour of the attack, 8:00am, came and went without the order being given to advance. Colonel Liversedge had been promised tanks to protect his men as they ran through open ground toward the tangle of vegetation that covered the base of Suribachi.

Without tanks, his losses would be far worse than he was already expecting. But the tanks had not arrived. (They were short of fuel and shells, he found out later.) So, Liversedge decided, the attack would have to go on anyway.

When the order was passed around the regiment that they were to charge forward without tanks, raw dread swept through the men. One soldier, Lieutenant Keith Wells, was reminded of the atmosphere in his father's slaughterhouse, when cattle realize they are about to be killed. Showing uncommon courage, Wells led by example. Despite a fear so deep he could feel it as a physical weight bearing down on him, he broke cover and began to run toward the mountain slope. He expected to be cut down in seconds. But, as he ran on, he could see hundreds of other Marines following on behind him, given courage by his bravery. Suribachi erupted into a dazzling flash of fire, and shells and bullets scythed down the charging Marines. But the men had been trained to advance at all costs, and gradually they reached the base of the mountain. Among those wounded was Lieutenant Wells, his legs peppered with shrapnel. His wounds were sufficiently bad to merit pain-killing morphine from a medic who treated him, but Wells still refused to leave his men. He directed them to destroy the blockhouses and machine-gun nests that lay at the foot of Suribachi, until loss of blood made him delirious. Gradually, men with flame-throwers were able to get close enough to do their hideous work. When the tanks eventually appeared to back up the assault, the Japanese front line on the mountain began to crumble at last.

Throughout the day, the companies and platoons of the regiment inched further up the mountain – by nightfall some had even penetrated behind Japanese lines. They lay low amid the parachute flares, and searchlights from offshore ships that combed the mountain with penetrating brilliance, fearing that every moving shadow was an approaching Japanese soldier.

On the fourth day, the Marines continued to creep forward, sometimes hearing their enemy in tunnels and command posts beneath them, but more often than not only locating a Japanese strong point when a hail of fire was unleashed on them. By now the Marines had strong tank and artillery support, and the Japanese inside Suribachi were blown and burned to oblivion. In the fading light, Japanese soldiers, increasingly aware that they were now cut off from any possible retreat, staged a breakout. One hundred and fifty suddenly broke cover, in a desperate dash down the mountain, only to be slaughtered by Marines who were getting their first sight of the soldiers who had visited such torment on them. Only 25 made it back to the Japanese lines.

At the dawn of day five, Liversedge sensed a major morale-raising coup was in his grasp. Although he suspected that many Japanese soldiers probably remained inside Suribachi, their strength as a fighting force was gone, and it might now be possible to capture the mountain outright. If he was wrong, it could prove to be a very costly gamble.

The day's fighting began with another air attack: carrier planes smothered the top of the mountain in napalm. After that, Suribachi seemed oddly quiet. Had all the remaining Japanese fled? There was only one way to find out. A four-man patrol was sent up the mountain's 168m (550ft) summit, each man fearing his life expectancy was measured in seconds, and that death was a footstep away. But the enemy never did open fire, and the commanding officer at the base of the mountain, Colonel Chandler Johnson, decided to risk a 40-man platoon. Lieutenant Schrier, the officer given the task of leading these men, was summoned before Colonel Johnson. He gave him a small American flag. "If you get to the top," said Johnson tactlessly, "put it up."

As Schrier's platoon snaked higher up the mountain, they caught the eye of every man on the beach and island close enough to see them. Then word got around. Even those offshore, in the vast armada that surrounded the island, trained their binoculars and telescopes on the thin line of men. At any second, both the platoon and their thousands of spectators expected the remaining Japanese on Suribachi to open up and cut them to ribbons.

The platoon advanced gingerly, and with great caution. At every cave they came to, they tossed in a grenade, in case it contained enemy troops. But, after forty tense minutes, they stood breathless at the top, not quite believing they were still alive. At 10:20am they raised the Stars and Stripes on the summit, using a piece of drainage pipe as a flagpole. When the flag went up, a huge cheer rose from the throats of the thousands of Marines who had been watching below. Offshore, warships sounded their horns, and men onboard hollered in triumph. "Our spirits were very low at that point," recalled one soldier, Hershel "Woody" Williams, "because we had lost so many men and made so little gain. The whole spirit changed." Although the fighting was far from over, seeing the American flag flying over Iwo Jima's highest point convinced every Marine that they were there to stay.

Around the flag, Marines stood uneasily, posing for army photographer Louis Lowery. With the flag fluttering in a strong breeze, and their silhouettes standing out on the top of the mountain, they would soon be the target for every enemy sniper and artilleryman within range. One of the soldiers present recalled, "It was like sitting in the middle of a bull's-eye."

Sure enough, the cacophony touched off by the raising of the flag had alerted the Japanese. The ragged soldiers left on the mountain began to emerge from hiding places. They tossed grenades or loosed off a few rounds toward the Marines, who dived for cover and began to fight back. But, amazingly, no one was hurt, and soon the mountain settled down again to a sullen silence.

There were indeed still several hundred Japanese troops left on Suribachi, but they had lost the will to carry on.

"...LIKE RUNNING THROUGH RAIN
AND NOT GETTING WET."

Strange as it seemed to the American Marines, most chose to kill themselves rather than fight to the death or surrender.

Watching the flag-raising from the beach below was "Howling Mad" Smith, and none other than the US Secretary of the Navy, James Forrestal, a man so important that he would later have a large aircraft carrier named after him. (The *USS Forrestal* saw service in both Vietnam and the first Gulf War.) Forrestal instantly understood the significance of that moment for the reputation of the Marines. He turned to Smith and said: "The raising of that flag on Suribachi means a Marine Corps for the next 500 years."

Forrestal decided he had to have the flag as a souvenir, but when his request reached Chandler Johnson, the colonel spat, "To hell with that!" He was determined to keep it for the Marines. With an undignified race on to be first to grab the flag, Johnson craftily decided that a much bigger replacement flag was called for. One was quickly located from a large landing craft just off the beach. Significantly, this flag had itself been rescued from one of the ships sunk at Pearl Harbor.

"...LIKE RUNNING THROUGH RAIN AND NOT GETTING WET."

So it was that Captain Dave Severance, and six men from Easy Company's second platoon walked into history. Like Lieutenant Schrier's men before them, they worked their way up the hill with great caution, reaching the summit around noon. A large iron pipe was found to serve as a flagpole, and stones were piled up to hold the heavy pole in place. Near the summit was Associated Press photographer Joe Rosenthal. On an impulse, he went over to record the scene. He was still preparing his equipment when the flag was raised by six Marines. Rosenthal instinctively pointed his camera and clicked the shutter without even checking the shot in his viewfinder. Thus, in one four-hundreth of a second, the most famous American photograph of the war was taken. At the time, no one could possibly have grasped the significance of this particular moment. No one cheered. After all, it was just a replacement flag. The men of Easy Company returned to the fighting, their task complete. Of the six who raised the flag, three would subsequently die in the continuing battle to capture the island.

Rosenthal sent his roll of film off on a flight to Guam, a thousand miles to the south. Here it was developed and printed up, passed through army censors, and finally reached the desk of John Bodkin, the local Associated Press picture editor. It was his job to decide which shots were worth transmitting back to the bureau in America. Bodkin knew immediately he had a shot in a million. "Here's one for all time!" he told his staff. Sure enough, within two days of the shot being taken, it was on the front page of almost every American paper. Its arrival on picture desks was timely. At that moment, Iwo Jima was currently the most written about hot spot of the entire war, and public interest was massive. Rosenthal's shot became an icon, and prints were sold in their millions, to be framed and placed on workplace or living room walls, next to shots of sons and fathers in uniform. The image even appeared on 137 million postage stamps. After the war, a huge statue based on the photograph became the US Marine Corps memorial in Washington.

Perhaps the same worldwide fame would have greeted Louis Lowery's shot of the first, actual, raising of the flag, had it reached newspaper picture desks first. But it didn't. Army shots always took a much slower route back home than those of commercial news organizations.

"...LIKE RUNNING THROUGH RAIN
AND NOT GETTING WET."

Kuribayashi and his high commanders had been correct in assuming the American public would be shocked by Marine casualties. They were. Within two days there had been more casualties than in the entire five-month campaign at Guadalcanal, in the South Pacific, earlier in the war. It was unquestionably the American military's costliest operation so far. But the picture of the flag being raised less than a week into the campaign seemed to offer a major vindication. It said, quite incontrovertibly, that whatever their losses, the Marines at least were winning.

But that was only part of the story. Suribachi may have been the most strategically useful spot on the island, but its conquest was mainly symbolic. Another month of slow, agonizing, fighting dragged on before the Japanese were wiped out. Of the 21,000 men under Kuribayashi's command, only 216 were taken prisoner. The last two of these surrendered in 1949, when they found a scrap of newspaper reporting on the American occupation of Japan. They had kept themselves hidden in the maze of defensive tunnels inside the mountain for almost four years, pilfering food from US army supplies to keep from starving.

The American casualties were also horrific. Few of the Marines who landed on the first day escaped unscathed. Altogether nearly 6,000 were killed, and over 17,000 were wounded. Kuribayashi's men had sold their lives with at least one or two American casualties. Survival seemed a matter of pure luck. Lloyd Keeland, caught up in the initial bombardment on the first day of the landing, fought for 36 days, although he was injured several times. He survived a night-time sword attack, waking up to hear a Japanese soldier attacking the man next to him. On another occasion, he stood talking to a soldier who was shot in mid-conversation. After the battle, on a troop ship home, Keeland was haunted by nightmares of combat, one time waking to find he was strangling the man in the next bunk.

But the battle had served its purpose. Japanese fighter planes no longer harassed the American bombers that passed over the island. In the final months of the war some 2,400 damaged *B-29s*, which would otherwise have crashed into the sea, were able to land at Iwo Jima. The 27,000 US airmen on board these huge bombers were saved from a near certain death.

THE DESTROYER OF WORLDS

1939-1945

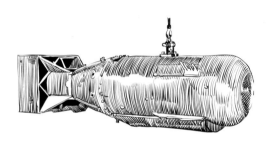

IMAGINE THE SCENE. Marooned in a research laboratory bunker hidden away in the desert, a group of scientists are concocting a strange experiment involving a bomb and the splitting of atoms. They are tampering with the very fabric of the universe itself, in an ultra-secret operation known as the *Manhattan Project*. It is the middle of the night, and thunderous rain and howling winds lash the landscape.

The soldiers sent to guard the scientists are in a state of high agitation. Some have overheard that the explosive device they are about to detonate is so powerful it could actually set the atmosphere on fire, incinerating all life on Earth.

The chief scientist, a tall, wiry-looking man called Oppenheimer, is chain-smoking, his inquisitive face tense with anxiety. He knows that when the experiment begins he will unleash the most powerful force in history. Oppenheimer is so unsure of what will happen he feels like a deep-sea diver under a huge depth of water, crushed by the weight of his responsibilities. The laboratory clock ticks away the final seconds of the countdown. Scarcely breathing, he raises a trembling hand to press the firing button, and takes a giant step into the unknown.

Outside, a good 9km (5 miles) away, the experiment springs into terrible life. The steel tower the bomb perches on is vaporized in an instant, and the desert beneath is scorched to glass. Night turns to day. It is as if the Sun has suddenly appeared with a colossal roar and mighty rush of wind. The brightness slowly fades to be replaced by a vast, billowing mushroom cloud of fire and smoke that reaches 12,000m

(40,000ft) into the sky. Oppenheimer staggers out of his bunker and stands transfixed, overawed by his monstrous creation. He mouths the words of the Hindu *Bhagavad Gita*:

"I am become Death
The destroyer of worlds."

It sounds like an old black and white horror film, but it all happened. The place was Alamogordo, New Mexico. The date, July 16, 1945.

Robert Oppenheimer, then 41, was the leader of a team of scientists who had just constructed and detonated the world's first atomic bomb. The *Manhattan Project* had been an enormously complex and costly undertaking. Oppenheimer's team had three major problems. They had to create material to make a bomb, ensure it worked, then perfect a method of delivering this weapon to its target. Starting with an initial budget of $6,000 in February 1940, this had escalated to $2 billion by the summer of 1945.

Getting the project started had been difficult. Even today,

most people are baffled by the processes of atomic physics. Sixty years ago, the subject was completely alien. Scientists bidding for government funds would explain, for example, that each atom of uranium contained 200 million volts of electricity. Officials would greet such information with open-mouthed disbelief or even scorn. Only a letter to the US President from the world's most famous scientist, Albert Einstein, eventually persuaded the US Government to begin funding research into an atomic bomb.

By 1945 those working on the project included some of the most distinguished scientists from America, Canada and Britain. Most significantly, Oppenheimer's team also contained several refugees from Nazi Germany, Fascist Italy and other countries in occupied Europe. Among them were Niels Bohr, Enrico Fermi and Lise Meitner: three of the world's leading nuclear pioneers.

Since the beginning of the century, it had been known that powerful forces lurked within atoms. During the 1930s, scientists in both America and Germany had discovered the process of nuclear fission – where atoms are split apart to release energy. It soon became clear that such a process could be used to create an immensely powerful bomb. But only very few materials are suitable for fission. One is uranium 235, a substance obtainable from uranium ore. Another is plutonium, an entirely man-made material, produced inside a nuclear reactor. Acquiring even small amounts of both substances requires a costly, difficult and time-consuming process, involving massive amounts of electrical power. Both uranium 235 and plutonium are such powerful explosives that a sphere of either material the size of a large orange would produce a detonation equivalent to 20,000 tons of TNT – then the most commonly used explosive in shells and bombs.

The process of developing such a dangerous weapon was tricky. Some of Oppenheimer's team referred to their experiments as *tickling the dragon*. But due to the skill and caution exercised by these world-class scientists, there were no fatal disasters during development. By the summer of 1945 the *Manhattan Project* had developed two kinds of bomb. One, known as the gun-type, would produce a nuclear explosion by firing a small piece of uranium into a larger piece. The other kind, known as the implosion type, fired several high-explosive charges into a plutonium core. In terms of factories, research and development labs, national resources and manpower, Oppenheimer's operation almost matched the scale of America's car industry. Despite employing 600,000 people, it was all top secret. Vice-President Harry Truman only found out about the *Manhattan Project* when he became President, after the death of Franklin Roosevelt in April 1945.

What drove the American government to fund such a vast enterprise was the fear that their German and Japanese enemies would produce a similar weapon before they did. Once the fission process had been discovered, it was only a matter of time before someone produced an atomic bomb. But, fortunately for the world, Germany and Japan never really got close to developing a workable bomb – although the Allies didn't realize this until the war was over. Hitler's rabid anti-Semitism had led to the exclusion of immensely gifted German-Jewish scientists from German universities. Indifferent to the consequences, Hitler remarked: "If the dismissal of Jewish scientists means the annihilation of contemporary German science, we shall do without science for a few years." Although

German nuclear physicists made essential discoveries during the 1930s and 40s, they were hampered by lack of funding. Some, fully aware of the evils of their government, falsified results to delay development. In 1943, just to make sure, British commandos destroyed a German laboratory in Norway, where atomic research was being carried out. The Japanese, similarly, lacked both the funding and resources ever to stand a serious chance of developing their own weapon.

Oppenheimer himself was fascinating, if not entirely likable. He was tall, gaunt, and had a mischievous, pixie-like face. In many photographs it looks as if a playful quip is about to spring from his lips. But he could be crushingly unpleasant too – humiliating colleagues in lectures and discussion groups with biting sarcasm. In lesser mortals such conduct would be dismissed as despicable, but with Oppenheimer, people made allowances. Before the war began he established a reputation as one of the greatest scientists of his age. Despite the flaws in his character, he managed to build a brilliant team of physicists at the California Institute of Technology. He did much the same with the *Manhattan Project*. As an American

Jew, he was particularly driven to produce such a weapon before the Germans did.

The breadth of his intelligence was astounding. His scientific studies encompassed both the infinitesimally tiny – atomic particles – and the astronomically vast – black holes. And Oppenheimer didn't stop there. Along with positrons and neutron stars, he also had space in his brain for French literature, ancient Greek, music, art and politics. His politics brought him no end of trouble. Many of his close family and friends, including one ex-girlfriend, were actively left wing and even communists. This was not unusual in America in the 1930s, especially among more liberal-minded academics and students. Oppenheimer was never a communist himself, but his remarkable career was nearly stalled on several occasions by government officials who had come to think of communism as some kind of infectious disease of the mind. They saw Oppenheimer as a security risk, fearing he would betray atomic weapons secrets to Soviet Russia.

By the time the bomb was ready to use, Germany had been defeated. But Japan was still fighting on fiercely, even though she had no hope of winning the war. In April, 1945,

US troops had landed on the Japanese island of Okinawa and fought for 82 days against fanatically determined resistance. America's leaders feared an invasion of the Japanese mainland would cost upwards of half a million American lives. The bomb was now ready, so they decided to use it. First, an ultimatum was issued to the Japanese government, warning of "the prompt and utter destruction" of their country if they did not surrender. It was debated whether or not to provide a demonstration to the Japanese, to let them know what the bomb could do. But this was rejected as impractical. The industrial city of Hiroshima, in the south of Japan, was chosen as its first target. One reason for its selection was that it had been barely touched by previous bombing raids, so it would be easy to determine how much damage had been caused directly by the atomic bomb.

The crew of the B-29 *Superfortress*, *Enola Gay*, stationed at Tinian air base in the Mariana Islands in the Pacific, were chosen to deliver it. "The bomb you are going to drop is something new in the history of warfare," they were told at their mission briefing. "It is the most destructive ever produced." Only a few of the 12 strong crew actually knew the exact nature of the bomb, and among them was weapons specialist Captain William Parsons. He had been sent directly from the *Manhattan Project* to oversee the mission. Parsons persuaded his commanding officer to let him finish assembling the bomb once they were in the air. The previous day he had watched four *B-29s* crash on takeoff at Tinian. Such a crash with a fully activated atomic bomb would have wiped out the entire island in one blinding flash.

So, dangerously overloaded with her sinister cargo, *Enola Gay* lumbered off the runway at Tinian, just missing running into the sea. Flying alongside were two other *B-29s* packed with cameras and scientific instruments. It was 2:45 on the morning of August 6.

Fifteen minutes into the 2,400km (1,500 mile) flight to the city, Parsons clambered down a steel ladder into *Enola Gay*'s bomb bay. Here he gingerly inserted explosive charges into the bomb, which had been given the codename *Little Boy*. It was now fully assembled. A few hours later, just as the Sun was coming up over the North Pacific, Parsons made a final trip to the bay. Here he replaced three green plugs in the bomb with three red ones. *Little Boy* was now armed and ready. Pilot Colonel Tibbets chose this moment to inform his crew they were carrying the world's first atomic bomb.

At 8:12am, *Enola Gay* began its bombing run. The sight of three tiny, silver *B-29*s high above Hiroshima caused little consternation below, and the city went about its early morning business as usual. In the glass nose of the aircraft, bombardier Major Thomas Ferebee peered through his bomb sight, calling out small directional commands to Tibbets. The plane was heading directly for the Aioi bridge in the middle of the city. The bridge formed a distinctive T-shape, linking an island in the Ohta river with the city either side of its banks.

At 8:15am the bridge appeared directly in the lines of Ferebee's sight. The bomb was released from the plane. *Enola Gay*, immediately much lighter, lurched up in the air. *Little Boy*, complete with a message from the ship that delivered it to Tinian – "Greetings to the Emperor from the men of the *Indianapolis*" – plummeted to earth.

The bomb had a three-stage detonation sequence, to guard against premature explosion. The first switch was triggered when it left the plane. The second was activated by air pressure when it reached 1,500m (5,000ft). The third, which would set it off, was operated by an on-board radar set to register 576m (1,890ft) above the ground. This was considered the height at which it would do the greatest damage. *Little Boy* was a uranium gun-type bomb – different in design from the one that exploded at Alamogordo. Such a bomb had never been tested. It was possible it would not even work. But it did work – very well indeed.

At 8:16am, 43 seconds after it had fallen from the *B-29*, *Little Boy* exploded above a hospital, some 250m (820ft) off target. Instantaneously, with a blinding flash of light, the air was superheated, scorching the surrounding area to 3,000°C (5,400°F) – more than half the temperature of the surface of the Sun. Buildings and people simply vanished. In some places, shadows were all that remained of some Hiroshima residents. Their outlines had been caught on a wall or pavement for the fraction of a second before their bodies were vaporized. Birds dropped from the sky in flames. Further away, buildings were flattened, and people caught in the open were turned to charcoal statues, their fingertips glowing with eerie blue flames. A mile or so from the explosion, a train full of commuters was flung away from the track like a discarded toy. In those first few seconds, perhaps 80,000 people were killed. Then, as if this was not enough to suffer, air rushed back to replace that blown away by the initial blast. This created a hurricane-force tornado that sucked people and rubble into its swirling, dark heart.

High above, once they had recovered from the shockwave that tossed their plane like a cork on a wave, the crew of *Enola Gay* gazed down in awestruck wonder. Navigator Theodore Van Kirk noted that the city looked like a pot of boiling, black oil. The tail gunner described it as, "A bubbling mass...with that red core." Two-thirds of the city had been destroyed. When the fires died down, a strange black rain of ash and radioactive dust fell. In the weeks and years to come, another 80,000 Hiroshima residents would die of radiation poisoning.

That same day, the Americans called on Japan to surrender. A broadcast from the President warned of "a rain of ruin from the air, the like of which has never been seen on this Earth." But the Japanese were too stunned to react. Hiroshima had been so utterly annihilated, accurate reports of its fate could not be sent to Tokyo. When news did finally reach Japan's leaders, it was dismissed as a wild exaggeration.

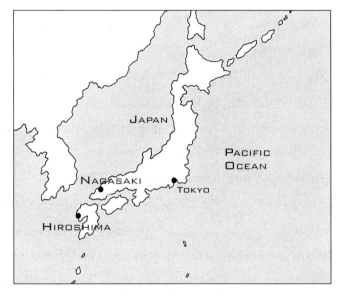

Map showing Hiroshima and Nagasaki,
targets for the US atomic bombs

On August 9, another bomb was dropped, this time on the city of Nagasaki. It was a plutonium implosion-type device – the same kind tested at Alamogordo. It had much the same effect as the Hiroshima bomb, both in the damage it caused and the number of people it killed.

Still, powerful Japanese leaders, especially the war minister General Korechika Anami, argued that the war should go on. But eventually, Emperor Hirohito intervened to stop the fighting, declaring, "The time has come when we must bear the unbearable." Even then, army officers tried to stage a coup, with the intention of continuing the war. It failed. Anami committed ritual suicide, together with scores of other high-ranking soldiers who could not bear the shame of defeat. Fighting stopped on August 15. On September 2, Japanese government ministers went aboard the *USS Missouri*, anchored in Tokyo bay, and signed the documents of surrender. It was six years and a day after the Second World War had begun.

The dropping of atomic bombs on Hiroshima and Nagasaki were two of the most significant events of the war. At the time, the decision provoked heated debate among America's military and political leaders. Sixty years later, that debate still continues.

Some American generals were matter of fact about the whole thing. "I'll tell you what war is about..." said Major-General Curtis LeMay. "You've got to kill people, and when you've killed enough, they stop fighting."

Future president and one of America's most famous generals, Dwight Eisenhower, disagreed strongly: "The Japanese were ready to surrender, and it wasn't necessary to hit them with that awful thing." Admiral William Leahy, another high-ranking military commander, was even more vociferously opposed to the bombing: "…in being the first to use it, we had adopted the ethical standards common to barbarians in the Dark Ages."

Surprisingly, an argument for using the bombs came from the Japanese themselves. One leading politician, Hisatune Sakomizu, was quite clear about it: "If the A-bomb had not been dropped we would have had great difficulty to find good reason to end the war."

But for ordinary American soldiers the bombs were a fantastic release. Paul Fussell, then a 21-year-old officer preparing for the invasion of Japan, now a history professor, recalled: "When the bomb dropped and news began to circulate that the invasion of Japan would not, after all, take place, that we would not be obliged to run up the beaches near Tokyo assault-firing while being mortared and shelled… we cried with relief and joy. We were going to live. We were going to grow up to adulthood after all."

From Technicolor to black and white...

IN GREATNESS OR IN EVIL, the chief characters of the Second World War – Winston Churchill, Franklin Roosevelt, Adolf Hitler, Joseph Stalin – dwarf almost all other political leaders of modern times. The set piece moments of the war – the Battle of Britain, Pearl Harbor, *Operation Barbarossa*, Stalingrad, the D-Day landing and the A-bomb attacks – are among the most significant events of the 20th century.

The Holocaust, the Nazi destruction of the European Jews, is arguably one of the foulest evils in history.

Without doubt, it was the most horrific conflict ever fought. But, despite the scale of the war, its hardship and suffering, and its astronomical casualties, many people who lived through it, especially those from winning nations, look back on it as the greatest days of their life. For them, the battlefront campaigns, front-line or home front comradeship, wartime romance and eventual victory are all remembered in a blur of glorious Technicolor. The rest of their lives seemed to be lived out in dull black and white. One woman, Edith Kup, who worked for the RAF, expressed it like this: "It took me years to settle down to civilian life. I had changed and no longer spoke the same language as my family. Life seemed slow, dull and pointless. We had lived on the knife edge for so long, seen dreadful sights and lost many friends. Our responsibilities had been great, but it had been exciting and we had worked as close-knit teams. I wouldn't have missed it for the world."

Edith Kup worked in an operations room, helping to direct fighter aircraft to intercept enemy bombers. But those who actually fought in combat had even more vivid memories. Broadcaster and writer Ludovic Kennedy recalled his part in the hunt for the Bismarck as, "the most exciting five days of my life."

But this excitement and comradeship was often bought at a terrible price. Many soldiers who had been through the war never spoke of their experiences to their friends and family back home. John Bradley was a navy corpsman (paramedic) attached to the US Marines. He was one of the men who hoisted the Stars and Stripes over Iwo Jima. For the rest of his life he was haunted by the death of a close friend who had been with him on the island. Shortly after parting company from Bradley, this man had been seized by Japanese soldiers and slowly and grotesquely tortured to death over three days. It was a fate that could so easily have befallen Bradley himself.

For years after the war, Bradley would weep in his sleep, and kept a long knife at his bedside. Others took refuge in drink, to dull the grief they felt for fallen comrades, or to blot out memories of the terrible things they had done to other men. Many survivors of the war felt a heavy weight of guilt for having come home, when so many braver and better men – so they felt – had perished.

One small poem by John Maxwell Edmonds was popular with both American and British troops, who would engrave it on makeshift cemetery plaques close by their battlefields:

When you go home,
Tell them of us and say,
"For your tomorrows
These gave their today."

Those who fought the war, and who lost family and friends, liked to think they were fighting for a better tomorrow. The Cold War that followed, and the nuclear standoff between the United States and the Soviet Union, was a bleak end to the conflict. But the idea of a world controlled instead by the inhuman regimes of Nazi Germany and Imperial Japan is a truly haunting one.

Usborne Quicklinks

For links to exciting websites where you can watch a film clip from *The Battle of the Somme*, see vintage photographs of American soldiers arriving in France, send secret messages using a virtual Enigma machine and find out more about the First and Second World Wars, go to the Usborne Quicklinks Website at **www.usborne-quicklinks.com** and enter the keywords "war stories".

Internet safety

When using the Internet, make sure you follow these safety guidelines:

• Ask an adult's permission before using the Internet.

• Never give out personal information, such as your name, address or telephone number.

• If a website asks you to type in your name or email address, check with an adult first.

• If you receive an email from someone you don't know, don't reply to it.

The information in this book came from hundreds of different sources; books, websites, newspaper articles, radio and television documentaries. The author would especially like to acknowledge and recommend the following sources:

The First World War

General information

The First World War: An Illustrated History by A.J.P. Taylor (Penguin, 1970) is a highly readable account of the conflict by a world famous historian.

The Great War by Correlli Barnett (Penguin, 2000) is another accessible introduction.

The following three books are all haunting first-hand accounts of individuals who fought or lived through the war:

Death's Men – Soldiers of the Great War by Dennis Winter (Penguin, 1978)

1914-1918: Voices and Images of the Great War by Lyn Macdonald (Penguin, 1991)

Voices from the Great War by Peter Vansittart (Pimlico, 1998)

Older readers might like to dip into Paul Fussell's deeply moving *The Great War and Modern Memory* (Oxford University Press, 2000).

The following books were also useful for these chapters:

The Angels of Mons

The First Casualty by Phillip Knightley (Prion Books, 2001)

Myths & Legends of the First World War by James Hayward (Sutton Publishing, 2002)

1914: The Days of Hope by Lyn Macdonald (Penguin, 1989)

Strange meetings

Silent Night: The Remarkable 1914 Christmas Truce by Stanley Weintraub (Simon and Schuster, 2001)

The great zeppelin campaign

Zeppelins of World War One by Wilbur Cross (Paragon House, 1991)

The Zeppelin in Combat by Douglas H. Robinson (Schiffer Publishing Ltd, 1994)

The Battle of Jutland

Jutland: The German Perspective by V.E. Tarrant (Cassells and Co., 1995)

The Battleships by Ian Johnston and Rob McAuley (Channel 4 Books, 2000)

The first day of the Somme

Somme by Lyn Macdonald (Macmillan, 1983)

1914-1918: Voices and Images of the Great War by Lyn Macdonald (Penguin, 1991)

Accrington Pals by William Turner (Wharncliffe Publishing, 1987)

The cellar house of Pervyse

The Cellar House of Pervyse: A Tale of Uncommon Things from the Journals and Letters of the Baroness T'Serclaes and Mairi Chisholm (A&C Black, 1917)

The Virago Book of Women and the Great War edited by Joyce Marlow (Virago, 1998)

Nightmare at Belleau Wood

The Doughboys – America and the First World War by Gary Mead (Penguin, 2000)

Poetry of the First World War

The war produced some extraordinary and moving poetry, be found in such books as:

Up the Line to Death by Brian Gardner (ed) (Methuen, 1964)

Some Corner of a Foreign Field by James Bentley (ed) (Little, Brown and Co., 1992)

History through Poetry – World War One by Paul Dowswell (Hodder Wayland, 2001)

The Poems of Wilfrid Owen Wordsworth Editions Ltd., 1994

The War Poems of Siegfried Sassoon (Faber & Faber, 1999)

For links to websites, where you can read poems from the First World War online, go to the Usborne Quicklinks Website at **www.usborne-quicklinks.com** and type in the keywords "first world war". For safe Web surfing, please follow the safety guidelines given on the Usborne Quicklinks Website.

The Second World War

General books

There are thousands of books on the Second World War. Here are two particularly useful ones. Time-Life's *Shadow of the dictators* (1989) gives a good introduction to both the rise of Hitler and the Second World War, and is illustrated with evocative photographs.

The Reader's Digest *The world at arms* (1989) is a massive, highly illustrated and authoritative account of the war.

The first and final voyage of the *Bismarck*

Although there are several recent books which deal with the Bismarck's ill-fated voyage, *Pursuit* by Ludovic Kennedy (Cassell Military paperbacks, 1974) is a brilliant, even-handed and compassionate account.

The discovery of the Bismarck by Robert D. Ballard (Hodder and Stoughton, 1990) tells the story both of the voyage and the discovery of the ship by marine archaeologists 50 years later. It is full of fascinating photographs.

Death of a salesgirl

Susan Ottaway's *Violette Szabo – The life that I have* (Leo Cooper, 2002) is a clear, solid and up-to-date account of this often romanticized figure.

Cracking Enigma

Hugh Sebag-Montefiore's *Enigma – The battle for the code* (Weidenfeld & Nicolson, 2000) is a readable history of this complex subject and contains first-hand accounts from surviving members of *U-110*.

The book-keeper's storage problem and **The lost hero**

There are reams of books on the Holocaust.

Never again – *A history of the Holocaust* by Martin Gilbert (Harper Collins, 2000) tells the story in a readable, highly illustrated, comprehensive account.

Nazi hunter – *The Wiesenthal file* by Alan Levy (Constable & Robinson, 2002) is also a very accessible introduction.

John Bierman's *Righteous Gentile* (Penguin Books, 1981) and Danny Smith's *Lost hero* (Harper Collins, 2001) are two solid biographies of Raoul Wallenberg.

Roman Vishniac's *To give them light* (Viking, 1993) is a collection of photographs documenting the vanished world of Eastern European Jews before the war.

The war of the rats

There are two especially readable accounts of the epic Battle of Stalingrad: Antony Beevor's *Stalingrad* (Penguin, 1998) and William Craig's *Enemy at the gates* (Penguin, 2000).

"...like running through rain and not getting wet."

One of the most recent titles on the much-covered battle at Iwo Jima, James Bradley and Ron Powers' *Flags of our fathers* (Bantam Doubleday Dell, 2000) is a beautifully written but harrowing account, which may not be suitable for younger readers.

The destroyer of worlds

Jack Rummel's *Robert Oppenheimer: Dark Prince* (Facts on File Inc., 1992) is a gripping introduction to the Manhattan Project and its leading personality.

From Technicolor to Black and White...

The quote by Edith Kup comes from *The women who won the war* by Dame Vera Lynn (Sedgewick & Jackson, 1990).

ACKNOWLEDGEMENTS

Cover (top right) © Stapleton Collection/CORBIS, (middle and top left) © Bettmann/CORBIS; p13 Imperial War Museum (IWM) Q 81730; p41 Hulton Archive/Getty Images; p49 IWM HO 26; p 80 IWM SP1708; p 93 IWM Q 70167; p114 IWM Q 68201; p149 IWM Q106001; p179 US National Archives and Records Administration; p189 IWM Q8467; p193 IWM MH13154; p221 IWM ZZZ 3130C; p240 IWM HU16541; p278 IWM MH 29100; p289 USHMM; p296 IWM HU 5140; p 343 IWM HU 3213; p354 ullstein bild Berlin; p371 USHMM, Courtesy the Thomas Veres Archive; p385 IWM NYP 59700; Backcover © Stapleton Collection/CORBIS.

THE VIEWS OR OPINIONS EXPRESSED IN THIS BOOK, AND THE CONTEXT IN WHICH THE IMAGES ARE USED, DO NOT NECESSARILY REFLECT THE VIEWS OR POLICY OF, NOR IMPLY APPROVAL OR ENDORSEMENT BY, THE UNITED STATES HOLOCAUST MEMORIAL MUSEUM.

Every effort has been made to trace and acknowledge the copyright holders of material in this book. If any rights have been omitted, the publishers offer their apologies and will rectify this in any future editions following notification.

'The Venlo Snatch' and 'Eye of the morning' are based on stories written by Fergus Fleming in Usborne's *Tales of Real Spies*.